A WORKBOOK IN DEMOGRAPHY

ROLAND PRESSAT

Translated by E. Grebenik
in collaboration with C. A. M. Sym

METHUEN & CO LTD
11 New Fetter Lane   London

First published in 1966 by Dunod Publishers, Paris
English translation first published in 1974
by Methuen & Co Ltd
11 New Fetter Lane, London EC4P 4EE
© 1974 Methuen & Co Ltd
Printed in Great Britain by
Butler & Tanner Ltd, Frome and London

ISBN 0 416 11880 1 (hardback)
ISBN 0 416 78160 8 (paperback)

CONTENTS

PREFACE TO THE ENGLISH EDITION

The statistical approach is essential in demographic studies, but the methods employed are largely specific to demography. In other words, the subject that has come to be called demographic analysis does not normally form part of a general treatise on statistical methods.

However, the specificity of the methods employed is neither the only characteristic, nor the principal difficulty in the statistical study of populations. The main difficulty for the beginner lies in the extreme variety of situations that he will find in practice. Advanced students of the subject should therefore be confronted with examples which are as close as possible to the subjects treated by research workers. Nor must there be any neglect of the many points of detail which the latter have to deal with and solve during the course of their work.

That is the object of this book. It was written with the needs of the students of the University of Paris in mind, but the examples are obviously not confined to specifically French problems. The variety of approaches and viewpoints to which reference has been made above, and which is an essential part of demographic instruction, makes it necessary to refer to many and diverse problems and data which are met with in the demography of the world as a whole.

I am particularly grateful to Professor Grebenik for a translation that enables the English-speaking student to feel himself thoroughly at home. I am equally in Professor Grebenik's debt for his encouragement of the project: it could not be better commended to the English reader.

ROLAND PRESSAT

I

THE CONCEPT OF
A POPULATION

1

Medical manpower and population

In this chapter the concept of a population as an aggregate of birth cohorts is introduced. The subpopulation of medical practitioners is used as an example and is subdivided into birth cohorts.

No special techniques are required to deal with the problems set out in this chapter, other than the last, in which stable population analysis must be used. This chapter thus provides an introduction to a method of approach that is fundamental in demographic analysis.

However, the problems are not purely of academic interest. The methods shown may be used to study a variety of subpopulations, e.g. the population of graduates, teachers, agricultural workers, etc.

Data

On 1 January 1959 the age distribution of French medical practitioners actively practising their profession was as follows:

Age last birthday	Numbers
Under 25	200
25–29	7 200
30–34	7 700
35–39	8 200
40–44	4 100
45–49	5 100
50–54	4 300
55–59	2 450
60–64	1 950
65–69	1 550
70 and over	1 950
All ages	44 700

Problem 1

Represent these data graphically and comment on them.

Answer

The numbers in the table may be represented graphically in a diagram which is similar to the traditional age pyramid (Fig. 1.1). As both sexes are treated together, only half the usual pyramid is shown. The age group '70 and over' is drawn on a base of ten years. Since it is not possible to give a lower limit for the 'Under 25' age group, this has been omitted from the age pyramid altogether. The shape of the pyramid will depend on the age distribution of the French population as a whole, and on the conditions of medical education in France.

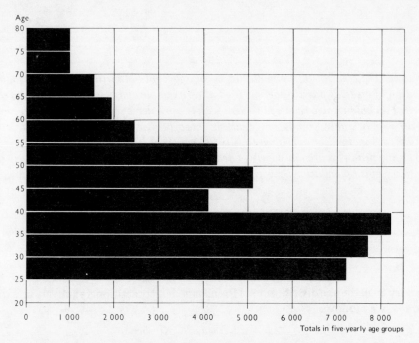

Fig. 1.1   *Age pyramid of French medical practitioners, 1 January 1959*

The successive increases in the first three age groups reflect the progressive entry of new recruits to the medical profession. The youngest age group (up to ages 25–29) contains only a fraction of those who will ultimately practise medicine, because some will not have qualified yet. On the other hand, it may be assumed that in the 35–39 age group virtually all medical students will have completed their training.

However, two other factors influence the shape of the pyramid in Fig. 1.1:

(1) The age composition of the French population as a whole.
(2) The relative importance of medical practitioners in different birth cohorts.

For instance, if medicine were to become more attractive as a profession, the increase in numbers in successive age groups that have been commented upon could well be different. It is conceivable that the differences may disappear altogether. It will be shown later that there is some evidence that such a change has in fact taken place.

On the other hand, little importance needs to be attached to changes in the numbers in different birth cohorts, except in the 40–44 age group. In that group the small number of doctors is almost certainly due to the shortfall in births in four of the five annual birth cohorts making up this group – those of 1914–18.

In the upper part of the pyramid numbers decline much faster than in the corresponding section of the pyramid for the whole French population; the fall is particularly pronounced at ages 55–59. Here again the First World War was probably responsible, for there were heavy losses in manpower and many students in these cohorts abandoned their medical studies before qualifying. But this is not the full explanation: at ages 55–59 there is a relatively small number of medical practitioners, even though the relevant birth cohorts (1899–1903) were not greatly affected by the war.

The highest part of the pyramid shows the effects of retirement. Medical practitioners, however, retire relatively late in life, and the influence of retirement only shows itself in the very highest age group ('70 and over').

Problem 2

Calculate the number of medical practitioners per 100 000 population in each age group. Represent your results in a diagram and comment.

Answer

Table 1.1 gives the total French population, the population of medical practitioners, and the ratio of the latter figure to the former. The last column is shown diagrammatically in Fig. 1.2. In this diagram ages *decrease* from left to right, so that the points represent successive birth cohorts.

Table 1.1 *Population of France and medical practitioners, 1 January 1959*

Age	Population (000s)	Medical practitioners	Medical practitioners per 100 000 population
Under 25		200	
25–29	3254	7200	221
30–34	3224	7700	239
35–39	3054	8200	269
40–44	1971	4100	208
45–49	2943	5100	173
50–54	2914	4300	148
55–59	2739	2450	89
60–64	2231	1950	87
65–69	1808	1550	86
70 and over*	2509	1950	78

* Population aged 70–79

The proportion of medical practitioners in each cohort is nearly constant from age 55 onwards (youngest birth cohort: 1903). Taking account of retirements among older medical practitioners, it is not impossible that the proportion of doctors may actually have been higher in the earliest cohorts (especially among those aged 70 and over). The age group 50–54 is quite distinct. As we move from left to right, the proportion rises for the next three age groups (down to ages 35–39). The proportion then falls, but this decline is explained in part, and possibly entirely, by the fact that some medical practitioners in these groups will not yet have completed their professional education.

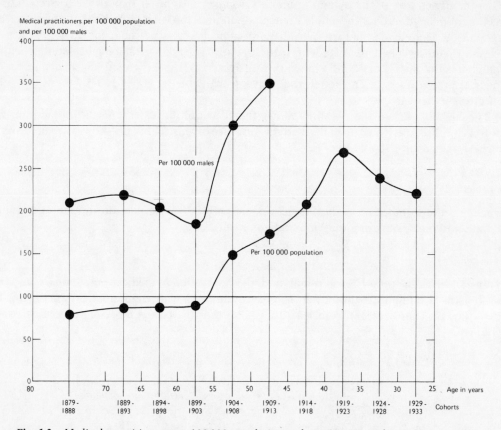

Fig. 1.2   *Medical practitioners per 100 000 population and per 100 000 males, 1 January 1959*

Note that entry into and exit from the profession are only two of the factors, albeit the most important ones, which make it impossible to obtain a correct estimate of the proportion of medical practitioners in each age group – particularly in the extreme age groups. Differential mortality among medical practitioners would affect the ratios. Excess mortality among doctors would cause their numbers to decline faster with increasing age than amongst persons not medically qualified. This would lead to an underestimation of the proportion of medical practitioners in each cohort, and the underestimate would be particularly pronounced in the older cohorts, because of the cumulative effect of excess mortality. If mortality were lower than in the general population there would, of course, be an overestimate. Differential migration rates would have similar consequences. As aliens are unable to practise medicine in France, a high rate of immigration would lead to an apparent lower proportion of medical practitioners among those birth cohorts that contain the bulk of the migrants. However, data on mortality and migration differentials are lacking, and the effects of such differentials will therefore be ignored; they are unlikely to be important and would not in any case affect the trends that have been observed in successive cohorts.

Among the cohorts born before 1904 no definite trend appears. In these cohorts the practice of medicine was almost wholly confined to males, and this suggests that it would be more appropriate to calculate the ratio of medical practitioners per 100 000 males, rather than per 100 000 population. Such ratios would be expected to show a different trend. The proportion of men will vary with the age of the cohort, because of the excess mortality of males; further, the majority of the birth cohorts considered here have been affected by the war, which has influenced the proportion of men in the population. The series of ratios based on the male population is therefore likely to differ from that based on the population as a whole. The two series are shown side by side in Table 1.2. The cohort 1899–1903 stands out (see also Fig. 1.2). The proportion of medical practitioners in this cohort is smaller than among older cohorts, and also much smaller than that in the next younger cohort (births of 1904–8). A more detailed study might show the extent to which the conditions to which the 1899–1903 cohort was subjected during its lifetime – particularly the First World War – affected the attractiveness of medicine or medical studies. It is possible that this phenomenon is not restricted to the medical profession, and that a smaller proportion of the younger people in this birth cohort received a university education.

Table 1.2 *Proportion of medical practitioners in some birth cohorts*

Age group	Birth cohorts	Medical practitioners per 100 000 population	100 000 males
45–49	1909–1913	173	350
50–54	1904–1908	148	301
55–59	1899–1903	89	186
60–64	1894–1898	87	204
65–69	1889–1893	86	218
70–*	1879–1888	78	210

* Taken as 70–79 years.

Problem 3

Extrapolate the trend from the three points relating to the cohorts 1904–8, 1909–13, 1914–18. Redraw the diagram in Problem 2 on a semi-logarithmic scale, i.e. graph the logarithms of the proportions. Hence estimate the proportion of medical practitioners per 100 000 population in the cohorts 1924–8, 1929–33 and 1934–8. Use your results and the data for 1 January 1959 to estimate what proportion of those who will ultimately practise medicine do so at ages 25–29, and at ages 30–34.

Answer

Fig. 1.2 is redrawn in Fig. 1.3 with the proportion of medical practitioners shown on a logarithmic scale. This transformation immediately reveals a much simpler trend: the points representing the three cohorts 1904–8, 1909–13 and 1914–18 are nearly collinear. This implies an exponential rate of growth in the proportion of medical practitioners, which was not apparent from an examination of the diagram on an arithmetic scale. The point corresponding to the 1889–93 cohort is very nearly on the same line, that representing the 1919–23 cohort lies a little way above it.

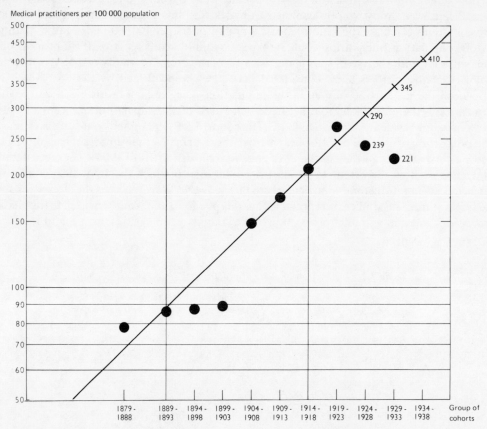

Fig. 1.3   *Medical practitioners per 100 000 population and per 100 000 males, 1 January 1959*

It seems reasonable to use this line for purposes of extrapolation, since it is based on a relatively large number of recent cohorts. The final proportion of medical practitioners per 100 000 population could be read off this line as follows:

Cohort 1924–8	290	(as against 239 on 1 January 1959)
Cohort 1929–33	345	(as against 221 on 1 January 1959)
Cohort 1934–8	410	

The extrapolation therefore suggests that 82·4% (= 239/290) of those who will ultimately practise medicine do so at ages 30–34 and 64·1% (= 221/345) at ages 25–29.

Problem 4

Estimate the number of medical practitioners on 1 January 1964, by applying the appropriate proportions of medical practitioners to population projections at the appropriate ages. The necessary proportions are those obtained in Problems 2 and 3; for the age group 70–80 you may assume a ratio of 80 medical practitioners per 100 000 population.

Answer

It will be necessary to construct a table similar to Table 1.1. The basic data are the projected populations and the proportion of medical practitioners in different age groups. The required number may then be obtained by multiplying the population in each age group by the appropriate ratio.

The proportions are those obtaining on 1 January 1959 in different birth cohorts, rather than in age groups. This is justified, provided that the proportion of medical practitioners in a birth cohort remains constant with increasing age. In Problem 2 it has been shown that this ratio may be affected by several factors, the two most important being entry into and withdrawal from the profession. But these affect only the youngest and oldest cohorts, and account has been taken of this. A round figure of 80 per 100 000 population has been assumed for the age group 70–79. This is roughly equal to that applying at these ages in 1959 (78 per 100 000), and lower than that for the age group 65–69 at the same date, even though this age group forms an important constituent of those who will be 70–79 years old in 1964. For age groups 20–24, 25–29 and 30–34, the fractions estimated to be practising medicine at these ages (obtained in Problem 3) have been applied to the estimated proportion of medical practitioners in the same

Table 1.3   *Projection of medical practitioners to 1 January 1964*

Age group	Projected population (000s)	Ratio	Number of medical practitioners
25–29	3022	263	7 950
30–34	3252	284	9 240
35–39	3206	290	9 300
40–44	3021	269	8 130
45–49	1933	208	4 020
50–54	2843	173	4 920
55–59	2759	148	4 080
60–64	2524	89	2 250
65–69	1980	87	1 720
70–79	2565	80	2 050
			53 660

extrapolation. This yields the following proportion of medical practitioners per 100 000 population, where the ages are those on 1 January 1964:

$$
\begin{array}{ll}
\text{25–29 years} & 0{\cdot}263 = 0{\cdot}410 \times 0{\cdot}641 \\
\text{30–34 years} & 0{\cdot}284 = 0{\cdot}345 \times 0{\cdot}248 \\
\text{35–39 years} & 0{\cdot}290 = 0{\cdot}290 \times 1{\cdot}000 \text{ (assumed)}
\end{array}
$$

In calculating the proportions it has been assumed that the conditions of medical study and of entry into the medical profession remain unchanged over time. The projection yields a total of 53 660 medical practitioners aged 25 and over on 1 January 1964. If account is taken of the small number of medical practitioners aged less than 25 (there were 200 such in 1959, but predictions for this particular age group are very unreliable), a round figure of 54 000 practising medical practitioners of all ages is arrived at.

Note that a cohort approach was essential to answer this problem; data given by age alone would have been insufficient.

Problem 5

Calculate the mean annual rate of increase of the population of French medical practitioners for the period 1959–63. Compare this rate with the corresponding rate for the entire French population and account for the difference.

Answer

The number of medical practitioners on 1 January 1964 is equal to the number of 1 January 1959 multiplied by 54 000/44 700. This fraction may be put equal to $(1+r_m)^5$, where r_m is the mean annual rate of growth:

$$
5 \log(1+r_m) = \log 54\,000 - \log 44\,700,
$$

which yields

$$
r_m = 0{\cdot}0385.
$$

From past population projections (which have, however, been overtaken by events) the total French population on 1 January 1964 could have been obtained by multiplying that of 1 January 1959 by 46 202 000/44 788 000. Putting this expression equal to $(1+r)^5$, where r is the mean annual rate of increase, we obtain $r = 0{\cdot}0062$. Thus, the annual rate of growth of the population of medical practitioners was over six times that of the population as a whole. This difference in the rate of growth is due to the continuous increase in the proportion of medical practitioners in successive birth cohorts.

Problem 6

Calculate the number of persons in the population per medical practitioner on the assumption that the proportion of practitioners in different age groups remains constant at the level attained by the 1934–8 cohort.

Answer

The limiting situation in which the ratio of medical practitioners in different birth cohorts will remain fixed will take approximately half a century. But by that time the different cohorts will, in the main, have been subject to lower rates of mortality than those given by the French life table of 1959. However, different cohorts will have experienced different mortality rates and, for this reason alone, the French population will not have reached stability. Complete stability in a mathematically rigorous sense will in any case only be attained at infinity.

Even though future declines in mortality will probably be relatively small, mortality conditions in a stable population will not be the same as those given by a *current* life table. In the answer to this problem one of the life tables with the lowest mortality currently available – that for Norwegian females in 1951–5 – will be used to represent the limiting stable conditions of mortality. The reader is reminded that this table will be used to estimate the effect of a fixed proportion of medical practitioners in individual birth cohorts on the proportion of medical practitioners in the whole population.

The annual rate of increase of 1% in the stable population is of the same order of magnitude as the rate of 0·0062 found in the answer to Problem 5 (this rate of between 0·006% and 0·007% per annum is in any case likely to increase as the age composition of the French population changes).

The method of calculating a stable population, when the annual rate of growth and the life table, are known, is not dealt with here; it is discussed in detail in my book *Demographic Analysis* (London 1972). The population used here also appears in the examples given in that work.

Table 1.4 *Number of medical practitioners in a stable population*

Age group	Stable population*	Medical practitioners Per 10 000 population	Numbers
25–29	7083	26	18
30–34	6710	34	23
35–39	6348	41 ⎫	
40–44	5991	41 ⎪	
45–49	5634	41 ⎬	115
50–54	5262	41 ⎪	
55–59	4863	41 ⎭	
60–64	4419	35	15
65–69	3896	20	8
70–79	5672	10	6
			185

* This stable population contains a total of 100 000 persons, grows at an annual rate of 0·01 and is subject to the mortality conditions given by the Norwegian life table for females for 1951–5 ($e_0 = 74·7$ years).

The number of medical practitioners in this stable population is given in Table 1.4. This is of the same type as Table 1.3, but contains different data. A constant proportion of 410 medical practitioners per 100 000 population in each age group is assumed, but account is taken of progressive entry into and withdrawal from the profession. At ages 25–29 only 64·1% and at ages 30–34 82·4% of all future doctors have begun practice. It is also assumed that withdrawal from the profession will begin earlier and be proportionately heavier than in the past. This is a likely development as retirement will become easier, but the figures used must only be regarded as approximations.

The following proportions have been assumed:

> 41 medical practitioners per 1000 in age group 55–59
> 35 medical practitioners per 1000 in age group 60–64
> 20 medical practitioners per 1000 in age group 65–69
> 10 medical practitioners per 1000 in age group 70–79

This assumption implies that withdrawal only becomes numerically important after the age of 65 years, and that only one-quarter of medical practitioners continue in practice between the ages of 70 and 80.

The final figure is 185 medical practitioners per 100 000 population, or one practitioner for every 541 persons. This compares with actual figures of one practitioner for every 1002 persons in 1959 and one practitioner for every 856 in 1964. The ratio of 541 persons per practitioner is nearly equal to that obtaining at present in the USSR, which is the most advanced country in this particular field. It is therefore perfectly feasible to maintain the proportion of medical practitioners at a level equivalent to that likely to be attained in the 1934–8 birth cohort (i.e. 410 doctors per 100 000 population). The continuous increase in the demand for medical services which is being brought about by advances in therapeutic techniques and the more widespread use of medical services would suggest that it is not impossible that even higher proportions of medical practitioners per head of population might be achieved.

2

Mortality and migration in a cohort

In this chapter the development of a cohort through time will be traced, and two forces that affect its numbers will be considered: mortality and migration. Some important concepts will be introduced: current mortality, cohort mortality, and measures of the frequency of certain events (in this case, migration) in the absence of disturbing factors (in this case, deaths).

The purpose of these problems is not to instruct the reader in detailed techniques of measurement, but to make him aware of the value of a cohort or longitudinal approach, i.e. of looking at observations over a period of time. In demographic analysis such an approach is always useful, and sometimes, indeed, essential.

Problem 1

In the census taken on 10 May 1954 the population of the Département Saône-et-Loire was reported, as shown in Table 2.1.

Table 2.1

	Population	
Year of birth	Males	Females
1954	1693	1671
1953	4600	4493
1952	4478	4586
1951	4651	4423
1950	4854	4603

Represent these data graphically by means of an age pyramid.

Answer

Whilst our data are given in birth cohorts, an age pyramid normally represents the population by age groups. On 1 January of any year, age groups and birth cohorts coincide, but we are concerned with the population on 10 May. To represent the numbers in Table 2.1 in the form required it is necessary to note:

(1) The birth cohort of 1954 forms part of the age group 0–1 (age last birthday 0). It will represent approximately 130/365 of the youngest age group, 130 being the number of days from 1 January to 10 May.
(2) Part of the 1953 cohort will be aged 0, and the other part aged 1 last birthday. The cohort will be divided between these two groups approximately in the ratio 235:130. In the absence of any supplementary information, the division of the cohort into two different age groups can only be made in proportion to the lengths of the two periods 10 May to 31 December and 1 January to 10 May. This is equivalent to assuming a uniform distribution of births over time.

Because the first cohort only represents 130/365 of the age group, the numbers must be multiplied by 365/130 in order to reconvert them to an annual basis. This product will be the base of the lowest rectangle in the age pyramid. We obtain:

$$\text{Males: } 1693 \times \frac{365}{130} = 4753 \qquad \text{Females: } 1671 \times \frac{365}{130} = 4692.$$

The resulting age pyramid (Fig. 2.1) is somewhat unusual. The indentations of the pyramid are not shown at exact years of age, because age groups and birth cohorts do not coincide. The diagram does, however, accurately represent the given data.

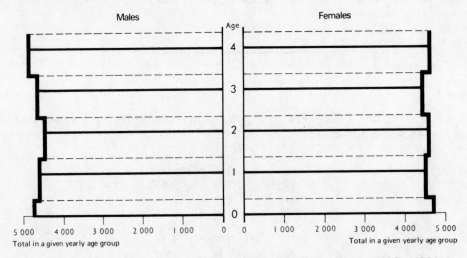

Fig. 2.1   *Population of the French Département Saône-et-Loire, 10 May 1954*

To obtain a more conventional age pyramid it will be necessary to convert the cohorts into age groups. In this case the numbers in any particular age group would contain the survivors of two different birth cohorts.

The construction of such a **pyramid** would be simple, if the observations were given in a double classification, showing both the ages of persons and the birth cohorts to which they belong. In this example, however, it is necessary to allocate the numbers in each cohort to one of two age groups. The simplest allocation is proportionate to the length of the periods in which the births could have taken place. Thus the 4600 males of the 1953 cohort are divided into $4600 \times 235/365 = 2962$ aged 0 last birthday, and $4600 - 2962 = 1638$ aged 1 last birthday. The total number aged 0 last birthday will therefore be $1693 + 2962 = 4655$. On this basis we obtain the age distribution shown in Table 2.2 and the associated diagram Fig. 2.2.

Table 2.2   *Estimated population of the Départe-ment Saône-et-Loire by single years of age, 10 May 1954*

Age last birthday	Population	
	Males	Females
0	4652	4564
1	4521	4553
2	4589	4481
3	4782	4539

The areas between lines corresponding to completed years of age are the same in Fig. 2.2 as in Fig. 2.1. But the shape of the population pyramid in Fig. 2.2 appears more conventional.

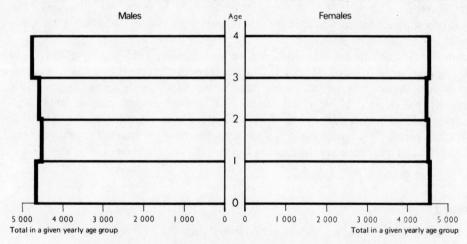

Fig. 2.2   *Population of Saône-et-Loire by age, 10 May 1954*

Table 2.3

Age last birthday	Population	
	Males	Females
0	4654	4387
1	4565	4468
2	4467	4576
3	4647	4418
4	4851	4601

Problem 2

The National Institute of Statistics estimates the age distribution of the same population of 1 January 1955 as set out in Table 2.3.

Explain how Table 2.3 may be obtained from Table 2.1 in Problem 1.

Answer

The data in Table 2.3 relate to age groups on 1 January which are equivalent to birth cohorts. The transition from Table 2.1 to Table 2.3 proceeds therefore by taking account of entries to and exits from each cohort between the two dates. Entries consist of births and in-migration, exits of deaths and out-migration.

In all cohorts, except that of 1954, the numbers vary little. Thus for males:

$$1953: 4600 - 4565 = 35$$
$$1952: 4478 - 4467 = 11$$
$$1951: 4651 - 4647 = 4$$
$$1950: 4854 - 4851 = 3$$

Differences diminish as one goes back in time. These figures suggest that mortality is the only important attrition factor, or, at least, that net migration is zero. Knowledge of the organization of French statistics leads to the conclusion that the estimates for 1 January 1955 were obtained by subtracting from the population observed on 10 May 1954 the deaths during the interval.

But in the 1954 cohort not all members alive on 1 January 1955 had been born on 10 May 1954. The number in that cohort on 1 January is therefore obtained by adding to the number enumerated at the census all births taking place between 10 May 1954 and 1 January 1955, and subtracting the deaths taking place during that period among children who had been enumerated at the census and among those who were born after census day. The difference between the census figure and that for 1 January is much larger than in the other cohorts, and there has been an increase since the census of $4654 - 1693 = 2961$ boys and $4387 - 1671 = 2716$ girls.

Problem 3

In Table 2.4 below are shown the estimated populations in two other age groups.

Table 2.4

Age	Population	
(completed years)	Males	Females
45–49	17 746	17 155
50–54	17 860	17 545

Compare the number of males in these groups with the new-born of the same cohort in Saône-et-Loire. Compute the number of survivors (l and l') corresponding to 100 000 new-born.

You are given the following data:

Annual births in Saône-et-Loire

1899: 7233	1903: 6620	1907: 5868
1900: 6960	1904: 6459	1908: 6167
1901: 7179	1905: 6497	1909: 6147
1902: 7090	1906: 6337	1910: 5906

Answer

The group aged 45–49 on 1 January 1955 had their last birthday in 1954. They therefore belong to birth cohorts lying between $1954 - 45 = 1909$ and $1954 - 49 = 1905$, i.e. to the quinquennial cohort 1905–9. Similarly, the age group 50–54 represents the birth cohort of 1900–4.

The required ratios between those numbers and the appropriate births are shown in Table 2.5. For 100 000 new-born, there are therefore $l = 52\,058$ persons in the cohort 1900–4 and $l' = 57\,216$ in the cohort 1905–9.

Table 2.5 *Number of males in Saône-et-Loire*

Cohort	Births	Number in quinquennial cohort		Ratio
		At birth (1)	1 Jan. 1955 (2)	(2):(1) × 100 000
1900	6960			
1901	7179			
1902	7090	34 308	17 860	$l = 52\,058$
1903	6620			
1904	6459			
1905	6497			
1906	6337			
1907	5868	31 016	17 746	$l' = 57\,216$
1908	6167			
1909	6147			

Problem 4

Calculate the arithmetic mean of l and l' in Problem 3. Interpret this quantity.

Answer

$$\tfrac{1}{2}(l + l') = 54\,637 = \bar{l}$$

$\bar{l}$ may, as a first approximation, be regarded as the ratio of survivors to the total number of registered births in the corresponding cohort, in the same way as l and l'. However, in the last two cases, the group of survivors corresponded exactly to the births to which they were related. In the case of $\bar{l}$ the correspondence is no longer exact, as would have been the case if the numerator had consisted of the total of survivors and the denominator of the total of births. The results are not very different, however, and $\bar{l}$ may be regarded as a more accurate approximation of the ratio of survivors on 1 January 1955 to births taking place towards the middle of the period 1900–9, i.e. around 1 January 1905.

In a closed population in which there was no migration, this ratio would represent the probability that a male born about 1 January 1905 would survive to his 50th birthday. However, the existence of migration affects the value of $\bar{l}$. In the case of France, emigration is particularly important, and $\bar{l}$ should be smaller than that probability. Note that in the absence of immigration $\bar{l}$ is the chance that a male born in Saône-et-Loire about 1 January 1905 would still be living there on 1 January 1955. This topic will be investigated in more detail later.

Problem 5

Find two approximations for $\bar{l}$, from the French life tables for 1898–1903 and 1908–13 respectively. Comment on your results.

Answer

It has been shown in the previous answer that, in the absence of migration $\bar{l}$ may be interpreted as the probability of a new-born male surviving to birthday 50. If there is migration, it is necessary to modify this interpretation. The life table data with which $\bar{l}$ must be compared are probabilities of survival. The result of this comparison is shown below; the probabilities are given per 100 000 new-born.

Life table 1898–1903	53 818
Life table 1908–13	58 320
Arithmetic mean	56 069
$\bar{l}$	54 637

$\bar{l}$ lies between the probabilities of survival given by the two life tables and is slightly below their arithmetic mean.

This suggests that the arithmetic mean (56 069 per 100 000) may be interpreted as the probability of surviving to birthday 50, corresponding to the mortality conditions prevailing on or about 1 January 1906, the date midway between the two extremes to which the two life tables relate (1 January 1898 and 31 December 1913). The chance of a new-born male surviving to birthday 50 would be 0·56069, provided that mortality had remained at a constant level over fifty years. This will be written $_{50}p_0$.

If the mortality of the Saône-et-Loire were not very different from that of France as a whole, the figure of 0·56069 might be compared with that yielded by $\bar{l}(=0·54637)$ for males born about 1 January 1905, a date that is very close to the mean date of the two life tables. Thus:

1 On the assumption of constant mortality and no migration, the chance of surviving to birthday 50 would be 0·56069 for those born about 1 January 1905.

2 Considering that mortality had declined during the last fifty years, and in the absence of migration, the number of survivors per 100 000 would be expected to be higher than 56 069.

3 As only 54 637 persons actually survived for every 100 000 new-born, it is clear that emigration has taken place and has more than cancelled the reduction in the mortality of that cohort.

Problem 6

On the assumption that mortality in Saône-et-Loire is not very different from that for France as a whole, and that this mortality is given by the following life tables:

For 1905–13 by the life table for 1908–13
For 1920–4 by the life table for 1920–3
For 1925–34 by the life table for 1928–33
For 1935–44 by the life table for 1933–8
For 1945–54 by the life table for 1950–1

Calculate the probability of a new-born male in Saône-et-Loire born in 1905 surviving to birthday 50.

Answer

The male generation life table for boys born in 1905 will be constructed on the assumption that the mortality of Saône-et-Loire is equal to that for the whole of France. The generation life table is constructed by splicing together appropriate segments of the different current life tables. The necessary computations are set out in Table 2.6. The successive life tables yield probabilities of surviving from 0 to 15, 15 to 20, 20 to 30, 30 to 40, and 40 to 50 years. The final generation life table will consist of the survivors l_0, l_{15}, l_{20}, l_{30}, l_{40} and l_{50}. This final figure will give the chance of a new-born male in Saône-et-Loire in 1905 surviving to his 50th birthday as 0·64239. This probability will be written $_{50}p'_0$.

Problem 7

Compare the results obtained in Problems 5 and 6. What conclusions may be drawn?

Answer

Three probabilities relating to new-born males born in or about 1905 may now be compared:

$$\bar{l} = 0·54637 \qquad _{50}p_0 = 0·56069 \qquad _{50}p'_0 = 0·64239$$

The following two conclusions suggest themselves:

(1) The gain in survivorship caused by the decline in mortality is evident. 100 000 boys born in about 1905 and subjected to the mortality prevailing at about the date of their births would yield only 56 069 survivors at birthday 50. The fall in mortality since 1905 has raised this figure to 64 239.
(2) On the assumption that there is no difference between the mortality of migrants and non-migrants, the 54 637 men aged 50 on 1 January 1955 are the survivors of

$$\frac{54\,637}{_{50}p'_0} = \frac{54\,637}{0·64239} = 85\,053 \text{ births.}$$

This number may be compared with the radix of the birth cohort in Saône-et-Loire

(100 000). Thus, in the absence of mortality, net emigration between birth and 50th birthday may be estimated as $100\,000 - 85\,053 = 14\,947$, or approximately 15%.

The important concept of the frequency of a particular event in the absence of mortality will be made more explicit in later chapters, and particularly in Chapter 11. It will be sufficient to mention here that the theoretical figure of 14 947 out-migrants (a net figure, which does not take account of out-migrants who are later replaced by new in-migrants) contains a certain number whose emigration was prevented by premature death. In other words, the figure will exceed the true number of out-migrants.

Table 2.6 *Calculation of a cohort life table*

Current life table used	Date	Age (x)	l_x in life table used	$_n p_x$	Cohort life table for births of about 1905	
					x	l_x
1908–13	1905	0	100 000	0·79627	0	100 000
	1920	15	79 627		15	79 627
1920–3	1920	15	83 650	0·97935	20	77 983
	1925	20	81 923			
1928–33	1925	20	84 900	0·94782	30	73 914
	1935	30	80 470			
1933–8	1935	30	83 103	0·93231	40	68 911
	1945	40	77 478			
1950–1	1945	40	8 794	0·9322	50	64 239
	1955	50	8 198			

Conversely, the difference between the 64 239 survivors estimated on the assumption that mortality alone was responsible for the reduction in numbers and the observed figure $\bar{l} = 54\,637$ provides an estimate of the number of net out-migrants surviving to their 50th birthdays. In addition to the $64\,239 - 54\,637 = 9602$ out-migrants who have survived, others will have migrated from the Département, but do not appear in the calculations because they died before 1 January 1955.

Writing E_f for the net number of emigrants it is seen that $9602 < E_f < 14\,947$ per 100 000 births in the Département.

Even though this figure differs from the proportion calculated by using statistics of migration, the ratio of 15% of out-migration in the absence of mortality yields a good estimate of the intensity of out-migration from the Département. But, as there will have been some in-migrants during the period as well, the interpretation of this figure is somewhat difficult.

Note that the calculations provide a method of estimating net migration in an area. They would have been even more valuable if figures of deaths actually registered in the different cohorts could have been used, instead of estimates of cohort mortality.

3

The population of the Soviet Union

When analysing demographic data it is frequently necessary to make a choice between different methods of computation. It is not always possible to provide rigorous criteria for the choice of one method over another, and this makes for difficulties for the beginner.

The analysis of published Soviet statistics resulting from the 1959 census of the Soviet Union illustrates the kind of estimating procedures that it is sometimes necessary to employ. The techniques used are not very complex: all that is necessary is to use all the information available and to ensure that the results are consistent between themselves.

Though such methods may not be very satisfying intellectually, they often illustrate connections between different variables that would not have been immediately evident, so that the problems treated in this chapter have considerable instructional value.

Data

Statistical data relating to the population of the Soviet Union are fragmentary, and a process of reconstitution becomes necessary whenever a more detailed analysis is required. The only statistics showing the age and sex distribution of the population published after the census of 15 January 1959 are shown in Tables 3.1 and 3.2 below.

Table 3.1 *The population of the Soviet Union on 15 January 1959, by age (data in 000s)*

Age last birthday	Population	Age last birthday	Population
0– 9	46 363	35–39	11 590
10–15	17 133	40–44	10 408
16–19	14 675	45–49	12 264
20–24	20 343	50–59	19 146
25–29	18 190	60–69	11 736
30–34	18 999	70 and over	7 972

Table 3.2   *The population of the Soviet Union by sex and age, 15 January 1959 (data in 000s)*

Age last birthday	Males	Females
0– 9	23 608	22 755
10–19	16 066	15 742
20–24	10 056	10 287
25–29	8 917	9 273
30–34	8 611	10 388
35–39	4 528	7 062
40–44	3 998	6 410
45–49	4 706	7 558
50–54	4 010	6 437
55–59	2 906	5 793
60–69	4 099	7 637
70 and over	2 541	5 431
Not known	4	4
All ages	94 050	114 777
0–31	62 729	62 489

From these data the population by sex and age in the conventional quinquennial age groups (0–4, 5–9, etc.) will be estimated up to the age of 60. In Table 3.3 a series of rates, which will be used in this estimation, is shown.

Table 3.3   *Vital rates in the Soviet Union, per 1000*

	1954	1955	1956	1957	1958
Birth rate	26·6	25·7	25·2	25·4	25·3
Death rate	8·9	8·2	7·6	7·8	7·2
Infant mortality rate	68	60	47	45	41

To simplify the calculations it will be assumed throughout that the situation on 15 January 1959 is identical with that on 1 January 1959.

Problem 1

Calculate the annual rate of natural increase for each year between 1954 and 1958. Find the total population of the Soviet Union on 1 January of each of these years. Deduce the annual numbers of births, distinguishing between each sex, on the assumption that the masculinity ratio at birth is 105:100.

Answer

The rate of natural increase (r) is the difference between the birth rate (b) and the death rate (d): $r = b - d$. For the years in question we obtain:

$$1954: 0·0177$$
$$1955: 0·0175$$
$$1956: 0·0176$$
$$1957: 0·0176$$
$$1958: 0·0181$$

As the population on 1 January 1959 is known (by assumption it is equal to that on 15 January of that year), the population on 1 January of each of the five preceding years may be estimated from the rates of natural increase. It will be necessary to assume that net migration was zero, which is almost true for the USSR.[1]

There is one further slight difficulty. It is usual to compute the rate of natural increase with the mean population for the year as a base, and not with the population at the beginning of the year. In other words, it would be wrong to write $P_1 = P_0(1+r)$, where P_0 and P_1 stand for populations on successive new year's days. This equation would have yielded P_0 immediately, once P_1 and r were known. With the same notation, the equation for r is

$$r = \frac{P_1 - P_0}{\frac{1}{2}(P_1 + P_0)}.$$

This equation can be used to estimate the population on 1 January of a given year (P_0) from a knowledge of the population on 1 January of the succeeding year (P_1) and r. The equation may be manipulated to yield

$$P_0 = P_1 \frac{2-r}{2+r}.$$

In Table 3.4 the multipliers $(2-r)/(2+r)$ are shown. These are applied to populations on successive new year's days to yield an estimate of the population at the beginning of each of the years 1954 to 1958. The calculation begins with the figure for the beginning of 1959, i.e. 208 827 000 persons.

Table 3.4 *Estimation of annual births by sex in the Soviet Union*

	1.1.1954	1.1.1955	1.1.1956	1.1.1957	1.1.1958	1.1.1959
r	0·0177	0·0175	0·0176	0·0176	0·0181	
$2-r$	1·9823	1·9825	1·9824	1·9824	1·9819	
$(2-r)/(2+r)$	0·98246	0·98265	0·98255	0·98255	0·98206	
Population (000s)	191 139	194 551	197 986	201 502	205 081	208 827
Mean population	192 846	196 268	199 744	203 291	206 954	
Birth rate (b)	0·0266	0·0257	0·0252	0·0254	0·0253	
Births in 000s (B)	5130	5044	5034	5164	5236	
$0·512B$	2627	2583	2577	2644	2681	
$0·488B$	2503	2461	2457	2520	2555	

The annual number of births (B) is obtained by multiplying the mean population by the birth rate (b); male and female births are estimated by using the proportions $0·512:0·488$, equivalent to a sex ratio at birth of $105:100$.

---

[1] It is, however, estimated that, between 1956 and 1964, 400 000 Poles left the Soviet Union to return to Poland. This exceptional migration will be ignored.

Problem 2

Estimate the number of male and female survivors on 1 January 1959 of the five birth cohorts calculated in Problem 1. It will be necessary to estimate the infant mortality rate for the period 1954–8. By using the Model Life Tables in the United Nations *Population Studies*, No. 25, this rate may be used to obtain probabilities of survival for the five cohorts.

Answer

The infant mortality rate for the period 1954–8 may be calculated in two different ways: (*a*) as the arithmetic mean of the rates for each individual year of the period, or (*b*) by relating the total number of infant deaths during the period to the number of births in the same period.

Method (*b*) is equivalent to computing a weighted mean of the annual rates, the weights being the proportions of births in any given year to the total number of births in the quinquennium. Provided that annual numbers of births remain fairly constant (as is the case here), the two methods yield practically identical results. From the theoretical point of view method (*a*) is to be preferred as giving a better measure of infant mortality. Method (*b*), however, is more useful for achieving the aim of this calculation.

For ease of computation, therefore, we calculate the arithmetic mean of the five rates, which comes out as 52·2 per 1000. In the UN Model Life Tables, this corresponds to a figure lying between Level 85 and Level 90. In the former case the arithmetic mean of the infant mortality rates for males and females is 60·9 per 1000 (a weighted mean of the male and female rates using coefficients 0·512 and 0·488 would have been preferable on theoretical grounds, but the difference between the weighted and the unweighted mean is negligible). The arithmetic unweighted mean for Level 90 is 45·9. Soviet infant mortality in 1954–8 is therefore a little nearer Level 90, if 'distance' between different levels may be measured by differences in infant mortality rates. In the calculations that follow Level 85 will, however, be used for two reasons. In the first place the tables will be employed to calculate the survivors of births who will form the age group 0–4. This will involve using death rates at ages over 1 year. These rates were relatively high in the Soviet Union and probably exceeded those corresponding to the equivalent level of infant mortality in the Model Tables. In other words, if mortality under the age of one year in the USSR were nearer to Level 90, it is likely that among children aged over 1 year mortality rates would be nearer to Level 85, and possibly to an even lower level.[1]

In the second place there are reasons for believing that infant mortality in the Soviet Union is somewhat underestimated (see the paper cited in the footnote). This would provide a partial explanation for the discrepancy between infant mortality and death rates at ages over 1 year. But it reinforces the conclusion that Level 85 is the proper one to choose. Once the choice of level has been made, the calculation of the population aged 0–4 by sex on 1 January 1959 follows directly and is shown in Table 3.5.

Table 3.5

	Males	Females
Births 1954–8	13 112 000	12 496 000
Probability of survival (Level 85)	0·9262	0·9380
Population aged 0–4 on 1 January 1959	12 144 000	11 721 000

[1] See 'Les premières tables de mortalité de l'Union Soviétique (1958–9)', *Population*, **18**, 1 (1963), pp. 65–92.

Problem 3

The number of births in 1943 was 2 900 000. This cohort between birth and 1 January 1959 has been subject to the mortality defined by the UN Model Life Table with an expectation of life at birth of 50 years. How can this assumption be verified? Assume that the sex ratio at birth was 105 males to 100 females, and calculate the number of survivors on 1 January 1959 by sex.

Answer

It is not possible to justify rigorously the assumptions made in this question. Contrary to widely held beliefs, there is no demographic procedure that will compensate completely for insufficiency or lack of observed data. In this problem the gaps in the data are considerable, and the Model Life Table selected has been chosen after examining a number of items of information. It would be difficult to justify the choice of this particular table beyond showing that it gives reasonable results, particularly as the results obtained will not be used in further studies.

In 1943, the middle year of the war, the territory of the Soviet Union was in large part under enemy occupation, the war effort was total and losses were already very heavy. It has been estimated that the Soviet Union lost approximately 40 million people through excess mortality, lower birth rates and emigration.[1] In the absence of war a natural increase of the order of 15 million between mid-1941 and mid-1945 might have been expected. This is equivalent to an annual rate of increase of 0·02, on a base population estimated by Soviet demographers as 190·7 million in 1939 (within the boundaries of that year). All this suggests that a rounded figure of 180 million for the Soviet population in 1943 is a reasonable estimate.

It remains to try and estimate the birth rate for that year. The case of France during the 1914–18 period yields an interesting precedent. In the First World War her birth rate fell by nearly one-half. The situation in the Soviet Union in the Second World War probably differed from that of France in the First World War. The birth rate immediately before the war was very much higher. It was 32 per 1000 in 1936, and 37 per 1000 in 1937–8, following the restrictions on legal abortions, which had previously been fairly numerous. In contrast, the French birth rate before 1914 was only 18 per 1000. Moreover, the new mothers of 1943 were mainly women who were themselves born during the war of 1914–18 and the revolution. These cohorts were already small, and, other things being equal, the birth rate would be expected to be low. The 2·9 million births assumed in the problem would be equivalent to a birth rate of 16 per 1000, a little less than half the rate of 1937–8. This does not seem too unreasonable.

Model Life Tables of Level 60, which correspond to an expectation of life at birth of 50 years, can only provide a very rough approximation to the mortality of the 1943 birth cohort. Model Life Tables are constructed from current life tables for populations with an age structure very different from the population corresponding to that of the cohort tables, particularly when mortality was changing rapidly. This is true of the present example: the very unfavourable conditions during the war will almost certainly have resulted in a very high mortality during the early years of life. Conditions then returned to normal, and later still considerable progress was made in reducing mortality. Thus, the value of $_5q_{15}$ in the Soviet life table of 1958–9, which relates mainly to the cohorts of 1939–43, comes to 0·00777 for men and 0·00471 for women. These values suggest that Level 95 ($e_0 = 68·2$ years) would be appropriate for men, and Level

[1] 'La structure par âge de la population de l'U.R.S.S.', *Population*, **15**, 5 (1960), pp. 894–8.

100 ($e_0 = 70\cdot2$ years) for women. This is a much lower level of mortality than that of the model table that has been proposed. On the other hand, the approximate calculations described in Chapter 4 suggest that in 1938–9 the expectation of life at birth in the Soviet Union may have been 46·3 years, a figure midway between Levels 50 and 55. With the continued progress in the reduction of mortality, an expectation of life at birth of 50 years would seem reasonable for 1943. But even if no account were taken of the increase in violent deaths caused by the war, the mortality situation almost certainly deteriorated between 1938–9 and 1943. The infant mortality of the 1943 cohort (infant deaths in 1943 and 1944) probably exceeded the already high figure of 150 per 1000 registered in 1939 (for 1940 the value given is 184 per 1000). It would, therefore, *a fortiori*, be higher than the infant mortality of Level 60, with $e_0 = 50$ years, which was suggested for these calculations (at that level $q_0 = 0\cdot135$ approximately).

As mortality conditions improved very rapidly after the end of the war, the cohort of 1943 would have been subject to diminishing risks of death (setting aside the falling probability of death due to the age of the cohort). It would probably have fallen below the values given by Level 60 which has been chosen to represent the overall mortality of the cohort between ages 0 and 15. In Table 3.6 the progress of this cohort is shown; in the table only the last line is based on firmly established data – the others do no more than indicate orders of magnitude. The table indicates that the choice of Level 60 to describe overall mortality between ages 0 and 15 is not unreasonable; mortality was at first higher and later lower than the values suggested by this level. The weight of q_0 in this overall mortality is such that it is right to choose a level nearer to that applying at the beginning than at the end of the period studied.

Table 3.6   *Mortality in the birth cohort of 1943 in the Soviet Union (based on UN Model Life Tables)*

Age last birthday	Period	Mortality level		
		Number	e_0	
0	1943–4	40	40	
5	1948–9	70	55	Level used for
10	1953–4	80–85	62	ages 0–15: 60
15	1958–9	95–100	69	$e_0 = 50$

Table 3.7   *Survivors of the 1943 birth cohort at 1 January 1959, Soviet Union (numbers in 000s)*

Number of births		Probability of survival	Number aged 15 on 1 January 1959
Total	By sex		
B = 2900	Males: $B_m = 0\cdot512B$ = 1485	0·775	1151
	Females: $B_f = 0\cdot488B$ = 1415	0·793	1122

The computation of the number of male and female survivors on 1 January 1959 follows directly, provided that the probability of survival to birthday 15 is taken as equivalent to the probability of a member of the birth cohort surviving for 15 years. Any attempt at a more refined calculation would give a spurious appearance of accuracy, considering the approximate nature of the data used.

Problem 4

From the data given calculate the sex ratio at different ages in the Soviet population, and represent these figures graphically. Comment on your results, and compare them with previous estimates. Estimate separately the numbers of men and women for the age groups for which this has not been done previously.

Answer

To calculate the various sex ratios, it will be sufficient to divide the number of men in Table 3.2 by the corresponding figure for women. Note, however, that the figures given for the age group 0–31 make it possible to split the age group 30–34. The following results are obtained:

Age	Males	Females
30–31	4082	4432
32–34	4529	5956

It is thus possible to compute the sex ratios of Table 3.8, which are represented graphically in Fig. 3.1. It has been assumed that the ratio at age 0 is 1·05.

Table 3.8 *Ratio of males to females in the Soviet population, 1 January 1959*

Age	Ratio	Age	Ratio
0– 9	1·037	40–44	0·624
10–19	1·021	45–49	0·623
20–24	0·978	50–54	0·623
25–29	0·962	55–59	0·502
30–31	0·921	60–69	0·537
32–34	0·760	70 and over	0·468
35–39	0·641		

The sex ratio falls very abruptly after age 31. In the 30–34 age group it changes from 0·921 for ages 30–31 to 0·760 for ages 32–34; thereafter the values are all very low – in general there is barely more than one man for every two women. The value in the 55–59 age group is particularly low.

The abnormal sex structure of the Soviet population is well brought out when compared with populations with a less troubled history. It is also possible to compute the sex ratios in different stationary populations that would result from normal excess male mortality. In the stationary population, defined by Level 50 ($e_0^0 = 45$), the following values are found (values for the Soviet Union are those given in brackets):

25–29	0·982	(0·962)
35–39	0·983	(0·641)
60–69	0·885	(0·537)

The increase in the ratio at ages 35–39 is due to excess female mortality in childbirth.

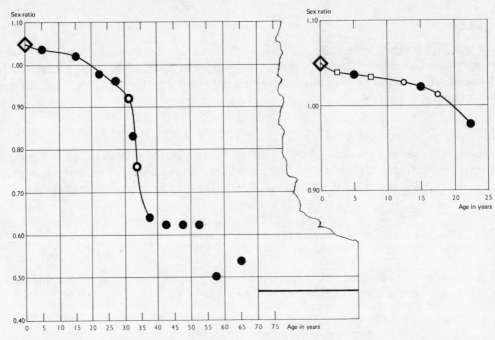

Figs. 3.1 and 3.2   *Sex ratio by age in the Soviet population, 1 January 1959*

The Soviet Union therefore has a severe deficit of men in all age groups over 32 years. Up to that age the situation appears normal, except possibly at ages 30–31, but the real change appears at the age of 32. The first male cohort that is in deficit, the 32-year-olds, was born in 1926 and had reached the age of 19 in 1945. The sex ratio shows the effects of a very destructive war. For older cohorts, particularly the age group 55–59, the effects of the First World War and the subsequent revolution are also very apparent (the sex ratio for the 50–59 age group is lower than that for the 60–69 group).

In Fig. 3.2 the values of the ratio are shown on a larger scale for ages up to 20–24. The preceding calculations lead to the values in Table 3.9, where the numbers are again given in thousands. These ratios do not coincide completely with the values read off the diagram – given the low accuracy of the diagrammatic representation, this is only to be expected.

Table 3.9

Age group	Males	Females	Sex ratio: males/females	
			Calculated	Read from diagram
0–4	12 144	11 721	1·036	1·040
5–9	11 464	11 034	1·039	1·034
15	1 151	1 122	1·026	1·021

The values read off the diagram may be used to estimate the numbers in the age groups 10–14 and 15–19. Having made an estimate of the number aged 15 last birthday of 2 273 000 (Table

3.7), the age group 10–14 becomes (in thousands) $17\,133 - 2273 = 14\,860$, and that aged 15–19 becomes $14\,675 + 2273 = 16\,948$. The sex ratios on the diagram are $1\cdot026$ and $1\cdot012$ respectively, so that the results shown in Table 3.10 follow.

Table 3.10   *Soviet Union, population aged 15–20 on 1 January 1959 (000s)*

Age group	Sex ratio	Males	Females
10–14	1·026	7525	7335
15–19	1·012	8525	8423

These data may be checked for consistency with those given in Table 3.2 for the age group 10–19. The following results are found (in thousands):

$$\text{Males} \begin{cases} \text{Table 3.10} & 16\,050 \\ \text{Table 3.2} & 16\,066 \end{cases} \text{Difference} = 16$$

For females, the magnitude of the difference is, of course, the same but it has the opposite sign. The comparison is satisfactory. However, if complete consistency between the data given and the results obtained were required, this could be obtained by keeping one of the columns in Table 3.10 and obtaining the second by subtracting from the data in Table 3.2 relating to the age group 10–19. In that case the following would be the result:

Age group		Males	Females
10–19	Table 3.2	16 066	15 742
10–14	Table 3.10	7 525	7 335
15–19	Difference	8 541	8 407

Table 3.11 shows the complete results.

Table 3.11   *Population of the Soviet Union by sex and age, 15 January 1959 (000s)*

Age group	Males	Females
0– 4	12 144	11 721
5– 9	11 464	11 034
10–14	7 525	7 335
15–19	8 541	8 407
20–24	10 056	10 287
25–29	8 917	9 273
30–31	4 082	4 432
32–34	4 529	5 956
35–39	4 528	7 062
40–44	3 998	6 410
45–49	4 706	7 558
50–54	4 010	6 437
55–59	2 906	5 793
60–69	4 099	7 637
70 and over	2 541	5 431
Unknown	4	4
Total	94 050	114 777

Problem 5

Construct an age pyramid for the Soviet population on 1 January 1959 and comment.

Answer

The required age pyramid is shown in Fig. 3.3. On the horizontal axis numbers are shown for quinquennial age groups, even though not all age groups are given by quinquennia. One is given in ten-year groups (e.g. 60–69), the numbers being divided by 2 to reduce them to quinquennial figures.

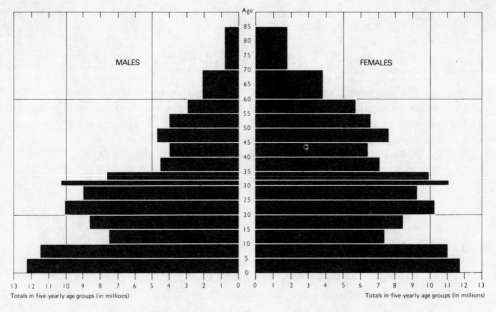

Fig. 3.3 *Population of the Soviet Union, 1 January 1959*

There is one open-ended group (70 and over). It is conventional to represent this as a number of quinquennial groups which must not be so large as to distort the appearance of the pyramid. In Fig. 3.3 it is represented by three quinquennial groups, which gives a reasonable shape.

As separate data are given for age group 30–31 and 32–34, these must be represented by rectangles of a width comparable to those of the quinquennial groups. There are 4 082 000 men aged 30–31, and the width of the rectangle is therefore given as $5/2 \times 4\,082\,000 = 10\,205\,000$.

The most striking feature of the pyramid is the imbalance between the sexes after age 32. This has already been commented on, when the sex ratios were considered. Note, however, that in spite of the imbalance, the general shape of the pyramid is not dissimilar for each sex.

There are three separate indentations in the pyramid, showing years of birth deficits, followed by larger numbers signifying a return to normal conditions, and possibly some making up of prevented births. Unfortunately, it is not possible to determine from quinquennial age distributions the exact cohorts that are deficient in births.

The oldest group that shows a deficit is that aged 35–44 (corresponding to the births of 1914–23, i.e. mainly those of the war and revolutionary period), the next is that aged 25–29 (births of 1929–33, a period when there was a large increase in the number of abortions in the Soviet Union), and there is finally the age group 10–19 (births of 1939–48), which shows the effect of the Second World War.

II

THE MEASUREMENT AND
COMPARISON OF MORTALITY

4

Measuring mortality in the Soviet Union

The Soviet Union provides an example of a country where, in the past, demographic statistics have either been irregular or non-existent. For instance, no life tables were published between 1926–7 and 1958–9. It therefore becomes necessary to use the fragmentary data that do exist to make better estimates which will be useful for comparative studies. In this chapter a series of age-specific mortality rates, which have been published, will be used to construct life tables.

Such tables will be constructed for 1938–9 and for 1958. The results for the latter year will be compared with those published in the official life tables for 1958–9 in order to check the accuracy of the estimates. Good agreement between these two sets of figures will be found, and this will serve as an encouragement to use age-specific death rates systematically for the construction of life tables. Reluctance to undertake this task is probably due to the view that the construction of life tables is a particularly complicated process. Difficulties appear intimidating when the subject is considered from the point of view of the actuary, but the demographer may legitimately have fewer fears and show greater courage.

Data

Age-specific death rates for both sexes combined relating to 1938–9 and 1958 were published for the Soviet Union in 1960. These data constitute the only detailed information available on recent Soviet mortality levels. The series in Table 4.1 will be used to construct approximate life tables.

Problem 1

To construct life tables it is necessary to divide the mortality of the 0–4 age group into two parts: infant mortality, and mortality between ages 1 and 4. Attempt such a division, making

Table 4.1 *Age-specific death rates per 1000, Soviet Union, actual territory*

Age	1938–9	1958
0– 4	75·5	11·8
5– 9	5·5	1·1
10–14	2·6	0·8
15–19	3·4	1·3
20–24	4·4	1·8
25–29	4·7	2·2
30–34	5·4	2·6
35–39	6·8	3·1
40–44	8·1	4·1
45–49	10·2	5·4
50–54	13·8	8·0
55–59	17·0	10·9
60–64	24·4	16·9
65–69	35·0	23·5
70 and over	78·6	62·4

use of the data given below (these are not exact, relating to the actual territory of the period, but are the only data available for an approximate solution):

(a) Infant mortality rate: 1938–9 0·185
      1958 0·0406

(b) Numbers of births: 1938–9 12 750 000
      1958 5 250 000

(c) Estimated population of the Soviet Union by age on 17 January 1939[1] and 1 January 1959 (Table 4.2).

Table 4.2 *Population of the Soviet Union, actual territory*

	Numbers	
Age	17 January 1939	1 January 1959
0	5 298 809	5 030 000
1	5 046 204	4 860 000
2	4 375 895	4 660 000
3	3 825 847	4 710 000
4	3 260 378	4 755 000
5		4 480 000

Answer

It is required to estimate the age-specific death rate for ages 1–4 from the data given in Roman type in Table 4.3. However, these data do not immediately yield the required information and a number of preliminary remarks are necessary.

[1]See F. Lorimer, *The Population of the Soviet Union: History and Prospects.*

The population on 17 January 1939 will be taken as equivalent to the mean population for the period 1938–9 (Fig. 4.1). The total numbers aged 0–4 may then be obtained by adding together the appropriate figures in Table 4.2. The number of deaths in that age group will be computed by applying the age-specific mortality rate (0·0755) to the total. By doubling this figure, the number of deaths over the two-year period is then estimated as 3 293 000. Subtracting the number of deaths of those aged less than 1 year (12 750 000 × 0·185 = 2 359 000) from that total yields an estimate of the number of deaths in the age group 1–4. When this figure is related to the appropriate mean population the age-specific death rate for 1–4 comes out as 0·0283, or 28·3 per 1000.

For 1958 the procedure is exactly the same, once the mean population for that year has been computed. This problem is, however, slightly more difficult than for the preceding period.

To estimate the mean population aged 0–4 in 1958 it is necessary to consider the two groups of cohorts G_1 and G_2 (see Fig. 4.1). G_1 is the total population aged 0–4 on 1 January 1959 and G_2 is the population aged 1–5, which one year earlier formed the age group 0–4. In calculating the

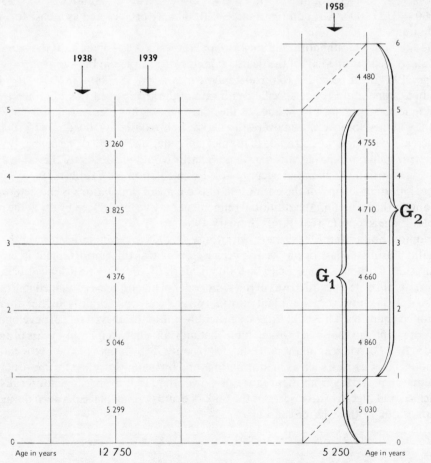

Fig. 4.1 Population at ages under 6 years and births in the USSR (both sexes, in 000s)

Table 4.3   *Estimation of age-specific death rates for ages 1–4 in the USSR (both sexes, numbers in 000s)*

	1938–9			1958		
Age	Population	Deaths	Death rate	Population	Deaths	Death rate
0–4	21 806	3293	0·0755	23 800	281	0·0118
0*	12 750	2359	0·185	5 250	213	0·0406
1–4	16 507	934	0·0283	18 825	68	0·0036

* The population aged 0 is taken as equivalent to the number of births taking place in that period. The rate used is therefore the classical infant mortality rate, and not the proper age-specific death rate that appears in the other two lines of the table.

arithmetic mean of these two numbers, $\frac{1}{2}(24\,015\,000 + 23\,465\,000) = 23\,740\,000$, one-half of the deaths that had occurred in the group G_2 since 1 January 1958 are ignored. These deaths will form a smaller proportion of the age group 0–4 than the age-specific central death rate, 0·0118. If this rate were applied to G_2, it would yield 277 000 deaths, and one-half of this figure is 138 000. The correct number will therefore lie between 23 740 000 and 23 740 000 + 138 000 = 23 878 000. A round figure of 23 800 000 may be accepted as a base for subsequent calculations.

The method for estimating the mean population aged 1–4 is exactly the same. It is not difficult to see that one-half of the deaths taking place in 1958 in the age group aged 2–5 on 1 January 1959 must be added to the arithmetic mean, $\frac{1}{2}(18\,985\,000 + 18\,605\,000) = 18\,795\,000$. The first estimate of the age-specific death rate of the group aged 1–4, obtained by using the arithmetic mean previously obtained as the equivalent of the mean population, yielded 0·0036. Deaths will therefore have been overestimated by approximately $0·0036 \times 18\,605\,000 = 67\,000$. By increasing the previous estimate of the mean population by 30 000 one probably comes near to the true value; moreover, this new denominator would yield exactly the same age-specific death rates within the limits of accuracy of the calculation (see Table 4.3).

The important feature in the estimation of these mean populations is the determination of the cohorts they contain. An additional refinement may be introduced by using the numbers in the oldest age group (5 years) on 1 January 1958.

A comparison of the 1938–9 rates with those of 1958 gives an indication of the decline in mortality during the last twenty years; because of the war this improvement in fact occurred during the last fifteen years. In 1938–9 infant mortality in the USSR lagged behind that of Europe: a rate of 185 per 1000 was of the same order of magnitude as obtained in France before 1870. In 1958, however, the infant mortality rate was only slightly higher than in other developed countries. The slight excess is probably due to the uneven rate of development of the different peoples in the Soviet Union. Note that mortality between 1 and 4 years of age has been reduced by 87%, whereas infant mortality fell by only 78%. At ages below 1 year mortality due to 'endogenous' causes, such as malformations and birth injuries, plays an important part. The reduction in mortality from these causes is slower than that from 'exogenous' causes, such as bronchitis and digestive diseases. But the bulk of deaths taking place between the ages of 1 and 4 years is due to these latter causes.

Problem 2

Convert the rates given in Table 4.1 (other than those for the age group 0–4) and the estimated rates for the age group 1–4 to q_x values by using the Reed-Merrell tables.

Answer

The Reed-Merrell tables link central death rates for quinquennial or decennial age groups with q_x values for the same intervals For ages 1–4 the tables are based on American conditions and make allowance for the under-enumeration of young children in the American censuses of 1910, 1920 and 1930. For this reason a more generally applicable table has been used for this age group.[1]

There is no difficulty in using these tables; q_x values may be looked up in much the same way as logarithms in a table of logarithms. Linear interpolation will always have to be used (the Reed-Merrell tables rates are given per 1000 – in this chapter rates will be given per 10000).

The infant mortality rate will be taken as an estimate of q_0, the probability of dying within one year of birth. The results are shown in the life tables which have been constructed in answer to the next problem.

Problem 3

Construct life tables from the series of probabilities found in the answer to Problem 2. Compute the expectation of life at birth assuming that $e_{70}^0 = 9$ years in 1938–9 and 11 years in 1958 in the Soviet Union.

Table 4.4   *Life tables in the Soviet Union* (*both sexes combined*)

1938–9			Age	1958		
l_x	$_nq_x$	$_nd_x$	x	l_x	$_nq_x$	$_nd_x$
10 000	0·1850	1850	0	10 000	0·0406	406
8 150	0·1074	875	1	9 594	0·0143	137
7 275	0·0272	198	5	9 457	0·0055	52
7 077	0·0129	91	10	9 405	0·0040	38
6 986	0·0169	118	15	9 367	0·0065	61
6 868	0·0218	150	20	9 306	0·0090	84
6 718	0·0232	156	25	9 222	0·0109	101
6 562	0·0267	175	30	9 121	0·0129	118
6 387	0·0335	214	35	9 003	0·0154	139
6 173	0·0398	246	40	8 864	0·0203	180
5 927	0·0498	295	45	8 684	0·0267	232
5 632	0·0668	376	50	8 452	0·0393	332
5 256	0·0818	430	55	8 120	0·0532	432
4 826	0·1154	557	60	7 688	0·0813	625
4 269	0·1616	690	65	7 063	0·1113	786
3 579			70	6 277		

$n = 1$ for $x = 0$; $n = 4$ for $x = 1$; $n = 5$ for $x \geq 5$

[1] Such a table has been published in the Appendix to R. Pressat, *Demographic Analysis*. London, Arnold, 1972.

Answer

The method of computing life tables from probabilities of death is well known. The results of the calculations are shown in Table 4.4. It will be necessary to establish a formula for the expectation of life at birth, when the only information about mortality at ages over 70 is the expectation of life at that age.

In calculating the total number of years lived by a cohort of new-born (l_0) there are two components:

(1)   The number of years lived up to age 70:

$$l_1 + 4l_5 + 5(l_{10} + l_{15} + \ldots + l_{70}) + \tfrac{1}{2}(l_0 - l_1) + 2(l_1 - l_5) + 2\tfrac{1}{2}(l_5 - l_{10} + l_{15} + \ldots + l_{65} - l_{70}).$$

This expression reduces to:

$$\tfrac{1}{2}l_0 + 2\tfrac{1}{2}l_1 + 4\tfrac{1}{2}l_5 + 5(l_{10} + l_{15} + \ldots + l_{65}) + 2\tfrac{1}{2}l_{70}.$$

(2)   The number of years lived after age 70, i.e. $l_{70}(e_{70})$.
      Thus:

$$e_0 = \tfrac{1}{2} + \frac{1}{l_0}\left[2\tfrac{1}{2}l_1 + 4\tfrac{1}{2}l_5 + 5(l_{10} + l_{15} + \ldots + l_{65}) + (e_{70}^0 + 2\tfrac{1}{2})l_{70}\right].$$

Introducing the values found into these expressions, the expectation of life at birth for 1938–9 comes out as $e_0 = 46\cdot3$, and for 1958 as $e_0 = 67\cdot8$.

These values confirm the impressions obtained from the comparison of infant mortality rates. There has been a considerable reduction in mortality between 1938–9 and 1958, or, more accurately, between 1945 and 1958. Mortality levels in the Soviet Union at present are close to those of the most advanced countries, whereas twenty years ago the expectation of life at birth was less than that found for France in 1900.

Problem 4

Comment on the age patterns of mortality in 1938–9.

Answer:

The comparisons that have been made appear to show that infant mortality in 1938 was higher than would have been expected from a knowledge of general mortality levels, given the expectation of life at birth. The order of magnitude of the infant mortality rate (0·185) is the same as in France before 1870, whereas the expectation of life at birth is comparable to that achieved in 1900, a period when infant mortality in France had already fallen considerably.

This distortion in the age pattern of mortality is confirmed by a rapid comparison with the Model Life Tables of the United Nations (see Table 4.5). The models used are those shown in *Population Studies* No. 22.

The nearest level of the Model Life Tables is Level 22 ($e_0 = 46\cdot8$ for both sexes combined). At this level $q_0 = 0\cdot150$, whereas the observed value in the Soviet Union was 0·185, a rate lying between Level 25 (0·180) and Level 26 (0·190). The value of $_4q_1$ is greatly in excess of that given

Table 4.5 *Mortality in the Soviet Union and in UN Model Life Tables*

Function	Value in Model Life Table $e_0 = 46\cdot8$ (Level 22)	Situation in the Soviet Union 1938	
		Computed values $e_0 = 46\cdot3$	Nearest level of Model Life Table with similar q-values
q_0	0·150	0·185	25–26
$_4q_1$	0·0747	0·1074	26
$_5q_5$	0·0235	0·0272	23–24
$_5q_{10}$	0·0166	0·0129	18–19
$_nq_x$ $(x>10)$			$>13, >20$

by the Model Life Table with Level 22, and corresponds closely to that defined by Level 26. There is still some relative excess mortality between ages 5 and 10, and it is only after age 10 that the probabilities are consistently lower than those given by Level 22. Thus, the relatively high mortality in the USSR immediately before the Second World War was due to a particularly high death rate among children aged less than 10. If mortality at these ages had corresponded to the level of adult mortality, the expectation of life at birth would have been five to seven years higher (Model Life Table Level 19 represents Soviet mortality after age 10 fairly well, and yields $e_0 = 52\cdot7$).

Problem 5

Compare your abridged life table for 1958 with the tables for 1958–9 published by Soviet statisticians in 1962.

Answer

Life tables for the period 1958–9 were computed and published by Soviet statisticians in 1962, following the publication of age-specific death rates for 1958. It is therefore possible to compare the life table obtained in answer to previous problems with those of calculations that might be expected to be more accurate. It is true that the periods to which the two calculations relate are not exactly the same, but the differences should not be great.

The official Soviet publications contain a separate life table for each sex, and one for both sexes combined. It can easily be demonstrated that the third table has not been calculated as an appropriately weighted average of the separate tables for each sex. The expectation of life at birth for both sexes combined is given as 68·6 years. A weighted average of the expectations for each separate sex, with weights 0·512 and 0·488 respectively, corresponding to the sex ratio at birth, yields $(0\cdot512 \times 64\cdot4) + (0\cdot488 \times 71\cdot7) = 68\cdot0$. Without much difficulty it is possible to establish that the table for both sexes combined has been computed from probabilities of dying in the various age groups of the population taken as a whole. Because there is a large deficit of men at ages over 31 (see Chapter 3), the probabilities calculated in this way are significantly lower than would have been the case if the normal method of weighted averaging had been used in which the age composition is that resulting from two associated stationary populations for each sex, with 105 male births for every 100 female births. This method gives greater weight to the higher mortality of men than is the case when using the actual sex structure of the Soviet population with its abnormally high proportion of women beyond the age of 31, as a result of wars and internal disturbances. This is the reason why the expectation of life at birth for both sexes combined, estimated by the Soviet statisticians, is higher than would have been obtained by the normal method (68·6 against 68·0 years).

Which of the tables should be compared with the table calculated in answer to a previous problem for 1958? This table was computed by using probabilities of dying for both sexes in combination and will therefore reproduce the same situation as the table constructed by the Soviet statisticians. If, therefore, the purpose of the exercise were to test the accuracy of the method of computation, the proper comparison is with the Soviet table for both sexes combined.

But there is some interest in comparing the table with the table for both sexes computed by the weighted average method. In Table 4.6 are given three values, one for the table computed above, one for the official Soviet table and one for the table calculated by the weighted average method. For the sake of simplicity only probabilities of dying are shown, together with expectations of life at birth and at age 70.

Table 4.6 *Probabilities of dying, USSR, both sexes combined (computations using different methods)*

Age x	$0.512\ l_x^m$	$0.488\ l_x^f$	l_x	$_n d_x$	$_n q_x$ 1958–9 (a)	$_n q_x$ 1958–9 (b)	$_n q_x$ 1958
0			10 000	407	0·0407	0·0406	0·0406
1	4893	4700	9 593	152	0·0158	0·0158	0·0143
5	4814	4627	9 441	49	0·0052	0·0057	0·0055
10	4783	4605	9 392	43	0·0046	0·0046	0·0046
15	4760	4589	9 349	57	0·0061	0·0062	0·0065
20	4723	4568	9 291	84	0·0090	0·0090	0·0090
25	4668	4539	9 207	101	0·0110	0·0108	0·0109
30	4600	4506	9 106	119	0·0131	0·0126	0·0129
35	4519	4468	8 987	148	0·0165	0·0153	0·0154
40	4420	4419	8 839	190	0·0215	0·0199	0·0203
45	4293	4356	8 649	248	0·0287	0·0265	0·0267
50	4127	4274	8 401	354	0·0421	0·0386	0·0393
55	3889	4158	8 047	498	0·0619	0·0560	0·0532
60	3556	3993	7 549	672	0·0890	0·0816	0·0813
65	3126	3751	6 877	891	0·1296	0·1231	0·1113
70	2607	3379	5 986				
e_{70}					12·3	12·6	11
e_0					68·0	68·6	67·8

Series (a) is obtained by the normal method from the preceding columns of the table. Series (b) is that given in the Soviet tables for both sexes combined. All computations are based on a radix of 10 000.

There is good agreement between Series (b) and the table calculated for 1958. Many of the $_n q_x$ values are practically identical, and the only important discrepancies found are those for the age groups 1–5 and 65–70 years. At age 70 the expectation of life used, which is taken from the French life table for 1950–1, is considerably lower than that given by the Soviet table. However, the difference is probably spurious, for it is known that mortality at advanced ages is underestimated in the USSR.[1]

The differences between the q_x values are not important and could have been caused by differences in the statistical information on which the two calculations are based. The very good agreement of the table as a whole indicates that the approximate method used for computing abridged life tables gives acceptable results, which may be used in place of the original data for purposes of comparison.

The differences between Series (a) and Series (b) arise because after the age of 30 the q_x values in Series (a) are systematically higher than in Series (b) – often considerably so. Between the ages of 50 and 65 the excess is of the order of 10%. This is in accordance with expectation and bears out the remarks made above regarding the computational procedures used.

[1]See R. Pressat, 'Les premières tables de mortalité de l'Union soviétique (1958–9)', *Population* (1963), No. 1.

5

The comparison of mortality

This chapter deals with the methods commonly used to compare the mortalities of populations as a whole. In the examples given the age patterns of mortality will be very different from one another, but the crude death rates of the populations will be close. In at least one of the examples considered, any attempt to differentiate between the general mortality levels of the populations would be virtually useless.

It will become apparent that it is frequently preferable to carry out elaborate analyses in order to arrive at qualified conclusions, rather than to use procedures of limited scope with the intention of drawing final conclusions.

Data

It is proposed to compare the mortality of one population, *D*, in which the level of living is high, with that of a population, *U*, belonging to an undeveloped country. Table 5.1 gives the sex-age-specific death rates for the two populations.

Table 5.1 *Age-specific death rates*

	D		U	
Age	*Males*	*Females*	*Males*	*Females*
0	0·0332	0·0255	0·0542	0·0411
1–4	0·0012	0·0010	0·0033	0·0035
5–14	0·0006	0·0004	0·0009	0·0006
15–24	0·0015	0·0006	0·0013	0·0009
25–34	0·0019	0·0011	0·0027	0·0017
35–44	0·0037	0·0022	0·0041	0·0031
45–54	0·0097	0·0051	0·0073	0·0050
55–64	0·0229	0·0118	0·0158	0·0099
65–74	0·0516	0·0307	0·0345	0·0245
75–84	0·1013	0·0751	0·0697	0·0554
85+	0·2026	0·2025	0·1985	0·1618

Problem 1

Compare these data diagrammatically, using a semi-logarithmic scale. Comment.

Answer

The data of Table 5.1 have been plotted in Figs. 5.1 and 5.2. Rates at age 0 have been interpreted as central death rates, and not as infant mortality rates. Thus the diagram begins at age 0·5, midway between birth and 1st birthday. Unless the rates are interpreted in this way, Problem 3 in this chapter will not make sense. The rates of the last, open age group have been omitted from

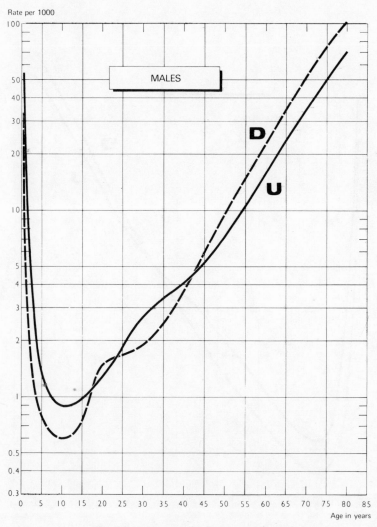

Fig. 5.1 *Age-specific death rates (males)*

the diagram, because it is not possible to attach a central age to this group. Moreover, these rates do not reflect age-specific mortality as well as do the others.

At younger ages the death rates in *U* exceed those of *D*. After the age of 45 for males and 50 for females the order is reversed. The situation for males is further complicated by the abnormally high age-specific rates for the age group 15–24 in *D*. Mortality in *U* is lower in this group; the high mortality level in *D* is probably due to accidental deaths. Note that in the later stages of life the lower mortality of *U* relative to *D* is more pronounced among men than among women. This would suggest that the general level of mortality of males in the two populations is more alike; among females *D* appears to show a generally lower mortality. This point will be discussed further below.

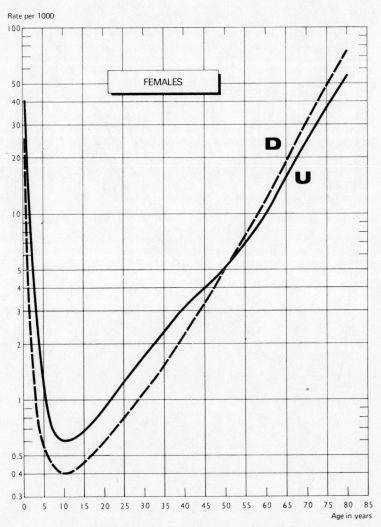

Fig. 5.2   *Age-specific death rates (females)*

Problem 2

Compare the general level of mortality in the two countries: (i) by applying the sex-age-specific death rates of D to population U, (ii) by applying the sex-age-specific death rates of U to population D. The sex-age structure of U is shown in Table 5.2. Population D is that of the United States on 1 July 1959. Comment.

Table 5.2 *Sex-age structure of population U,*
1 July 1959

Age	Males	Females
0	35 700	34 800
1– 4	143 900	140 000
5–14	328 100	320 600
15–24	202 400	216 200
25–34	120 700	142 200
35–44	114 700	123 300
45–54	93 600	87 200
55–64	63 500	60 400
65–74	50 200	47 600
75–84	9 000	12 800
85 and over	900	1 700

Answer

The procedure is, of course, that of standardization: it consists of applying the age-specific death rates of the two populations to be compared to a standard population. In this example the standard population is actually one of the two populations to be compared. In Method 2(a) U will be the standard population, in Method 2(b) it will be D.

Because the total numbers of deaths in populations D and U are not given, and because the two sexes must be compared separately, there will be altogether eight series of calculations, which are shown in Table 5.4.

Table 5.3 shows the crude death rates corresponding to the various possible combinations of age-specific death rates and populations. The principal diagonals of these tables show the differences between the actual death rates of these two populations: 0·01078 and 0·00798 for D, against 0·00687 and 0·00515 for U.

Table 5.3 *Death rates per 1000 population*

		Males		Females	
		D	U	D	U
Age-specific rates of	D	0·01078	0·00736	0·00798	0·00475
	U	0·00912	0·00687	0·00746	0·00515
Conclusion		$U_m < D_m$	$U_m < D_m$	$U_f < D_f$	$U_f > D_f$

The remaining entries are the standardized death rates. For males, whatever population is used as a standard, the advantage always lies with population U. For females the use of different

Table 5.4 Calculation of total number of deaths in the different populations with various age-specific death rates
(all numbers given in 000s)

	Males						Females				
Death rate D	Population D		Population U		Age	Death rate D	Population D		Population U		
	No.	Deaths	No.	Deaths			No.	Deaths	No.	Deaths	
0·0332	1930	64076	35·7	1185	0	0·0255	1865	47558	34·8	887	
0·0012	8152	9782	143·9	173	1– 4	0·0010	7849	7849	140·0	140	
0·0006	17941	10765	328·1	197	5–14	0·0004	17191	6876	320·6	128	
0·0015	12201	18302	202·4	304	15–24	0·0006	11917	7150	216·2	130	
0·0019	11404	21668	120·7	229	25–34	0·0011	11638	12802	142·2	156	
0·0037	11634	43046	114·7	424	35–44	0·0022	12149	26728	123·3	271	
0·0097	10026	97252	93·6	908	45–54	0·0051	10468	53387	87·2	445	
0·0229	7396	169368	63·5	1454	55–64	0·0118	7962	93952	60·4	713	
0·0516	4667	240817	50·2	2590	65–74	0·0307	5361	164583	47·6	1461	
0·1013	1940	196522	9·0	912	75–84	0·0751	2553	191730	12·8	961	
0·2026	359	72733	0·9	182	85 +	0·2025	499	101048	1·7	344	
	87650	944331	1162·7	8558			89452	713662	1186·8	5637	
		0·01078		0·00736				0·00798		0·00475	

	Males						Females				
Death rate U	Population D		Population U		Age	Death rate U	Population D		Population U		
	No.	Deaths	No.	Deaths			No.	Deaths	No.	Deaths	
0·0542	1930	104606	35·7	1935	0	0·0411	1865	76652	34·8	1430	
0·0033	8152	26902	143·9	475	1– 4	0·0035	7849	27472	140·0	490	
0·0009	17941	16147	328·1	295	5–14	0·0006	17191	10315	320·6	192	
0·0013	12201	15861	202·4	263	15–24	0·0009	11917	10725	216·2	195	
0·0027	11404	30791	120·7	326	25–34	0·0017	11638	19785	142·2	242	
0·0041	11634	47699	114·7	470	35–44	0·0031	12149	37662	123·3	382	
0·0073	10026	73190	93·6	683	45–54	0·0050	10468	52340	87·2	436	
0·0158	7396	116857	63·5	1003	55–64	0·0099	7962	78824	60·4	598	
0·0345	4667	161012	50·2	1732	65–74	0·0245	5361	131344	47·6	1166	
0·0697	1940	135218	9·0	627	75–84	0·0554	2553	141436	12·8	709	
0·1985	359	71262	0·9	179	85 +	0·1618	499	80738	1·7	275	
	87650	799544	1162·7	7988			89452	667292	1186·8	6116	
		0·00912		0·00687				0·00746		0·0515	

standard populations yields different results. Such indeterminacy can always arise unless all the age-specific death rates in one population are lower than those in the corresponding age groups in the other. It becomes more likely if the ratios of the age-specific death rates in different age groups vary greatly. Thus, whereas in the case of males population U has a lower mortality than D, this conclusion is much less certain in the case of females. This reinforces the conclusions reached in the previous problem, when the age-specific rates were compared diagrammatically.

Problem 3

Using the Reed-Merrell tables, convert the age-specific death rates in Table 5.1 (except those of the 0–1 age group) into probabilities of dying. For the age group 0–1 undertake this conversion by using the relation existing between the central death rate and q_0 in the stationary population.

Answer

In a stationary population the central death rate at age 0 (m_0) and the probability of dying before the 1st birthday (q_0) are related by the equation

$$q_0 = \frac{2m_0}{2+m_0}.$$

Table 5.5 shows the relationship in the four populations under consideration.

Table 5.5   *Computation of q_0 from m_0*

	D		U	
	Males	Females	Males	Females
m_0	0·0332	0·0255	0·0542	0·0411
$2m_0$	0·0664	0·0510	0·1084	0·0822
$2+m_0$	2·0332	2·0255	2·0542	2·0411
q_0	0·0327	0·0252	0·0528	0·0403

The procedure for transforming the other central death rates into probabilities of dying is well known. The results are given in the life tables, the construction of which is considered in the next exercise.

Problem 4

Compute the four life tables corresponding to the four series of probabilities of dying obtained in Problem 3. Compare the life tables.

Answer

The life tables shown in Table 5.6 are derived from the q_x functions that were obtained previously from the Reed-Merrell tables. The various survivorship functions (l_x) are plotted in Fig. 5.3.

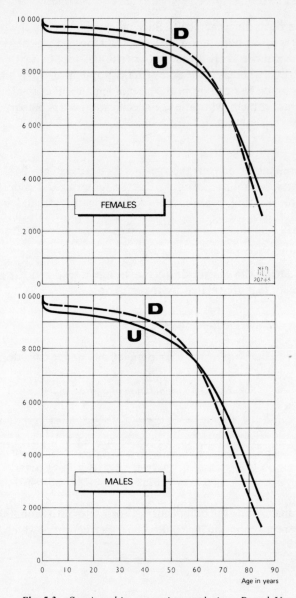

Fig. 5.3 *Survivorship curves in populations D and U*

The mortality of *U* is lower than that of *D* at the higher ages, and this permits the survival curves of *U*, which at first lie below those of *D*, to cross and finish above the *D* curves. In other words, to any age under about 60 (slightly less for men, slightly more for women) the probability of survival from birth is smaller in *U* than in *D*, but the reverse holds true for survival to higher ages. The chance of surviving to a very advanced age is thus higher for an inhabitant of *U* than for an inhabitant of *D*. This does not mean necessarily that the mortality of

Table 5.6 *Life tables by sex for populations D and U*

	D						U					
	Males			Females			Males			Females		
Age x	l_x	$_nq_x$	$_nd_x$	l_x	$_nq_x$	$_nd_x$	l_x	$_nq_x$	$_nd_x$	l_x	$_nq_x$	$_nd_x$
0	10 000	0·0327	327	10 000	0·0252	252	10 000	0·0528	528	10 000	0·0403	403
1	9 673	0·0048	46	9 748	0·0040	39	9 472	0·0131	124	9 597	0·0139	133
5	9 627	0·0060	58	9 709	0·0040	39	9 348	0·0090	84	9 464	0·0060	57
15	9 569	0·0149	143	9 670	0·0060	58	9 264	0·0130	121	9 407	0·0090	85
25	9 426	0·0188	177	9 612	0·0110	106	9 143	0·0267	244	9 322	0·0169	158
35	9 249	0·0364	337	9 506	0·0218	207	8 899	0·0403	359	9 164	0·0306	280
45	8 912	0·0931	829	9 299	0·0499	464	8 540	0·0708	605	8 884	0·0490	435
55	8 083	0·2080	1682	8 835	0·1123	992	7 935	0·1478	1173	8 449	0·0950	803
65	6 401	0·4157	2661	7 843	0·2699	2117	6 762	0·2985	2019	7 646	0·2210	1690
75	3 740	0·6655	2489	5 726	0·5489	3143	4 743	0·5209	2471	5 957	0·4393	2617
85	1 251			2 583			2 272			3 340		

U as a whole is lower than that of D. Standardization suggests that mortality in U as a whole is lower than in D for men, but does not lead to definite conclusions for women. Comparison will have to be continued by considering expectations of life at birth.

Problem 5

Compute the expectation of life at birth (e_0) for the four populations D_m, D_f, U_m and U_f, where the subscripts m and f stand for males and females respectively. It will be necessary to make some assumption about the expectation of life at age 85. For each of the populations assume two values of e_{85}^0 between which the unknown value is likely to lie. Calculate the corresponding four values of e_0^0 and justify your conclusion. What conclusions could be drawn about the median lengths of life?

Answer

The life tables in Table 5.6 terminate at birthday 85. It is necessary to make some assumption about the expectation of life at that age in order to obtain the expectation of life at birth.

In the absence of any information about this value in the four populations studied, it is necessary to use data from countries that have reliable statistics. These data relate to a wide range of periods in the past, and are thus likely to include the true values for the populations D and U. Except for France in 1952–6, where the tables calculated by the National Institute of Statistics were used, all the data considered have been taken from Paul Vincent's very thorough study[1] and are shown in Table 5.7.

***Table* 5.7**   *Expectation of life at birthday 85*

	Males	Females		Males	Females
France			*Switzerland*		
1920–9	3·14	3·60	1876–1914	3·09	3·25
1929–38	3·33	3·84	1912–48	3·30	3·63
1952–6	3·44	4·12			
Netherlands					
1910–25	3·58	3·85	Minimum	3·09	3·25
1925–39	3·73	3·95	Maximum	3·73	4·12

It will be seen that the differences between the minimum and maximum values are not very great (they are generally less than a year) and, by extending the range a little, 3 and 3·25 years will be taken as minimum values and 4 and 4·25 years as maximum values.

The mean expectation of life at birth is obtained from the equation

$$\frac{T_0}{l_0} = \frac{{}_{85}L_0 + T_{85}}{l_0}$$

where ${}_{85}L_0$ stands for the total number of years lived before birthday 85 and T_{85} for the number of years lived after that date.

[1] P. Vincent, 'La mortalité des vieillards', *Population* No. 2 (1951).

Moreover, $T_{85} = e_{85} l_{85}$, and

$$_{85}L_0 = l_1 + 4l_5 + 10(l_{15} + l_{25} + \ldots + l_{85}) + \tfrac{1}{2}(l_0 - l_1) + 2(l_1 - l_5)$$
$$+ 5(l_5 - l_{15} + l_{15} - l_{25} + \ldots + l_{75} - l_{85}),$$

which reduces to

$$_{85}L_0 = \tfrac{1}{2}l_0 + 2\tfrac{1}{2}l_1 + 7l_5 + 10(l_{15} + l_{25} + \ldots + l_{75}) + 5l_{85}.$$

These formulae lead to Table 5.8.

Table 5.8 *Calculation of expectation of life at birth*

	D		U	
	D_m	D_f	U_m	U_f
$\tfrac{1}{2}l_0$	5 000	5 000	5 000	5 000
$2\tfrac{1}{2}l_1$	24 182	24 370	23 680	23 992
$7l_5$	67 389	67 963	65 436	66 248
$10(l_{15} + \ldots + l_{75})$	553 800	604 910	552 860	588 290
$5l_{85}$	6 255	12 915	11 365	16 700
	656 626	715 158	658 336	700 230
Minimum value of T_{85}	3 753	8 395	6 819	10 855
Maximum value of T_{85}	5 004	10 978	9 092	14 195
Minimum value of T_0	660 379	723 553	665 155	711 085
Maximum value of T_0	661 630	726 136	667 428	714 425

The expectation of life at birth in D is between 66 and 66·2 years for males; the figures for U are between 66·5 and 66·7 years. For females the corresponding figures are between 72·4 and 72·6 years in D and between 71·1 and 71·4 years in U.

Thus, with an obvious notation, we have

$$D_m < U_m \qquad D_f > U_f$$

and the indeterminacy of the expectation of life data at age 85 makes no difference to these inequalities. Female life expectancy varies more between the two countries than does that of males. This makes it possible to come to firmer conclusions than before on the difference in general mortality, but the new results agree with our previous conclusions.

If the populations are arranged in order of median length of life, the value for U is higher than that for D, both for men and women. This may be seen from Fig. 5.3 by reading off the age corresponding to the 5000th survivor on each of the curves.

Though the information about the two populations is scanty, it may be concluded that two populations with very different standards of living may yet exhibit very similar overall mortality. The differences in age patterns are particularly interesting: mortality is lower at younger ages and higher at advanced ages in the population with the higher level of living. Male mortality is particularly favourable in the less developed country.

In the next chapter a study of mortality differences between northern and southern Italy will yield very similar results.

6

Mortality in northern and southern Italy, 1951–2

In this chapter life tables will be used to measure and compare different patterns of mortality. Life tables have become more useful for this purpose, since model life tables which may serve as standards have been constructed. The use of such model life tables is illustrated by an application to Italian regional life tables.

Data

Life tables for the period 1951–2 have been constructed for northern and southern Italy. The l_x functions from these tables are shown in Table 6.1.

Problem 1

Calculate the expectation of life at birth in the four populations. Arrange the populations in increasing order of expectation of life at birth and in increasing order of median length of life. Compare and comment.

Answer

The expectation of life at birth may be obtained by applying the formula:

$$e_0 = \tfrac{1}{2} + \frac{2\tfrac{1}{2}l_1 + 4\tfrac{1}{2}l_5 + 5(l_{10} + l_{15} + \ldots)}{l_0}.$$

The final age given in these tables is very high, and may effectively be considered as the last birthday, divisible by 5, attained by the different cohorts.

The median length of life may be obtained by linear interpolation on the l_x function. It is necessary to find M, such that $l_M = 50\,000$. For northern Italian males the median length of life

Table 6.1

	Northern Italy		Southern Italy	
Age	Males	Females	Males	Females
0	100 000	100 000	100 000	100 000
1	94 429	95 543	91 758	92 457
5	93 415	94 603	89 496	90 105
10	93 018	94 286	88 977	89 684
15	92 674	94 039	88 576	89 320
20	92 134	93 686	87 982	88 842
25	91 413	93 199	87 197	88 202
30	90 559	92 614	86 332	87 425
35	89 547	91 874	85 382	86 532
40	88 248	90 954	84 282	85 497
45	86 311	89 673	82 763	84 189
50	83 266	87 800	80 493	82 432
55	78 814	85 081	77 043	79 926
60	72 628	81 016	72 083	76 224
65	64 429	74 832	65 308	70 493
70	53 410	65 084	55 992	61 536
75	39 096	50 765	43 412	48 241
80	23 245	32 891	27 964	31 566
85	9 995	16 032	13 166	15 682
90	2 761	5 338	3 980	5 385
95	439	11 016	614	952
100	31	77	29	48

lies between 70 and 75 years, for $l_{70} = 53\,410$ and $l_{75} = 39\,096$; here M may be obtained from the formula:

$$M = 70 + 5\frac{l_{70} - 50\,000}{l_{70} - l_{75}} = 70 + \frac{5 \times 3410}{14\,314} = 71 \cdot 19.$$

The results are grouped together in Table 6.2 and are plotted in Fig. 6.1 for easier comparison.

Table 6.2　Mean and median length of life in Italy

	Males		Females	
	e_0	M	e_0	M
Northern Italy	64·67	71·19	69·16	75·21
Southern Italy	63·40	72·38	65·47	74·34

The direction of the differences between northern and southern Italy depends on whether the mean or the median length of life is compared: for males the mean length of life is shorter in southern Italy, but the median length is longer. The median length of life is in each case greater than the mean. The difference between north and south among females is much smaller between the medians than between the means. The reason why the differences for females are in the same directions for the medians and the means is that the difference in mean length of life is much larger among women: 3·69 years as against 1·27 years for men. Variation in mean lengths of life is greater than in median lengths.

The explanation for these differences lies in the fact that, in determining the median length of life, the age of the 50 000th death is taken (if $l_0 = 100\,000$). This age depends on the distribution of the 49 999 deaths that precede it, but much less so than the mean length of life. A particular value for the age of the 50 000th death is compatible with many different distributions of the first 49 999 deaths, which would yield quite different mean lengths of life.

In particular, it is possible to imagine a situation in which mortality is heavy at young ages, and particularly in the first year of life, but where this heavy mortality is compensated for by relatively low mortality in adult life. The median length of life might then be the same as in the

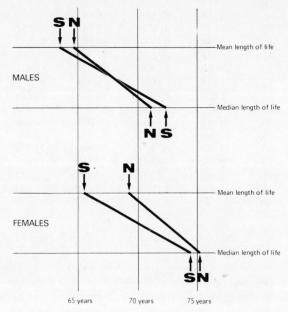

Fig. 6.1   *Mean and median length of life in northern Italy (N) and southern Italy (S), 1951–2*

case of a situation with a relatively low mortality at young ages, coupled with relatively high mortality of adults. But, in the second case, the mean length of life would be considerably higher. A displacement of deaths towards the older ages leads to an increase in the total number of years of life lived by the cohort, which has to be divided by the initial number of the cohort. Many other variations are possible, each of which will lead to differences between the mean and the median, which may be large or small.

The study of the age pattern of mortality, dealt with below, will illustrate the situation in the example studied.

Problem 2

Compare the mortality levels in the four populations, as measured by the expectation of life at birth, with those in the United Nations Model Life Table (UN *Population Studies* No. 22). What conclusions can be drawn about the mortality of northern and southern Italy?

Answer

A comparison between the mean lengths of life found in answer to the previous problem and the corresponding figures in the UN system of Model Life Tables is shown in Table 6.3. The Model Life Tables used are more detailed than those given in *Population Studies* No. 25. The range of life expectancies is much the same in both systems of tables, but there are forty tables in the former system and only twenty-five in the latter. The system of tables in *Population Studies* No. 22 is better adapted to mortality comparisons than that of No. 25, which was constructed specifically for the purpose of population forecasts.

Table 6.3   *Mean length of life and Model Life Tables*

	Males	Females
Northern Italy	64·67 (7: 64·33)	69·16 (6: 69·34)
Southern Italy	63·40 (8: 63·59)	65·47 (10: 65·30)

The first figure in each bracket is the level of the Model Life Table whose expectation of life is nearest to that found; the second figure is the expectation of life at birth in the Model Life Table.

These Model Life Tables, which have been computed from 158 national tables, yield norms for the sex-age pattern of mortality. Associated with each Model Life Table for the two sexes combined are two Model Life Tables, one for each sex, bearing the same number. The relations between male and female expectations of life in the table with the same index number define the norm of male excess mortality at different levels. Thus Level 17 for both sexes combined yields an expectation of life at birth of 56·72 years. The corresponding Level 17 table for males gives 55·20 years and for females 58·04 years. This means that at Level 17 male excess mortality leads to an excess in female length of life of 2·84 ($= 58·04 - 55·20$) years.

To compare sex-specific mortality in northern and southern Italy, it is necessary to find the level at which expectation of life at birth is closest to that which has been calculated. This is done in Table 6.3. The excess male mortality in the table should be nearly the same as the excess mortality found, if the mortality patterns for the two sexes are described by the same model. This is the case neither for northern nor for southern Italy. In the north male excess mortality is very high. Male mortality corresponds to Level 7, female mortality to Level 6, which is considerably more favourable.

In southern Italy, on the other hand, the relationship between male and female mortality is quite different. Male mortality approximates to Level 8, which is considerably more favourable than Level 10, the nearest to the mortality of women. Differences between male and female life expectancies at birth are small (2·07 years) and much lower than those usually observed. Fig. 6.2 shows the relationship between the actual excess mortalities and those in the Model Life Tables. The two points relating to the same region have a different abscissa, unlike the Model Life Tables which are constructed in such a way that the abscissa for the two sexes is the same.

Problem 3

Compare the Italian tables with the Model Life Tables by calculating probabilities of death at different ages: q_0, $_4q_1$, and then $_5q_x$, for $x = 5, 10, 15, \ldots 80$, to three significant figures. Plot

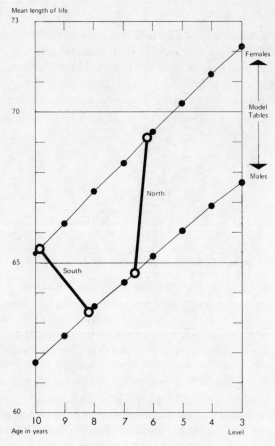

Fig. 6.2 *Mean length of life in northern and southern Italy (1951–2) and according to Model Life Tables*

these data on semi-logarithmic paper. Draw the two curves for males and for females on the same system of coordinate axes. Compare and comment.

Answer

The probabilities of death associated with life tables may be computed from the equation:

$$_nq_x = \frac{l_x - l_{x+n}}{l_x}.$$

The results are shown in Table 6.4. If it is desired to plot the age-specific mortality since birth, it is necessary to substitute $_5q_0$ for the two values q_0 and $_4q_1$ respectively, where $_5q_0$ is computed in the same way as the other probabilities.

The values of $_5q_0$ are as follows:

North: Males 0·0658   Females 0·0540
South: Males 0·105   Females 0·0989

Table 6.4   *Probabilities of dying in northern and southern Italy, 1951–2*

| Age | Males | | Females | |
x	Northern Italy	Southern Italy	Northern Italy	Southern Italy
0	0·0557	0·0824	0·0446	0·0754
1	0·0107	0·0247	0·00984	0·0254
5	0·00425	0·00580	0·00335	0·00489
10	0·00370	0·00451	0·00262	0·00384
15	0·00583	0·00671	0·00375	0·00535
20	0·00783	0·00892	0·00520	0·00720
25	0·00934	0·00992	0·00628	0·00881
30	0·0112	0·0110	0·00799	0·0102
35	0·0145	0·0129	0·0100	0·0120
40	0·0219	0·0180	0·0141	0·0153
45	0·0353	0·0274	0·0209	0·0209
50	0·0535	0·0429	0·0310	0·0304
55	0·0785	0·0644	0·0478	0·0463
60	0·113	0·0940	0·0763	0·0752
65	0·171	0·143	0·130	0·127
70	0·268	0·225	0·220	0·216
75	0·405	0·356	0·352	0·346
80	0·570	0·529	0·513	0·503

The difference in the mortality pattern between the north and the south is clearly apparent in the graphs of Figs. 6.3*a* and 6.3*b*. Mortality in the south is higher at younger ages, both among men and among women (up to age 30 for men and up to age 45 for women), and is lower thereafter. But the difference in mortality is not identical for the two sexes. The northern advantage at younger ages is less pronounced for men than for women. At older ages, on the other hand, the advantage of the south is greater for men than for women.

Thus, with advancing age, there is a reversal in the relative mortality situation between the north and the south of Italy. However, the overall mortality of men, as measured by life expectancy at birth, is not very different between the two regions, but for women the advantage of the south at higher ages is not sufficient to compensate for the higher mortalities experienced in early life.

As was shown in Table 6.2, life expectancy at birth in the two regions is nearly equal for men, and the median expectations of life are in the opposite rank order to the mean expectations; among women, on the other hand, the differences between north and south are quite considerable, and the relative mortalities of the two regions are in the same order, irrespective of whether mean or median expectations are compared.

Problem 4

What level among the Model Life Tables yields probabilities of death nearest to the values found in the preceding answer? Describe the mortality pattern in northern and southern Italy in the light of these figures.

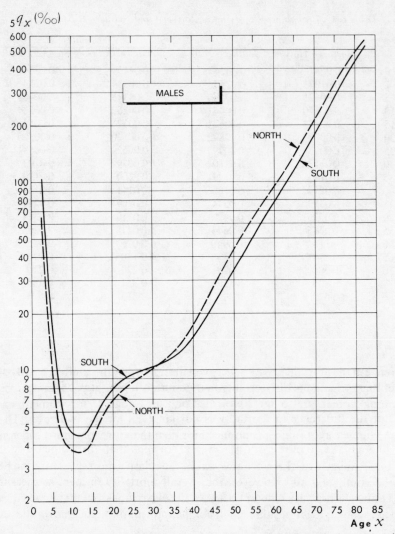

Fig. 6.3a *Five-yearly probabilities of dying in northern and southern Italy, 1951–2 (males)*

Answer

The examination of the age pattern of mortality in the two regions of Italy will be continued by finding that Model Life Table for which q_x values are closest to those calculated for northern and southern Italy. The procedure is similar to that adopted in Problem 2 for comparing expectations of life at birth, and the comparisons are shown in Table 6.5.

These data confirm the conclusions reached in the answer to Problem 3, but make it possible to examine the patterns in greater detail.

The reversal in the relative levels of male mortality after a certain age is seen to be due to an abnormally high mortality at ages under 5 in the south, and to a high mortality at ages over 40

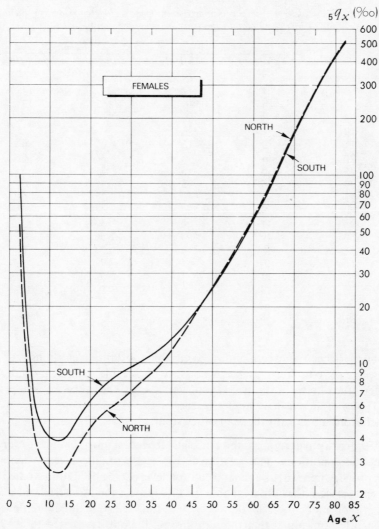

Fig. 6.3b   *Five-yearly probabilities of dying in northern and southern Italy, 1951–2 (females)*

in the north, though it is possible that the age pattern of mortality in one of the populations may have been close to that of the Model Life Table at all ages, and that only the age pattern of the second population was anomalous.

For women, the situation at the younger ages is very similar to that among men. In both parts of the country female mortality at these ages is relatively higher than that of males, in the sense of corresponding to a higher Level Model Life Table. At older ages female mortality in the north is described by a lower level table than that of males. Relative mortality does not begin to rise, in the sense described, until after women had reached the age of 55, whereas among men the rise becomes apparent after their 40th birthday. On the other hand, the older women in the

Table 6.5   *Model Life Table Levels approximating most closely to the expectation of life at birth and to q_x values in northern and southern Italy*

	Males		Females	
	North Italy	South Italy	North Italy	South Italy
All ages (e_0)	7	8	6	10
0	7	12	7	14
1	4	10	5	12
5	3	6	4	7
10	4	6	4	7
15	3	5	2	6
20	3	5	3	6
25	5	5	3	6
30	6	5	3	6
35	7	5	3	6
40	9	5	4	6
45	11	4	5	5
50	12	4	5	4
55	12	4	7	6
60	10	11	7	7
65	11	1	9	8
70	14	1	12	11
75	17	6	15	14
80	18	12	17	15

south do not experience the exceptionally favourable mortality conditions that apply to the men: after the age of 70 their experience is not very favourable. Female mortality in later life does not differ much between the two regions, and, as age advances, it is approximated by Model Life Tables of increasingly higher levels.

These conclusions agree with those of other studies.

1 The level of mortality at early ages, and especially the infant mortality rate, is very sensitive to socio-economic conditions. The relationship is less with the level of living (economic conditions proper) than with the general cultural level of the population studied and with the type of social services that are available. In this respect the industrialized and urbanized northern region is much more favourably placed than the rural and underdeveloped south.

2 It has frequently been found that the mortality of the old has ceased to fall in developed countries. In some areas, indeed, there has been an increase in recent years, following a long period of decline (Norway is an example). Mortality in later life is often higher than in economically less advanced populations, where a traditional way of life persists, and where the degree of urbanization and industrialization is low. The example of northern and southern Italy illustrates this kind of contrast. Two hypotheses have been put forward in explanation. It has been suggested that the stresses of life in industrialized societies have led to an increase in cardio-vascular disease. Alternatively, the very success in the struggle against premature death has led to a situation where those individuals who survive to an advanced age are particularly vulnerable, especially if their survival has been due to therapeutic measures which have postponed death. For this reason the fall in mortality rates in later life may cease and, indeed, give way to an increase. The argument is sometimes put

much more crudely: the effects of natural selection, which operated in the past through mortality in early life, no longer apply because of preventive measures.

In the case under consideration a climatic factor may also be relevant, the climate in southern Italy being more favourable than that in the north.

The present study is purely descriptive and does not permit definite conclusions to be reached, since the data are limited. But it is significant that the conclusions previously reached are confirmed when mortality differences between regions of the same country are studied.

Problem 5

What would be the expectation of life at birth among men in southern Italy, if mortality rates at ages 0–5 were the same as those that apply in the north?

Answer

Mortality in early life, particularly among those under 5 years of age, is the only black spot in the mortality of males in the south. It may be expected that, if excess mortality at these ages were eliminated, the general level of male mortality would be satisfactory. It is therefore of interest to calculate the expectation of life at birth for southern males on the assumption that up to their 5th birthday they were subjected to the more normal level of mortality as in the north of Italy. Writing l' for survivors in the north Italian table, and l'' for those in the southern table, the formula

$$e_0 = \tfrac{1}{2} + \frac{2\tfrac{1}{2}l_1 + 4\tfrac{1}{2}l_5 + 5(l_{10} + l_{15} + \ldots)}{l_0}$$

may be applied, by substituting for l_1 and l_5 the northern Italian values l'_1 and l'_5. From age 5 onwards the southern values are used, multiplied by an appropriate fraction to compensate for the effect of having used northern mortality up to that age. The fraction is given by

$$\frac{l'_5}{l''_5} = \frac{93\,415}{89\,496} = 1 \cdot 043\,79$$

and therefore:

$$l_{10} = \frac{l'_5}{l''_5}\, l''_{10},$$

$$l_{15} = \frac{l'_5}{l''_5}\, l''_{15},\ \text{etc.}$$

Finally,

$$e_0 = \tfrac{1}{2} + \frac{2\tfrac{1}{2}l'_1 + 4\tfrac{1}{2}l'_5 + 5 \times 1 \cdot 043\,79 (l''_{10} + l''_{15} + \ldots)}{100\,000}.$$

This formula consists entirely of known quantities. It is found that $e_0 = 66 \cdot 12$ years against the previously calculated value of $63 \cdot 40$ years. The gain in longevity is therefore $2 \cdot 72$ years and shows the importance of mortality in early life for the determination of life expectancy at birth.

III

SOME QUESTIONS ON MORTALITY

7

The disappearance of exogenous deaths in a population

In low-mortality populations most deaths take place at advanced ages, so that 'exogenous' deaths[1] have virtually disappeared. In the first three problems a situation is considered in which there are virtually no such deaths and where the level of mortality is lower than has been observed in most advanced countries. As the life table associated with this level of mortality is very simple, relationships between some of the variables of the table and the associated stationary population become easily apparent.

The two stationary populations considered give an indication of the possible future course of human mortality, though the second model studied in Problem 4 must be regarded as a very long-term projection.

Data

In a population with constant annual numbers of births, mortality has fallen to a level where 'exogenous' deaths have virtually disappeared. The infant mortality rate is 10 per 1000, and mortality between the 1st and 20th birthdays is zero.

Problem 1

If the expectation of life at age 20 is 60 years, what is the expectation of life at birth?

Answer

In Table 7.1 a mortality level which is consistent with the assumptions postulated (the value of

---

[1] *Translator's note:* The French terms *mortalité exogène* and *mortalité endogène* are not really translatable, but have been rendered as 'exogenous' and 'endogenous' mortality respectively. The expression *mortalité endogène* is used for deaths caused by congenital and degenerative diseases which are regarded as an indication of the biological minimum level of mortality. *Mortalité exogène* refers to all other deaths. This dichotomy has not been completely accepted by English-speaking demographers.

e_{60} is obtained from later calculations) is shown and compared with similar populations which have experienced exceptionally low mortality – namely, female populations in Norway, and the 'select' table of Bourgeois-Pichat, constructed on the assumption of no 'exogenous' deaths at all. The situation in Table 7.1 is practically identical with that described by Bourgeois-Pichat, except for the difference in the value of e_{60}. The Norwegian female life table for 1956–60 is the national table showing the lowest mortality levels observed so far, and does not differ greatly from the other two tables. As mortality continues to fall, Norwegian females could expect to experience death rates even lower than those shown in the other two tables, because these apply to both sexes combined (this is explicitly stated by Bourgeois-Pichat).

Table 7.1   *Some indices of mortality*

Age x	Table studied in this problem	Survivors Norwegian females 1956–60	'Select' table of Bourgeois-Pichat
0	10 000	10 000	10 000
1	9 900	9 827	9 890
20	9 900	9 751	9 875
e_{20}	60	57·49	58·2
60 $\{ l_{60}$	9 000	8 928	9 036
$\{ e_{60}$	23·6	20·06	20·8

The expectation of life at birth may be obtained from e_{20} by writing:

$$e_0 = \frac{{}_{20}L_0 + l_{20}e_{20}}{l_0}$$

where ${}_{20}L_0$ stands for the total number of years lived by the members of the cohort in the table between birth and their 20th birthdays. If

$$l_0 = 1000, \quad {}_{20}L_0 = 995 + 19 \times 990 = 19\,805,$$

whence

$$e_0 = \frac{19\,805 + 60 \times 990}{1000} = 79\cdot2.$$

The Norwegian table gives $e_0 = 75\cdot57$ and Bourgeois-Pichat's 'select' table gives $e_0 = 77\cdot2$.

Problem 2

Ninety per cent of all new-born children survive to their 60th birthday. Obtain an upper and lower limit for e_{60}.

Answer

Because the values of e_{20}, l_{20} and l_{60} are given, this puts certain constraints on e_{60}. It is obvious that

$$e_{20} = \frac{{}_{40}L_{20} + 900e_{60}}{990}$$

where $_{40}L_{20}$ stands for the number of years lived by the members of the cohort between their 20th and 60th birthdays. Given l_{20} and l_{60}, and remembering that the difference between these two values is small, means that $_{40}L_{20}$ does not vary greatly for different distributions of the ninety deaths taking place between these two ages $(l_{20}-l_{60}=90)$. Extreme values may be obtained as follows:

1 On the assumption that all the deaths take place immediately after the 20th birthday.
2 On the assumption that all the deaths take place immediately before the 60th birthday.

Assumption 1 yields

$$_{40}L_{20} = 40 \times 990 = 39\,600.$$

Assumption 2 yields

$$_{40}L_{20} = 40 \times 900 = 36\,000.$$

Because

$$e_{60} = \frac{990 \times 60 - {}_{40}L_{20}}{900},$$

the substitution of the extreme values gives $e_{60} = 22$ years and $e_{60} = 26$ years respectively.

These values are, of course, purely theoretical. It would have been possible to make some reasonable assumption about the mean length of life of those dying between the ages of 20 and 60, and thus to obtain an acceptable value for e_{60}. This is done in the following problem.

Problem 3

Find e_{60} on the assumption that those dying between ages 20 and 60 have lived on average for three-fifths of that period. Find the limiting age structure of this population in three large age groups: 0–19 years, 20–59 years, and 60 years and over. Find the birth rate of this population.

Answer

If it is assumed that the ninety members of the cohort dying between their 20th and 60th birthdays have lived on average for $40 \times 0.6 = 24$ years, it follows that $_{40}L_{20} = 900 \times 40 + 90 \times 24 = 38\,160$. Hence,

$$e_{60} = \frac{990 \times 60 - 38\,160}{900} = 23.6 \text{ years.}$$

If T_x denotes the population aged x and over, then in a stationary population T_x is equal to the number of years lived by the members of the cohort after their xth birthdays. In symbols, $T_x = l_x e_x$. A population with a constant annual number of births and unchanging mortality will become stationary in the long run. Hence,

$$T_0 \ = 1000 \times 79.205 = 79\,205,$$

$$T_{20} = \ 990 \times 60 \qquad = 59\,400,$$

$$T_{60} = \ 900 \times 23.6 \quad = 21240.$$

The total number required in the different age groups is found by differencing, and is shown in Table 7.2. This is a very elderly population: the age group 60 and over contains nearly double the percentage observed at present in Western populations. This age distribution would be obtained if total numbers were stabilized and the level of mortality were the minimum that could be achieved in the present state of medical knowledge. If the population were to decline, the proportion of elderly would have been even greater.

Table 7.2

Age group	Population Numbers	Population Percentages
0–19	19 805	25·0
20–59	38 160	48·2
60 and over	21 240	26·8
	79 205	100·0

In this stationary population the birth rate and the death rate will be equal, and both will be given by the reciprocal of the expectation of life at birth. This turns out to be 0·0126, or 12·6 per 1000.

Problem 4

If 'endogenous' mortality were to continue to fall until the expectation of life at age 60 became 40 years, and mortality before birthday 60 were to remain unchanged, what would be the expectation of life at birth, the percentage increase in the population, and the age structure of the population, once the transition had taken place? Comment on your results.

Answer

The value of $e_{60} = 40$ implies an increase of $40 - 23·6 = 16·4$ years. If mortality before birthday 60 were to remain unchanged, the total number of years lived by a cohort of new-born will increase by $16·4 l_{60} = 16·4 \times 900 = 14\,760$ years. Thus the expectation of life at birth would increase by $14\,760/1000 = 14·76$ years and would become $79·2 + 14·76 = 93·96$ years.

These 14 760 additional years of life will correspond to 14 760 persons aged 60 and over in the stationary population, which will grow to $79\,205 + 14\,760 = 93\,965$ persons, and the population would therefore increase by 14 760/79 205, or 18·6%. The new age distribution will be obtained by adding this number to the last line in Table 7.2, which would look as follows:

Age group	Population Numbers	Population Percentages
0–19	19 805	21·1
20–59	38 160	40·6
60 and over	36 000	38·3
	93 965	100·0

In this population those aged 60 and over are nearly as numerous as the age group 20–59. This provides a perfect example of the effect of the decline in the mortality of the aged on the age structure of a population.

8

High mortality in the past

Mortality levels in the past are difficult to describe, because levels were subject to random variations. Catastrophes – wars, famines and epidemics – had important effects on levels of mortality, and a 'normal' or 'average' mortality level is therefore difficult to define.

Past mortality will be studied by means of a theoretical model. It will be shown how excess mortality can be 'grafted' on a 'normal' level which would have obtained in the absence of major disturbances. By using both cohort and current analysis of mortality, the superiority of the first method over the second will be demonstrated.

Data

It is proposed to measure the effect of high excess mortality in the past on the life expectancy at birth of particular cohorts. It will be assumed that the 'normal' level of mortality is given by the table of Duvillard.

Problem 1

Assume that a short and sharp epidemic kills off one-third of the population in each age group. What is the expectation of life at birth for cohorts experiencing such excess mortality between the ages of 0–1 years, 1–2 years, 5–6 years, 10–11 years, 20–21 years, and 50–51 years?

Answer

Let the epidemic that has killed one-third of the population in each age group affect a given cohort between birthdays i and $i+1$. In such a case 'normal' mortality, q_N (note that the subscript does not refer to age), must be increased by an excess mortality, $q_E = 1/3$, between birthdays i and $i+1$.

In the absence of an epidemic the number of survivors, l_{i+1}, is obtained from l_i by applying the formula $l_{i+1} = l_i(1 - q_N)$. In the case of an epidemic the equation becomes $l'_{i+1} = l_i(1 - q_N)(1 - q_E) = l_{i+1}(1 - q_E)$.

As $q_E = 1/3$, $1 - q_E = 2/3$, so

$$l'_{i+1} = \frac{2}{3} l_{i+1}.$$

After birthday $i+1$ the mortality of the affected cohort returns to its normal level. Thus for values of $s > 0$,

$$l'_{i+s} = \frac{2}{3} l_{i+s}.$$

Expectation of life at birth is defined by

$$e_0 = \frac{T_0}{l_0}$$

where $T_0 = \frac{1}{2}l_0 + l_1 + l_2 + \ldots$ approximately.

In the case of an epidemic between birthdays i and $i+1$, T_0 may be written:

$$T_0 = \frac{1}{2}l_0 + l_1 + l_2 + \ldots + l_i + l'_{i+1} + \ldots + l'_\omega$$

where ω stands for the highest age attained by the cohort, or

$$T_0 = \frac{1}{2}l_0 + \sum_{x=1}^{i} l_x + \frac{2}{3} \sum_{x=i+1}^{\omega} l_x.$$

The computation of e_0 therefore requires the separate computation of the sums

$$\sum_{1}^{i} l_x \quad \text{and} \quad \sum_{i+1}^{\omega} l_x.$$

This is done in Table 8.1.

The reduction in the expectation of life at birth caused by the epidemic is naturally greater when the cohort is affected at younger ages. Duvillard's life table gives a life expectancy of 28·8 years at birth. It is seen that this figure is reduced by almost one-third if the epidemic affects the cohort between birth and the 1st birthday. If it affects the cohort between birthdays 50 and 51, the reduction is only 1·7 years ($28·8 - 27·1$), and the older the age at incidence the smaller the reduction becomes (see Fig. 8.1).

Table 8.1 *Life expectancy at birth in cohorts affected by an epidemic (normal $e_0 = 28·8$)*

	Age of incidence in years					
	0	*1*	*5*	*10*	*20*	*50*
$\sum_{1}^{i} l_x$	0	768	3 247	6 052	11 310	23 292
$\sum_{i+1}^{\omega} l_x$	28 259	27 491	25 012	22 207	16 949	4 967
$\frac{2}{3}\sum_{i+1}^{\omega} l_x$	18 839	18 327	16 675	14 805	11 299	3 311
$\frac{1}{2}l_0$	500	500	500	500	500	500
T_0	19 339	19 595	20 422	21 357	23 109	27 103
e_0	19·3	19·6	20·4	21·4	23·1	27·1

Expectation of life at birth

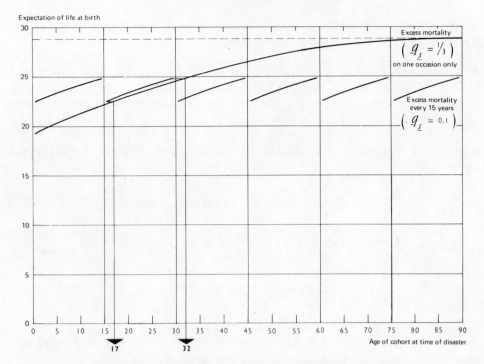

Fig. 8.1 *Expectation of life at birth by age at the moment of disaster*

Problem 2

A population is affected by a number of unspecified disasters of short duration (such as epidemics, famines, civil disorder). On each occasion these lead to the death of one-tenth of the population in each age group; these disasters follow each other at fifteen-year intervals. Compute the expectation of life at birth of cohorts subject to this excess mortality, on the assumption that the age of incidence of the first disaster is between ages 0–1, 1–2, 5–6, 10–11, 14–15.

Answer

The first disaster modifies the life table of the cohort in exactly the same way as in the previous problem:

$$l'_{i+1} = l_{i+1}(1 - q_E).$$

Here $q_E = 0.1$, so that

$$l'_{i+1} = 0.9 l_{i+1}.$$

Fifteen years later the resulting l_x is further modified by a second disaster of the same severity as the first which will happen when the cohort is between birthdays $i + 15$ and $i + 16$. Instead of l'_{i+16} the survivors will be

$$l''_{i+16} = (1 - q_E)l'_{i+16} = 0.9 l'_{i+16} = 0.81 l_{i+16} = (0.9)^2 l_{i+16},$$

and so on. If the age of incidence of the first disaster is between birthdays 0 and 1 ($i = 0$), the total number of years lived by the cohort will be:

$$T_0 = 500 + 0.9 \sum_{x=1}^{15} l_x + 0.81 \sum_{x=16}^{30} l_x + 0.729 \sum_{x=31}^{45} l_x + 0.656 \sum_{x=46}^{60} l_x + 0.590 \sum_{x=61}^{75} l_x + 0.531 \sum_{x=76}^{90} l_x$$

$$+ 0.478 \sum_{x=91}^{\omega} l_x.$$

This formula is modified without difficulty for other values of i ($i = 1, 5, 10, 14$), and the following results are obtained:

Age of incidence of first disaster	Expectation of life at birth
0– 1	22·5
1– 2	22·7
5– 6	23·4
10–11	24·2
14–15	24·8

Note that when disasters recur at fifteen-year intervals, the age when a cohort is first affected cannot be greater than 15. The calculations in this problem show the various possible effects of repeated excess mortality of this type on the expectation of life at birth.

Problem 3

What conclusions may be drawn from Problems 1 and 2?

Answer

The effect of repeated excess mortality of moderate intensity ($q_E = 0.1$) at fifteen-year intervals is never as great as the effect of a single very high excess mortality ($q_E = 1/3$), when this excess affects the cohort at very young ages. In Problem 2, the expectation of life at birth does not fall below 22·5 years. This value is higher than that obtained in Problem 1, provided that the excess mortality affected the cohort before the age of 17. On the other hand, a relatively moderate excess mortality of 0·1, repeated every fifteen years, prevents the expectation of life at birth from rising beyond 24·8 years. This is a lower value than would be caused by a single high excess mortality ($q_E = 1/3$) affecting the cohort after birthday 32 (see Fig. 8.1).

The two assumptions therefore lead to very different results, unless the single high excess mortality strikes the population between the ages of 17 and 32 years. Generally, the effect of a series of moderate excess mortalities ($q_E = 0.1$) repeated at fifteen-year intervals and affecting a cohort for the first time at age x is similar to that of a single high excess mortality ($q_E = 1/3$) affecting the cohort at age $x + 17$.

Assume next that high excess mortality happens once every ninety years. At that age only four out of 1000 new-born survive, so that the assumption is equivalent to saying that each cohort is affected only once. Fig. 8.1 has been drawn on this assumption. The expectation of life for ninety consecutive cohorts on this assumption becomes approximately $\frac{1}{2}(19\cdot3+28\cdot2)=24$ years, and $\frac{1}{2}(22\cdot5+24\cdot8)=23\cdot6$ years if it were assumed that a moderate excess mortality ($q_E=0\cdot1$) would be repeated every fifteen years.

Because the curves are convex towards the upper end of the diagram, estimates using the arithmetic mean tend to give too low a value for the complete set of ninety cohorts. This underestimation is greater in the example with a single high excess mortality, where the convexity of the curve is greater. It may therefore be concluded that the effect of a moderate excess mortality of 0·1 every fifteen years is likely to be greater than that of a high excess mortality of 1/3 striking each cohort once only.

Excess mortality reduces the expectation of life shown in Duvillard's table by between 4·8 and 5·2 years.

Problem 4

Construct current life tables for a year in which there is excess mortality on the assumptions in Problem 1 and Problem 2. Compute the expectation of life at birth in each case and comment.

Answer

Current life tables corresponding to the years in which excess mortality takes place may be computed by modifying the q_x values in Duvillard's table at all ages by introducing an additional excess of 1/3 or 1/10 respectively. It has been shown above that where this modification applies only to age i to $i+1$, this results in the substitution of $l'_{i+1}=2/3 l_{i+1}$, or $l'_{i+1}=0\cdot9 l_{i+1}$ for the values of l_{i+1} in Duvillard's table. For the construction of current tables this procedure must be applied at every age. This would yield the current table shown schematically below:

Duvillard's table	Current table	
	$q_E=1/3$	$q_E=1/10$
l_0	l_0	l_0
l_1	$2/3 l_1$	$9/10 l_1$
l_2	$(2/3)^2 l_2$	$(9/10)^2 l_2$
...	....	....
l_x	$(2/3)^x l_x$	$(9/10)^x l_x$

The values obtained are shown in Table 8.2.

Expectations of life at birth are respectively 1·8 and 5·7 years. These are extremely low values, which have never been found in any actual cohort. The assumption of this problem, in which a cohort is subjected to excess mortality at all ages, is much less illuminating than the assumptions of the previous problems where excess mortality affects the cohort only occasionally (between once and six times during the entire life of the cohort). It also yields different life expectancies at birth in the long run, namely

$$\frac{28\cdot8\times14+5\cdot7}{15}=27\cdot3 \text{ years, } \quad \text{and} \quad \frac{28\cdot8\times89+1\cdot8}{90}=28\cdot5 \text{ years,}$$

Table 8.2 *Current life table in a year of excess mortality*

$q_E = 1/3$				$q_E = 1/10$									
Age x	l_x	Age x	l_x	Age x	l_x	Age x	l_x	Age x	l_x	Age x	l_x	Age x	l_x
0	1000	10	10	0	1000	10	192	20	61	30	18	40	6
1	512	11	6	1	691	11	172	21	55	31	16	41	5
2	299	12	4	2	544	12	154	22	49	32	14	42	4
3	185	13	3	3	456	13	137	23	43	33	13	43	4
4	118	14	2	4	393	14	122	24	38	34	12	44	3
5	77	15	1	5	344	15	109	25	34	35	10	45	3
6	50	16	1	6	304	16	97	26	30	36	9	46	3
7	33	17	1	7	271	17	87	27	27	37	8	47	2
8	22			8	241	18	77	28	24	38	7	48	2
9	14			9	215	19	69	29	21	39	6	49	2
												50	2
												51	1
												52	1
												53	1
												54	1

instead of the values of 23·6 and 24 years obtained by applying the excess mortality to the history of an actual cohort.

It may be concluded that, although current life tables are a very useful instrument for studying mortality when variations in mortality are relatively small, as at present, they are much less valuable for the study of past mortality, where variations from year to year have often been very considerable.

9

The measurement of mortality when ages are mis-stated

This chapter is the middle one of three in which theoretical models are used to help in the better understanding of a real situation. The opportunity will also be taken here to demonstrate some other methods which have been found useful for other demographic problems.

A thorough understanding of the underlying relationships involved is essential to deal with these complex problems. The methods suggested will help in developing an analytic approach to the study of demography.

Data

In statistically underdeveloped countries age statistics are often defective, because old people tend to overstate their age. Such overstatement may take place either during a census or at death registration. The mortality of the old will therefore be underestimated in such populations. In this chapter methods will be demonstrated which will make it possible to estimate the errors caused by mis-statement of ages.

In all problems the French male life table for 1952–6 will be used.

Problem 1

Recompute the life table, taking account of births falsely registered as still births. Give results in the form of an abridged life table (ages 0, 1, 5, 10, 15, ... 100). Calculate the expectation of life at birth. Use 10 000 as the radix of the table.

Answer

According to French law births must be registered within three days of their occurrence. Children born alive, but dying before their birth is registered, are normally treated as still born. This practice reduces the number of infant deaths and the number of live births by an equal amount. But this reduction is relatively much more important in the case of infant deaths, so that French statistics tend to underestimate the infant mortality rate and the value of q_0 in the life table.

In the French male life table for 1952–6, with $l_0 = 100\,000$, the value given for l_1 is $95\,924$ if 'false still births' are ignored, and $l_1 = 95\,433$ if account is taken of them. Thus the survivorship function l_x for all values of $x \neq 0$ must be multiplied by $95\,433/95\,924 = 0.99488$ in order to correct the error introduced by 'false still births'. Table 9.1 has been constructed in this way.

Table 9.1   *French male life table for 1952–6, corrected for 'false still births'*

x	l_x	$_n d_x$	$_n q_x$	x	l_x	$_n d_x$	$_n q_x$
0	10 000	457	0·0457	50	8375	515	0·0615
1	9 543	77	0·0081	55	7860	709	0·0902
5	9 466	25	0·0026	60	7151	913	0·128
10	9 441	25	0·0026	65	6238	1157	0·185
15	9 416	51	0·0054	70	5081	1412	0·278
20	9 365	77	0·0082	75	3669	1519	0·414
25	9 288	89	0·0096	80	2150	1248	0·581
30	9 199	111	0·0121	85	902	679	0·755
35	9 088	148	0·0163	90	223	198	0·888
40	8 940	218	0·0244	95	25	24	0·960
45	8 722	347	0·0398	100	1		

The expectation of life at birth is computed by means of the usual formula:

$$e_0 = \tfrac{1}{2} + \frac{2\tfrac{1}{2}l_1 + 4\tfrac{1}{2}l_5 + 5(l_{10} + l_{15} + \ldots)}{l_0} = 64.70 \text{ years.}$$

The computation may be simplified by using the following reasoning. If no allowance were made for 'false still births' e_0 is found to be 65·04 years. The 95 924 survivors to their 1st birthday in this table come from 100 000 births. If allowance were to be made for 'false still births' the radix of the life table, R, could be obtained by writing $0.95433R = 95\,524$, where 0.95433 is p_0 when the practice of registering children dying before registration as still born is taken into account. It follows that

$$R = \frac{95\,924}{0.954\,33} = 100\,514.$$

In the corrected table

$$e_0 = \tfrac{1}{2} + \frac{l_1 + l_2 + \ldots}{R},$$

but in the proposed table

$$65.04 = \tfrac{1}{2} + \frac{l_1 + l_2 + \ldots}{100\,000},$$

so that $l_1 + l_2 + \ldots = 6\,504\,000 - 50\,000$. Substituting this value into the first formula:

$$e_0 = \tfrac{1}{2} + \frac{6\,504\,000 - 50\,000}{100\,514} = 64.71.$$

This result is practically the same as was obtained by using the previous method. Thus neglecting 'false still births' leads to an overestimation of the expectation of life at birth of 0·35 years.

Problem 2

Assume that ages are overstated at census and at death registration to an equal extent. Overstatement begins at age 50, at true age 55 it amounts to one year on average, at true age 60 to two years, at true age 65 to three years, etc. Use graphic interpolation on a semi-logarithmic scale to estimate the true annual probabilities of dying after age 50. Deduce the values of $_5q_{50}$, $_5q_{55}$, ..., etc., and compute the life table corresponding to these values.

Answer

What is the meaning of the function q_x, when ages are overstated? On the assumptions given in this problem, an individual will after his 50th birthday increase his stated age by six years for a real increase of five years. Therefore, an increase of one year in declared age will correspond to a real increase of only 5/6 of a year.

The function q_x calculated from census data and death registrations will have the following meaning:

(1) After birthday 50, real age, r, and declared age, x, will be linked by

$$r = 50 + \frac{5}{6}(x - 50)$$

which yields

$$r = \frac{5(10 + x)}{6}. \tag{1}$$

(2) Deaths, which form the numerator of the function q_x, and survivors who form the denominator are both understated to the extent of one-sixth of their true value. q_x, thus calculated, will therefore be the same at declared age x as at true age r. This is clear from the diagram in Fig. 9.1.

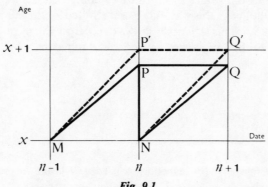

Fig. 9.1

If there were no overstatement of age, the population declaring their age as x at date n would be given by the flow across the segment NP'. Under the assumptions of the present problem, however, it will be the flow across segment NP ($= 5/6$NP'). In the absence of age overstatement deaths between birthdays x and $x+1$ would all lie in the parallelogram MNP'Q'. Overstatement, however, will mean that the deaths will be those in MNPQ, the parallelogram whose area is five-sixths of that of MNP'Q'.

Thus, overstatement of age beyond birthday 50 will not affect q_x at all. The value given for q_x will simply apply to true age r, where r and x are linked by **Equation (1)**.

This is by no means an obvious result. False declarations of age will deform the surfaces in the Lexis diagram which are used in computing probabilities of dying, and may affect their value. The fact that the values are not changed in this problem is due to the assumption that mis-statements of age take place both at census and at death registration *and to an equal extent*.

Thus, the probabilities of dying calculated when ages are overstated correspond to the real ages as given in Table 9.2.

Table 9.2 *Relation between 'declared' age and 'real' age, when ages are overstated*

'Declared' age	q_x value for 'real' age
50	q_{50}
56	q_{55}
62	q_{60}
68	q_{65}
74	q_{70}
80	q_{75}

For intermediate values in the first column of Table 9.2 graphic interpolation on a semi-logarithmic scale has been employed (see Fig. 9.2), for on such a scale the increase in the value of q_x with age is nearly linear. The ages shown on the abscissa are 'declared' ages (i.e. overstated) and for each of them (50, 56, 62, ...) the ordinate gives the corresponding value of q_x taken from the French male life table for 1952–6, i.e. $q_{50} = 0.0106$, $q_{55} = 0.0160$, $q_{60} = 0.0232, ...,$ etc. This procedure yields the values of q_x shown in Table 9.3 and, by completing the life table, the values of $_5q_x$ may be computed.

The values of $_5q_x$ obtained in this way may be substituted for the figures in Table 9.1, and this has been done in Table 9.4. This table also shows the correct values of $_5q_x$, and the percentage underestimation in these figures caused by age mis-statements.

Problem 3

Compute the percentage error in $_5q_x$ and comment.

Answer

It may be seen from the figures in the last column of Table 9.4 that the relative error increases up to the value of $_5q_{80}$, when it reaches 31% and falls thereafter.

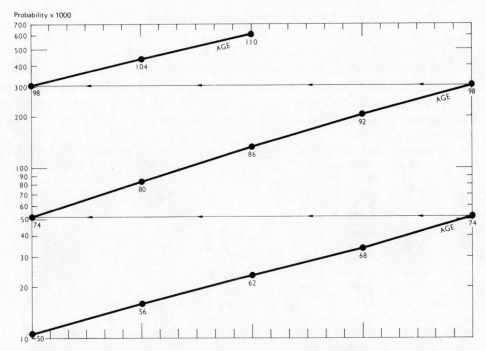

Fig. 9.2 *Estimation of annual probabilities of dying when ages over 50 are overstated*

It will be recalled from the previous problem, that if $_5q_x$ is the true value of the probability of dying within five years of birthday x, the mis-statement of ages leads to a situation in which $_5q_r$ must be taken as the correct value of $_5q_x$, where r and x are linked by Equation (1), i.e. $r = 5/6(10 + x)$. With this notation the relative error calculated in the last column of **Table 9.4** becomes

$$1 - \frac{_5q_r}{_5q_x},$$

provided x is greater than 50.

The fact that the relative error reaches a maximum value in this problem is due to the shape of the $_5q_x$ function, and probably depends also on the exact nature of age mis-statements. If $_5q_x$ varied linearly with x, there would not be a maximum. Normally, however, $_5q_x$ may be represented by an exponential function of x to a high degree of approximation, and in these circumstances a maximum relative error may be reached.

Problem 4

In the incorrect life table compute the values of e_{80}, e_{50} and e_0 and compare these with the corrected values. Why is the difference between the uncorrected and the corrected values so small at ages 50 and 0?

Table 9.3   *Computation of $_5 q_x$ values*

Age x	q_x	l_x	d_x	$_5 q_x$	Age x	q_x	l_x	d_x	$_5 q_x$
50	0·0106	10 000	106	0·0597	75	0·056	1000	56	0·289
51	0·0114	9 894	113		76	0·060	944	57	
52	0·0122	9 781	119		77	0·065	887	58	
53	0·0130	9 662	126		78	0·071	829	59	
54	0·0139	9 536	133		79	0·076	770	59	
		9 403					711		
55	0·0150	10 000	150+	0·0826	80	0·083	1000	83	0·401
56	0·0160	9 850	158		81	0·089	917	82	
57	0·0170	9 692	165		82	0·097	835	81	
58	0·0181	9 527	172		83	0·105	754	79	
59	0·0193	9 355	181		84	0·113	675	76	
		9 174					599		
60	0·0206	10 000	206	0·1114	85	0·122	1000	122	0·539
61	0·0220	9 794	215		86	0·133	878	117	
62	0·0232	9 579	222		87	0·143	761	109	
63	0·0248	9 357	232		88	0·154	652	100	
64	0·0262	9 125	239		89	0·165	552	91	
		8 886					461		
65	0·0279	10 000	279	0·1495	90	0·177	1000	177	
66	0·0298	9 721	290		91	0·190	823	156	
67	0·0317	9 431	299		92	0·205	667	137	
68	0·0337	9 132	308		93	0·220	530	117	
69	0·0361	8 824	319		94	0·233	413	96	
		8 505					317		
70	0·0388	10 000	388	0·2065	95	0·250	1000	250	
71	0·0418	9 612	402		96	0·266	750	200	
72	0·0449	9 210	414		97	0·283	550	156	
73	0·0485	8 796	427		98	0·305	394	120	
74	0·0519	8 369	434		99	0·325	274	89	
		7 935					185		

Table 9.4   *Life table with probabilities of dying underestimated*

Age x	l_x	$_5 q_x$	$_5 d_x$	Correct $_5 q_x$	Deficiency %
50	8375	0·0597	500	0·0615	2·9
55	7875	0·0826	650	0·0902	8·4
60	7225	0·1114	805	0·128	13
65	6420	0·1495	960	0·185	19
70	5460	0·2065	1127	0·278	26
75	4333	0·289	1252	0·414	30
80	3081	0401	1235	0·581	31
85	1846	0·539	995	0·755	29
90	851	0·683	581	0·888	23
95	270	0·815	220	0·960	15
100	50				

Answer

The required expectations of life may be computed from Tables 9.1 and 9.4 by using the formula:

$$e_x = 2\tfrac{1}{2} + 5 \frac{l_{x+5} + l_{x+10} + \cdots}{l_x}$$

where x is a multiple of five. For the expectation of life at birth, we use

$$e_0 = \tfrac{1}{2} + \frac{2\tfrac{1}{2}l_1 + 4\tfrac{1}{2}l_5 + 5(l_{10} + l_{15} + \cdots)}{l_0}.$$

The application of these formulae yields the values in Table 9.5.

Table 9.5   *Expectation of life at various ages*

Age	Life table Uncorrected	Corrected	Difference
0	66·8	64·7	2·1
50	24·8	22·4	2·4
80	7·4	5·2	2·2

The absolute value of the difference between the uncorrected table and the corrected table is practically identical at different ages. It is noteworthy that an overstatement of age after birthday 50 leads to an overestimation in the expectation of life at birth, which is nearly as large absolutely as the overestimation at age 50. This phenomenon may be explained as follows:

Write $_{50}L_0$ for the total number of years lived between birth and birthday 50 in both tables, and write e_x and e'_x for the expectations of life at age x in the corrected and uncorrected tables respectively. Then the total number of years lived after birthday 50 becomes $T_{50} = e_{50}l_{50}$ and $T'_{50} = e'_{50}l_{50}$ respectively. It follows that

$$e_0 = \frac{_{50}L_0 + e_{50}l_{50}}{l_0}$$

and

$$e'_0 = \frac{_{50}L_0 + e'_{50}l_{50}}{l_0}$$

so that

$$e'_0 - e_0 = (e'_{50} - e_{50})\frac{l_{50}}{l_0}.$$

Thus, differences between the expectations of life at birth and at age 50 will become closer to one another the more nearly l_{50}/l_0 is to unity – i.e. the smaller the mortality between birth and age 50. In this problem

$$\frac{l_{50}}{l_0} = \frac{8375}{10\,000} = 0\cdot8375$$

and $2\cdot4 \times 0\cdot8375 = 2\cdot01$. This result is not quite the same as was found in answer to the problem, but the difference is due to the rounding of figures in the comparison.

10

The distribution of deaths by age and the measurement of mortality

It is well known that the crude death rate of a population depends on its age distribution, as well as on the level of mortality. The age distribution does not depend on present mortality levels, and the crude death rate is, therefore, a poor index of mortality.

This is also true of other mortality indices, such as are studied in this chapter. Nevertheless such indices are often used. There is no better way of showing up the inadequacies of such measures than by applying them to model populations. Such populations can be made to represent a wide spectrum of real situations, and it can be demonstrated that these indices do not measure what they purport to measure.

Data

It has been suggested that the proportion of deaths taking place at ages 60 and over in a given year may be used as an index of mortality.

Problem 1

Discuss the reasoning on which such a measure may be based, and show why it does not properly measure mortality levels.

Answer

As mortality falls and the expectation of life increases, the distribution of deaths by age changes in different cohorts. Deaths at younger ages become progressively less frequent and are shifted to the later stages of life. Thus, *within a particular cohort*, the proportion of deaths taking place at ages over 60 is directly correlated with the expectation of life at birth and would provide a good index of mortality. For instance, the Model Life Tables in *Population Studies* No. 25 of the Population Division of the United Nations show the relations in Table 10.1.

Table 10.1 *Expectation of life at birth and proportion of deaths taking place at ages over 60*

Expectation of life at birth	20	30	40	50	60·4	70·2	73·9
Percentage of deaths at ages over 60		8·5	20·4	35·1	50·7	66·6	81·1	86·9

These relationships have led to the suggestion that the proportion of deaths taking place over the age of 60 *in a population* might be used as an index of mortality. However, although the distribution of deaths by age in part depends on mortality levels within the population, it will also be strongly influenced by the age distribution of the population, which is almost completely independent of the level of mortality. This will be illustrated by using different population models, all of which are subject to one and the same life table.

Problem 2

To illustrate the reservations made in Problem 1, calculate the proportion of deaths taking place at ages 60 and over in the stable population, subject to the mortality given by the French male life table for 1952–6, and with annual rates of increase of $+0·03$, $+0·02$, $+0·01$, 0, $-0·01$ and $-0·02$ respectively.

Answer

To answer the question posed, it is necessary only to calculate the distribution of deaths by age in the various stable populations, and not the stable populations themselves. One can begin by looking at the distribution of deaths by age in the stationary population associated with the French male life table for 1952–6. The data to be used can be found in the Statistical Appendix, but the results obtained in Table 9.1 in the previous chapter, where an abridged life table corrected for 'false still births' was constructed, would be even better for this purpose. The distribution of deaths by age may be obtained by differencing the survivorship column in that table. These differences are shown in the second column of Table 10.2. The deaths only add up to 9999 because there was one survivor to age 100.

To transform the distribution of deaths by age in a stationary population to that of a stable population, the methods used for calculating age distributions of stable populations may be applied.

Consider a particular date, D. Then in Fig. 10.1 those aged 0, 1–4 years, 5–9 years, etc., are survivors of those born in DA, AB, BC, ..., respectively. If the rate of increase of the stable population is r, the numbers at birth in each of these groups will be proportional to 1, $(1+r)^{-2·5}$, $(1+r)^{-7}$, ..., etc. As it is necessary to calculate deaths during a year centred at D, we shall replace deaths in the appropriate rectangle of Fig. 10.1 by the deaths at the same ages in the different birth cohorts. These may be obtained (per 10 000 births in DA) by multiplying the deaths in the stationary population by 1, $(1+r)^{-2·5}$, $(1+r)^{-7}$, ..., etc. These are the factors (multiplied by 10 000) shown in the column headed M in Table 10.2. Thus, for $r = 0·02$ and for the age group 50–54, it is necessary to calculate $(1·02)^{-52}$. By using logarithms:

log $1·02 = 0·00860$

(-52) log $1·02 = (-52) \times 0·00860 = -0·4472 = \bar{1}·5528$

whence $(1·02)^{-52} = 0·3571$.

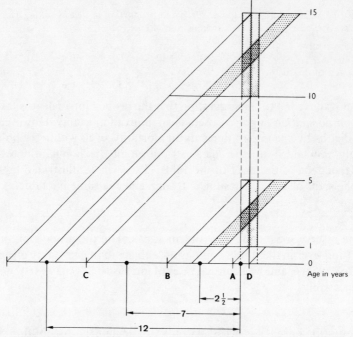

Fig. 10.1   *Deaths by age, age groups and groups of cohorts*

Table 10.2 shows the total number of deaths (T) in the populations considered, as well as the number of deaths occurring among persons above age 60 (T_{60}). The ratios T_{60}/T take the following values for different values of r:

r	0·03	0·02	0·01	0·00	−0·01	−0·02
T_{60}/T	0·409	0·526	0·630	0·715	0·782	0·833

The suggested index may therefore vary by 100% for populations with the same life table but with different rates of natural increase, i.e. different fertilities. Even if attention were confined to the rates of increase most commonly found – those between 0 and 0·03 – the range of the index is from 0·409 to 0·715.

It would be interesting to compute the value of this index for different rates of natural increase, for the whole range of UN Model Life Tables. This would make it possible to find the range of life tables corresponding to a given value of T_{60}/T for different values of r.

Problem 3

Calculate the mean age at death for the populations studied in the preceding problem. Comment on your results and discuss the difficulties in interpreting them.

Answer

It is possible to show how the distribution of deaths by age may vary in populations subjected to the same life table, by calculating the mean age at death.

Table 10.2 *Computation of mean age at death, and percentages dying at ages over 60 in some stable populations*

Age at deaths	Deaths in stationary population	Annual rate of increase of stable population														
		0·03			0·02			0·01			−0·01			−0·02		
		M	Deaths	D	M	Deaths	D	M	Deaths	D	M	Deaths	D	M	Deaths	D
0	457	10000	457	228	10000	457	228	10000	457	228	10000	457	228	10000	457	228
1– 4	77	9288	72	216	9517	73	219	9754	73	225	10254	75	237	10518	81	243
5– 9	25	8131	20	18	8706	22	22	9327	23	22	10729	27	28	11519	29	32
10–14	25	7014	18	62	7885	20	72	8875	22	86	11282	28	122	12743	32	144
15–19	51	6050	31	120	7142	36	150	8444	43	186	11863	61	288	14098	72	360
20–24	77	5219	40	160	6468	50	208	8034	62	272	12475	96	468	15596	120	616
25–29	89	4502	40	215	5859	52	295	7644	68	405	13117	117	765	17254	154	1060
30–34	111	3883	43	300	5306	59	426	7273	81	612	13793	153	1290	19088	212	1878
35–39	148	3350	50	441	4806	71	665	6920	102	1008	14504	215	2324	21117	313	3563
40–44	218	2890	63	696	4353	95	1096	6584	144	1736	15252	332	4456	23362	509	7176
45–49	347	2493	87	999	3943	137	1656	6265	217	2763	16038	557	7812	25845	897	13248
50–54	515	2150	111	1320	3571	184	2290	5961	307	4020	16864	868	12570	28592	1472	22430
55–59	709	1855	132	1606	3234	229	2948	5671	402	5423	17733	1257	18722	31631	2243	35090
60–64	913	1600	146	1920	2930	268	3684	5396	493	7128	18647	1702	27228	34943	3190	53748
65–69	1157	1380	160	2171	2653	307	4407	5134	594	8970	19608	2269	37843	38713	4479	78611
70–74	1412	1181	167	2184	2403	339	4634	4885	690	9884	20619	2911	46102	42828	6047	100758
75–79	1519	1027	156	1665	2177	331	3690	4648	706	8280	21682	3293	42675	47380	7197	98130
80–84	1248	886	111	832	1971	246	1936	4422	552	4576	22799	2845	26048	52416	6542	62992
85–89	679	764	52	221	1786	121	544	4208	286	1343	23974	1628	8483	57987	3937	21590
90–94	198	659	13	18	1617	32	72	4003	79	162	25209	499	1152	64150	1276	3060
95–99	24	569	1		1465	4		3809	9		26509	64		70969	170	
T	9999		1970			3133			5412			19458			39423	
A			444			447			453			465			471	
B			1441			2603			4880			18922			38885	
7·5 *B*			10807			19522			36600			141915			291637	
C			14948			28793			56876			238376			504486	
5 *C*			74740			143965			284380			1191880			2522430	
$T_{\bar{x}}$			85991			163934			321433			1334260			2814538	
$\bar{x}$	64·70		43·65			52·32			59·39			68·57			71·39	
$T_{60}\ (n_b)$	7152		806			1648			3409			15211			32832	
%	71·5		40·9			52·6			63·0			78·2			83·3	

Let $\bar{x}$ be the mean age required. Then $T\bar{x}$ will be the total number of years lived by those dying in a given year. By assuming that deaths are concentrated in the middle of an age group, it is found that

$$T\bar{x} = \tfrac{1}{2}d_0 + 3d_{1,4} + 7{\cdot}5d_{5,9} + 12{\cdot}5d_{10,14} + \ldots + 97{\cdot}5d_{95,99}.$$

For computational purposes it is easier to write this as

$$T\bar{x} = \tfrac{1}{2}d_0 + 3d_{1,4} + 7{\cdot}5 \sum_{5,10,\ldots} d_{x,x+4} + 5[d_{10,14} + 2d_{15,19} + 3d_{20,24} + \ldots].$$

Three values need to be computed:

$$A = \tfrac{1}{2}d_0 + 3d_{1,4}$$

$$B = \sum_{5,10,\ldots} d_{x,x+4}$$

$$C = d_{10,14} + 2d_{15,19} + 3d_{20,24} + \ldots.$$

The data used in these calculations will be found in the column headed D in Table 10.2, and at the bottom of this column the values of A, B and C are given. With this notation

$$\bar{x} = \frac{A + 7{\cdot}5B + 5C}{T}$$

While the expectation of life at birth in all six populations is 64·70 years, the mean age at death for the various rates of natural increase is given in the table below:

r	0·03	0·02	0·01	0·00	−0·01	−0·02
$\bar{x}$	43·65	52·32	59·39	64·70	68·57	71·39

The mean age at death in a given population may therefore differ very considerably from the expectation of life at birth (or mean duration of life), which depends only on the age-specific mortality rates of the population. The two concepts must therefore be carefully distinguished, even though at first sight they seem to be the same.

The two concepts have frequently been confused, particularly by those who estimate the expectation of life at birth on the basis of data relating to deaths only, e.g. from parish registers, funerary inscriptions, etc.

Here again, it would be valuable to calculate the relationship between the mean age at death and the rate of natural increase for different model life tables. This would yield an estimate of the range of life expectancies at birth which would be consistent with a given mean age at death in a population.

IV
RELATIONSHIPS BETWEEN NUPTIALITY AND MORTALITY

11

Nuptiality and mortality

This chapter attempts to clarify the considerations that have to be taken into account in a joint study of nuptiality and mortality.

This specific subject is an example of a much more general problem. Demographic phenomena cannot always be isolated, and the frequency of a particular vital event (in this case first marriages) often depends not only on the characteristic rates (in this case first-marriage rates) but also on a number of concurrent intervening variables (e.g. mortality, migration, etc.). In demographic analysis an attempt is made to isolate the 'pure' characteristics of a particular phenomenon from the study of data where other variables have intervened.

Data

A gross nuptiality table for spinsters has been calculated. The single survivors at birthday x, (S_x) are given below:

Age x	Single survivors S_x	Age x	Single survivors S_x
15	1000	35	200
20	860	40	150
25	520	45	125
30	310	50	120

Problem 1

Compute the series of first marriages associated with this nuptiality table and represent them graphically. Compute the mean age at first marriage.

Answer

The series of first (or spinster) marriages between successive birthdays is given in Table 11.1 by differencing the S_x column given above. The 880 first marriages, which take place between ages 15 and 50, on the assumption of zero mortality before age 50, are plotted in Fig. 11.1.

Table 11.1   *Distribution of first marriages by age and calculation of mean age at marriage*

Age x (1)	S_x (2)	First marriages $_5M_x$ (3)	Mean age at marriage in age group (4)	$(3) \times (4)$ (5)
15	1000	140	17·5	2 450
20	860	340	22·5	7 650
25	520	210	27·5	5 775
30	310	110	32·5	3 575
35	200	50	37·5	1 875
40	150	25	42·5	1 062·5
45	125	5	47·5	237·5
50	120			
		880		22 625·0

If it is assumed that the mean age at marriage in the age group x to $x+5$ is $x+2.5$, the mean age at marriage may be computed as shown in Column (5), and comes to $\bar{x} = 22\,625/880 = 25.7$ years.

Problem 2

Part of the life table for the female cohort studied is given below:

Age x	Survivors l_x	Age x	Survivors l_x
15	1000	35	858
20	972	40	818
25	935	45	776
30	897	50	728

What is the number of first marriages contracted before the age of 50 for 1000 girls reaching their 15th birthday? Calculate the age distribution of these marriages and compare it with the distribution found in the answer to Problem 1. Comment.

Answer

In any actual situation single survivors observed at birthday x (S'_x) are those who have not succumbed to either marriage or mortality, and it is obvious that $S'_x < S_x$. In order to find the relationship between these two functions, a number of assumptions will have to be made.

In the first place the mortality of single persons normally differs from that of the population as a whole. This difference will be neglected in this answer, and it will be assumed that the mortality of the single and of the married is the same and is given by the survivorship function l_x. For the sake of simplicity it will also be assumed that $l_{15} = 1$ (there would be no difficulty in using a life table for single persons, other than more complicated arithmetic).

In the second place some assumption must be made about the independence of mortality and nuptiality. If the two series were not independent, then it is possible that a higher chance of dying for an individual (which may be due to poor health or infirmity) might be associated with a lower chance of marrying. The calculation of probabilities of death and marriage would have to proceed by different methods, depending on whether or not independence is assumed. In this case, the simplest assumption – that of independence – will be made, even though in reality it is almost certainly false.

In the case of independence the chance of single survival will therefore be the product of the chance of surviving and the chance of not marrying in the gross nuptiality table. In this case:

$$\frac{S'_x}{S_{15}} = \frac{S_x l_x}{S_{15}}, \quad \text{or} \quad S'_x = S_x l_x.$$

To calculate the number of spinster marriages between two successive birthdays it is possible to reason as follows. Among the S'_x single survivors to birthday x, $S'_x(1-q_x)$ will survive to birthday $x+1$, and will therefore be subject to the risk of marriage for a whole year. This risk may be written n_x, and among the single survivors to birthday x there will therefore be $S'_x(1-q_x)n_x$ first marriages before birthday $x+1$. This reasoning assumes the independence of mortality and nuptiality.

If there were no marriages $S'_x q_x$ of the survivors to birthday x would die as single persons before birthday $x+1$. But the number of single deaths will be reduced by nuptiality. If it were assumed that all these women were to die immediately after their xth birthday, there would be no first marriages among such women; if they were all to die just before their $(x+1)$th birthday, the number of first marriages would come to $S'_x q_x n_x$. It will be assumed that the number of marriages actually taking place is the arithmetic mean of these two quantities and will therefore come to $\frac{1}{2} S'_x q_x n_x$. The total number of first marriages taking place between birthdays x and $x+1$, which will be written M_x, is therefore:

$$S'_x(1-q_x)n_x + S'_x \tfrac{1}{2}q_x n_x = S'_x(1-\tfrac{1}{2}q_x)n_x.$$

But, as we know that $S'_x = S_x l_x$, the equation becomes

$$M'_x = S_x l_x n_x (1-\tfrac{1}{2}q_x) = M_x \tfrac{1}{2}(l_x + l_{x+1}) \tag{1}$$

because $S_x n_x = M_x$ and $l_x(1-\tfrac{1}{2}q_x) = l_x - \tfrac{1}{2}d_x$, where d_x stands for the life table deaths between birthdays x and $x+1$. The last expression could be considered equivalent of $\frac{1}{2}(l_x + l_{x+1}) = l_{x+1/2}$. If only ages that are multiples of five are considered, Equation (1) is easily seen to become:

$$_5M'_x = {_5M_x}\tfrac{1}{2}(l_x + l_{x+5}). \tag{2}$$

This equation has been used to obtain the values shown in Table 11.2. The total number of first marriages comes to 817, against a figure of 880 shown in the gross nuptiality table which assumed that there was no mortality. The difference between these two values corresponds to the number of marriages that have been prevented by death.

The proportion of marriages prevented by death rises with age, and the distribution of first marriages by age in the net nuptiality table will therefore be different from the corresponding distribution in the gross nuptiality table, where zero mortality is assumed (see Fig. 11.1). The mean age at marriage is 25·4 years in the net table and 25·7 years in the gross table.

Table 11.2   *Computation of net nuptiality table*

Age x	l_x	$\frac{1}{2}(l_x + l_{x+5})$	$_5M_x$	$_5M'_x$
15	1000	986	140	138
20	972	953·5	340	324
25	935	916	210	192
30	897	877·5	110	97
35	858	838	50	42
40	818	797	25	20
45	776	752	5	4
50	728			
			880	817

Problem 3

Calculate the number, per 1000 women reaching their 15th birthday, of those who marry at least once before birthday 50, and those who do not marry. For each of these groups obtain the number surviving to birthday 50 and those dying before that age.

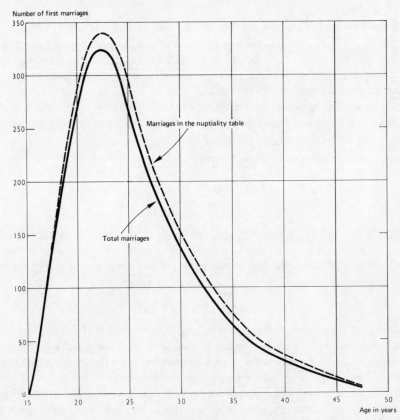

Fig. 11.1   *Distribution of marriages by age at marriage according to the nuptiality table and of actual marriages (per 1000 girls reaching the age of 15)*

Answer

In this problem it is possible to specify exactly the relationship between mortality and nuptiality.

The numbers italicized in Table 11.3 are those obtained in Problems 1 and 2. They relate to mortality ($l_{50} = 728$, $l_{15} = 1000$, and thus $l_{15} - l_{50} = 272$) and to the number of first marriages in the net nuptiality table (817). Only one further number (other than the complement of 817 to 1000) needs to be computed to complete the table.

Note that the computation of those dying as single persons before their 50th birthday is very similar to that of the previous problem.

Among the S'_x single survivors to birthday x, $S'_x(1 - n_x)$ would survive single to their $(x + 1)$th birthday, if there were no mortality. Because, however, the risk of dying between birthday x and birthday $x + 1$ is q_x, there will be $S'_x(1 - n_x)q_x$ single deaths.

On the other hand, if there were no mortality, $S'_x n_x$ women would marry between birthday x and birthday $x + 1$. Mortality will prevent some of these marriages from taking place. If women were all assumed to marry immediately after their xth birthday no marriages would be prevented by death; if, on the other hand, it were assumed that they would all marry just before birthday $x + 1$ there would be $S'_x n_x q_x$ spinster deaths. The arithmetic mean of these two will be taken as the best estimate of the number of spinster deaths among those who would have married, namely $\frac{1}{2}S'_x n_x q_x$.

The total number of spinster deaths (D'_x) between birthday x and birthday $x + 1$ is therefore $S'_x(1 - n_x)q_x + \frac{1}{2}S'_x n_x q_x = S'_x(1 - \frac{1}{2}n_x)q_x$ and this can be simplified without difficulty to

$$D'_x = d_x \tfrac{1}{2}(S_x + S_{x+1}) \tag{3}$$

where S_x is the single survivorship function of the gross nuptiality table with $S_{15} = 1$.

Note that $\frac{1}{2}(S_x + S_{x+1})$ may be written $S_{x+1/2}$.

If only ages that are multiples of five are considered, Equation (3) becomes:

$$_5D'_x = {_5D_x}\tfrac{1}{2}(S_x + S_{x+5}). \tag{4}$$

Equations (3) and (4) are analogous to Equations (1) and (2) of the previous problem. Summarizing the results up to the present, we have:

Among S'_x single survivors to birthday x in a cohort:

$S'_x(1 - \frac{1}{2}q_x)n_x$ will marry before birthday $x + 1$ (Problem 2).
$S'_x q_x(1 - \frac{1}{2}n_x)$ will die as spinsters before birthday $x + 1$.
$S'_{x+1} = S'_x(1 - n_x)(1 - q_x)$ will survive as spinsters to birthday $x + 1$.

Table 11.3 *First marriages and spinster deaths before birthday 50 in a cohort of 1000 women reaching birthday 15.*

	Married At birthday 50	Single	Total
Dying before 50	176	96	272
Survivors to age 50	641	87	728
Total	817	183	1000

To obtain the total number of spinster deaths before birthday 50, Equation (4) may be applied to yield

$$\sum_{x=15}^{45} \tfrac{1}{2}(S_x + S_{x+5})_5 D_x = 96.$$

This makes it possible to complete Table 11.3.

It would have been simpler to achieve this result by remembering that the proportion single among the 728 survivors to birthday 50 is equal to the proportion in the gross nuptiality table at that age: $87 = 728 \times 0\cdot120$. This is true provided that there is no differential mortality between married and single. This relationship will be used in the next chapter.

12
Nuptiality and mortality (continued)

In the previous chapter the relationships between nuptiality and mortality were considered without any reference to the conditions under which the data had been collected. This chapter begins with a discussion of the different measures that may be derived from data that are usually available (first marriages and deaths). It proceeds to discuss some theoretical points which will prove useful for further study.

Data

The following data were obtained in a census for a female cohort between their 25th and 26th birthdays:

1 At birthday 25 there were 4000 spinsters and 6000 ever-married members of the cohort.
2 Between birthday 25 and birthday 26 the following events were registered:
   First marriages: 380
   Spinster deaths: 56
   Deaths of ever-married women: 74

All members of the cohort remained under observation throughout the study.

Problem 1

Calculate the probability of survival from birthday 25 to birthday 26.

Answer

Table 12.1 shows the changes taking place in the cohort between the two birthdays. The required probability of survival is easily seen to be $p_{25} = 0.987$.

Table 12.1   *First marriages and deaths between birthdays 25 and 26*

	Single	Ever-married	Total
At birthday 25	4000	6000	10 000
First marriages	− 380	+ 380	
Deaths	− 56	− 74	− 130
At birthday 26	3564	6306	9 870

Problem 2

The proportion single at birthday 25 and birthday 26 will be used as an indicator of nuptiality in the cohort. Calculate these proportions. By interpreting them as the number single in a gross nuptiality table, compute the probability of marrying between birthdays 25 and 26.

Answer

The proportions single at birthdays 25 and 26 are respectively:

$$\frac{4000}{10\,000} = 0.4000 \quad \text{and} \quad \frac{3564}{9870} = 0.3611.$$

If these proportions are regarded as the single survivors in a gross nuptiality table, the probability of marrying between birthday 25 and 26 (n_{25}) is calculated in Table 12.2. It will be shown later that the calculation yields correct results only if it is assumed that there is no differential mortality between the married and the single. The truth of this assumption will be tested below.

Table 12.2

Age x	Single S_x	Marriages M_x	Probability of marriage n_x
25	4000	389	0.09725
26	3611		

Problem 3

Obtain another estimate of the probability of marriage by relating the number of first marriages to an appropriate number of spinsters at risk. Compare with the previous result and comment.

Answer

To calculate n_x directly, the procedure is as follows. If n_x is the probability required and S_x the number single at birthday x, and if there were no mortality, the total number of first marriages would be $S_x n_x$. However, only M_x marriages actually took place, because some were prevented by the D_x spinster deaths that occurred in the cohort.

If these D_x women had died immediately after their xth birthday, and if they had been subject to the same nuptiality rates as those who survived, the total number of marriages prevented by death would have been $D_x n_x$. If, on the other hand, they had all survived until just before their $(x+1)$th birthday, no marriage at all would have been prevented by mortality. Thus, the true number of prevented marriages lies between 0 and $D_x n_x$. The arithmetic mean of these two quantities may be taken as the best estimate of marriages prevented, so that $S_x n_x = M_x + \frac{1}{2} D_x n_x$, yielding:

$$n_x = \frac{M_x}{S_x - \frac{1}{2} D_x}.$$

This procedure is similar to that used in previous problems, though in this case the proportion rather than the absolute number of vital events is used. The data in Table 12.1 yield

$$n_{25} = \frac{380}{4000 - \frac{1}{2} 56} = 0.09567.$$

This value differs from that found in answer to Problem 2. It is not absolutely correct, as the number used in the denominator of the fraction is an estimate. Clearly, however, the true value must lie between

$$\frac{380}{4000} = 0.09500 \quad \text{and} \quad \frac{380}{4000 - 56} = 0.09635.$$

The answer found in Problem 2 was 0.09725 and lies outside this range. Clearly, the method used in the previous problem overstates the probability of marrying.

This result leads to a consideration of the assumption on which the method depends: that of equal mortality among the married and the unmarried. In an actual situation the unmarried will normally have a higher mortality (it will be shown later that this is the case here), and it is intuitively clear that this higher mortality will lead to an overestimation of the probability of marriage when the procedure outlined above is used.

This last statement will now be proved. Consider a cohort, in which l_x and S'_x are the number of survivors to birthday x, and the number of spinsters surviving to birthday x respectively (the prime in S'_x is used to avoid confusion with the number of single survivors in a nuptiality table, normally written S_x; this function in which $S_{15} = 1$ will be used later). Let n_x be the probability of first marriage, q_x and q'_x the probabilities of dying within a year of birthday x in the whole population and amongst spinsters respectively, and p_x and p'_x the respective complementary probabilities of survival.

In Problem 2, the proportion $P_x = S'_x / l_x$ was used, and the probability of marriage taken as:

$$n_x = \frac{P_x - P_{x+1}}{P_x} \tag{1}$$

If mortality and nuptiality were independent, it follows that

$$S'_{x+1} = S'_x (1 - n_x)(1 - q'_x) = S'_x p'_x (1 - n_x).$$

Also

$$l_{x+1} = l_x (1 - q_x) = l_x p_x,$$

whence

$$P_{x+1} = P_x(1 - n_x)p'_x/p_x.$$

Therefore, Equation (1) does not yield n_x, but $1 - (1 - n_x)p'_x/p_x$. This expression will only be equal to n_x, if $p'_x = p_x$, i.e. if there is no differential mortality between the single and the married. If $p'_x > p_x$, i.e. if spinsters are subject to an excess mortality, then $1 - (1 - n_x)p'_x/p_x > n_x$, as was stated.

If P_x were regarded as the proportion of women who, in the complete absence of mortality, had not married by birthday x, P_{50} or P_{60} might be interpreted as the proportion who never married. This can easily be seen to lead to an error. If l'_x were the number of survivors to birthday x in a single life table, i.e. one in which the probabilities of dying within a year of birthday x are q'_x, and in which $l'_x = l_x$ for ages up to 15, and if nuptiality and mortality were assumed to be independent, then

$$S'_x = S_x l'_x$$

As the number of survivors to birthday x in the cohort as a whole is l_x, it follows that $P_x = S'_x/l_x = S_x l'_x/l_x$. For instance, if P_{50} were known, then

$$P_{50} = S_{50} l'_{50}/l_{50}. \tag{2}$$

Thus, provided that there is an excess mortality amongst spinsters ($l'_{50} < l_{50}$) Equation (2) underestimates the true proportion single (S_{50}). This error would be particularly important in the case of men, for bachelors are subject to considerable excess mortality. This would become evident when the proportions P_{50}, P_{60}, P_{70}, ... in a particular cohort are examined. These proportions fall much more rapidly than would be the case if the only attrition factor were the nuptiality of elderly bachelors.

Problem 4

Compute the probability of a spinster dying between birthday 25 and 26 by relating spinster deaths to an appropriate number of spinsters at risk (the number exposed to risk will be obtained by analogy with Problem 3). Comment.

Answer

Just as some marriages will have been prevented from taking place by the deaths of those who would otherwise have married, so a number of women who would have died as spinsters will in fact be married at the time of their death, because of nuptiality. The reasoning is exactly the same as in the previous problem and leads to the equation: $Sq' = D + \frac{1}{2}Mq'$, whence $q' = D/(S - \frac{1}{2}M)$ (the subscripts x have been omitted for the sake of simplicity). The figures in Table 12.1 yield

$$q'_{25} = \frac{56}{4000 - \frac{1}{2}380} = 0.0147.$$

This is appreciably in excess of the probability of dying in the population as a whole, which is $1 - 0.987 = 0.013$. In this case the difference is not entirely due to uncertainty about the size of the denominator of the fraction. Even if the largest possible value (4000) had been used in the calculation of q'_{25}, a value of $56/4000 = 0.014$ would have been obtained. The excess mortality of spinsters would have been even greater if it had been compared with the mortality of ever-married women, rather than with the mortality of the whole population.

This confirms the conclusion of an excess mortality among single women that had already been suspected, when different methods of calculation yielded different values for the probability of a spinster death.

Problem 5

The calculations in Problems 3 and 4 are not entirely exact. If n and q' are written respectively for the probability of a spinster marrying or dying between birthday 25 and 26, and if w were the probability of leaving the single state, show that under certain assumptions

$$w = n + q' - nq'. \tag{1}$$

Show that this equation does not hold for the values of n and q' found in previous answers.

Answer

w is the probability of leaving the single state. A woman can leave this state through marriage or death. By the theorem of compound probability, it is clear that $w = n + q' - nq'$. If w were calculated from M marriages and D deaths, then $w = (M + D)/S$. But M and D have been shown to be equivalent to $n(S - \frac{1}{2}D)$ and $q'(S - \frac{1}{2}M)$ respectively. Substituting these values into the equation for w yields:

$$\frac{M+D}{S} = \frac{1}{S}\left[n(S - \tfrac{1}{2}D) + q'(S - \tfrac{1}{2}M)\right] = n + q' - \frac{nD + q'M}{2S}.$$

The last fraction in this expression does not reduce to nq', for $D = Sq' - \varepsilon$ and $M = Sn + \varepsilon$. Thus Equation (1) does not hold. Substitution of the numerical values that have been obtained will, however, show that the difference is not great.

Problem 6

It is suggested that n and q' should be calculated as follows. Let S be the number of spinsters at birthday 25 and let M and D be marriages and deaths between birthday 25 and 26 respectively. Separate M into two parts: M_1, first marriages of spinsters destined to survive to birthday 26; and M_2, first marriages of spinsters destined to die before birthday 26. Show that

$$M = Sn[1 - (1 - k)q]$$

where $0 < k < 1$. What meaning can be given to k?

Answer

Fig. 12.1 shows all possible situations for a single woman within a year of her birthday. However, the outcomes denoted A' and B' cannot be observed in practice. The occurrence of marriage (M) prevents the individual from dying as a single person, and the occurrence of death (D) prevents marriage. As all possible outcomes are shown in the diagram, it follows that

$$P(O) + P(A) + P(B) + P(A') + P(B') = 1$$

where $P(B)$ stands for the probability of B, and similarly for the other events. Clearly:

$$P(O) = (1 - n)(1 - q)$$

$$P(A) = n(1 - q)$$

$$P(B) = q(1 - n)$$

$$P[(A') + (B')] = n \cdot q$$

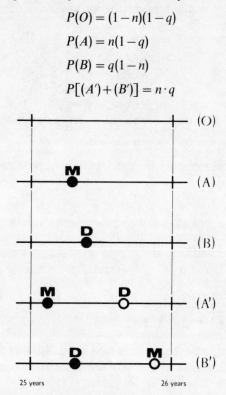

Fig. 12.1 *Different combinations of marriage (M) and death (D) of a single person, possible between birthday 25 and birthday 26*

The sum of these expressions is unity. But the last equation shows that $P(A') = knq$, where k is a fraction between zero and unity, and $P(B') = (1 - k)nq$. k may therefore be regarded as the probability that M will precede D, when both M and D happen. Its value will depend on the shape of the q and n functions. When these are both approximately linear, it may be shown that $k = \frac{1}{2}$, i.e. the chance of M preceding D is equal to that of D preceding M. It will follow that

$$M_1 = SP(A) = Sn(1 - q),$$

$$M_2 = SP(A') = Sknq,$$

so that

$$M = M_1 + M_2 = Sn[1 - (1 - k)q].$$

By analogy, the number of deaths of spinsters could be decomposed into two categories, D_1 and D_2, so that:

$$D_1 = SP(B) = Sq(1-n),$$
$$D_2 = SP(B') = Snq(1-k),$$

and

$$D = D_1 + D_2 = Sq(1-kn).$$

Problem 7

Check that Equation (1) in Problem 5 holds, provided n and q are calculated from the formulae established in answer to the preceding problem. Calculate n and q, if $k = \frac{1}{2}$, and compare their values with those found previously.

Answer

w, the probability of leaving the single state, is equal to $(M+D)/S$. If the values found in the previous answer for M and D are used,

$$(M+D)/S = n[1-(1-k)q] + q(1-kn) = n+q-nq.$$

The theorem of compound probability holds for these values.

If $k = \frac{1}{2}$, the equations are:

$$380 = 4000(1-\tfrac{1}{2}q)n$$
$$56 = 4000(1-\tfrac{1}{2}n)q.$$

These lead to the quadratic equation $2000q^2 - 3838q + 56 = 0$. There is only one root less than unity, $q = 0.01470$, from which $n = 0.0957$. These values may be compared with 0.01470 and 0.09567 found previously. Thus the present method, which is theoretically exact (in that the theorem of compound probabilities holds), gives results that are virtually indistinguishable from those obtained by the more approximate methods, and thus has little practical value.

Note that by putting $k = \frac{1}{2}$ one is led back to the formulae obtained in Chapter 11:

$$n = M/S(1-\tfrac{1}{2}q) \quad \text{and} \quad q = D/S(1-\tfrac{1}{2}n).$$

The reasoning used in Problem 6 leading to these results is very similar to that used in obtaining the formulae directly.

13

Marriages in France

In this chapter the theoretical results discussed in the previous two chapters are applied to an actual problem. Because good statistical data and other observational material are available, it will be possible to demonstrate how nuptiality can be studied to the fullest possible extent. Theoretical models of nuptiality are unsatisfactory, because each sex is studied in isolation. The inadequacy of this method will be demonstrated in the later problems of this chapter, when a projection of first marriages in France for the period 1960–75 will be attempted. It will be shown that inconsistent results will be obtained, because of the irregularity of the age distribution of the young population, and because of the entry of the larger birth cohorts of the immediate post-war period into the marriageable ages.

Problem 1

Compute the proportions single on 1 January 1955 in the different French male and female birth cohorts. Comment.

Answer

The required calculations present no difficulty whatever, and the results are shown in Table 13.1 for each year of age to 50, and then for ages 60, 70 and 80 only.

At first the proportions single decline very slowly with age, but the fall soon becomes more rapid (particularly between the ages of 21 and 26 for men, and 19 to 24 for women). For men the fall continues with advancing age, though at a much slower rate. For women the reduction in the rate of decline is much greater, and from age 42 onwards the proportions single become irregular, increasing at first and then diminishing again at higher ages. Further irregularities would in all probability have been found if calculations had been made for each year of age beyond the age of 50. As the principal reason for leaving the single state at younger ages is a first marriage, the decline in the proportion single with advancing age is an indicator of the age distribution of first marriages by age for each sex. But proportions single cannot be used as indicators of nuptiality with any accuracy, as will be shown in the succeeding sections.

Table 13.1   *Proportions single in France, 1 January 1955*

Cohort	Age on 1.1.1955	Proportions single per 10 000		Cohort	Age on 1.1.55	Proportions single per 10 000	
		Men	Women			Men	Women
1939	15		9987	1919	35	1385	1086
1938	16		9932	1918	36	1353	1068
1937	17	9997	9737	1917	37	1331	1031
1936	18	9949	9280	1916	38	1319	1015
1935	19	9794	8418	1915	39	1276	989
1934	20	9438	7304	1914	40	1232	966
1933	21	9156	6050	1913	41	1202	948
1932	22	7981	4907	1912	42	1174	951
1931	23	6704	4019	1911	43	1157	953
1930	24	5329	3203	1910	44	1138	955
1929	25	4401	2661	1909	45	1127	975
1928	26	3676	2224	1908	46	1102	987
1927	27	3186	1941	1907	47	1074	998
1926	28	2805	1755	1906	48	1047	1009
1925	29	2496	1585	1905	49	1016	1020
1924	30	2216	1465	1904	50	978	1031
1923	31	1945	1350	1894	60	696	1186
1922	32	1747	1255	1884	70	640	1010
1921	33	1566	1181	1874	80	593	977
1920	34	1438	1113				

Problem 2

The series of proportions obtained in Table 13.1 appears similar to the 'single survivors' column of a net nuptiality table. Indicate the principal differences between these two series.

Answer

Consider the significance of the proportion single within the same birth cohort at different ages. It is impossible to obtain an expression that in the study of nuptiality, would be analogous to the l_x column of a life table, for any individual remaining single will have avoided not only the risk of marriage, but will also not have succumbed to the risk of dying.

It will therefore be necessary to eliminate the effects of mortality. It would be possible to consider the marital status structure of a constant population (say 10 000) on the assumption of zero mortality (gross nuptiality); this is equivalent to calculating the proportion single at different ages. It has been shown in Chapter 11 that this procedure only yields correct results for the study of nuptiality if it is assumed that there are no mortality differences between the married and the single. However, this is never the case in practice. The single are always subject to higher mortality than the married, particularly single males, and the proportion single at more advanced ages, where there are few first marriages, will tend to be lower. Although the actual situation considered is more complex, the decline in the proportion single among men aged over 50 is largely explained by this factor. In the remainder of this answer, however, we shall ignore the bias introduced by this excess mortality, particularly since it is likely to have small effects at those ages where nuptiality is appreciable.

Consider the proportions single in Table 13.1. These proportions apply to as many different birth cohorts as there are ages in the table; they show the proportions never married on 1 January 1955 in thirty-nine different birth cohorts. They are the result of first marriages that had taken place in each of these cohorts before 1 January 1955. There is no reason for the results to be identical with those that would be obtained if one cohort only were considered at all ages. Identity between the two sets of proportions would be achieved only if the nuptiality of all the cohorts had been the same.

As these cohorts have experienced different nuptiality probabilities in the past, the series of proportions in Table 13.1 cannot satisfactorily describe the nuptiality of the population. Indeed, the method may yield inconsistent and impossible results, for the proportion single may actually increase with age at certain points in the table. This situation, which would, of course, be impossible within a single birth cohort, appears among women over the age of 41 in Table 13.1.

Moreover, the proportions single in Table 13.1 depend on the experience of the past in a different manner from those that would be obtained from the S_x column of a current nuptiality table. In the latter case the attrition factor is due to the additional marriages in different birth cohorts of a particular year; in Table 13.1 the decline in the proportions depends on the cumulative number of marriages that have taken place up to the date indicated. Moreover, these proportions, unlike corresponding proportions in a nuptiality table, do not reflect the nuptiality of a specific well-defined period. In particular they cannot be regarded as describing the situation in or about 1955.

Finally, the proportions in Table 13.1 relate to numbers in different cohorts at the same moment of time (in the Lexis diagram they would be represented as the flow across vertical segments). They relate to groups with the same age at last birthday. In a nuptiality table the S_x column is computed for the same group at a series of birthdays. In the Lexis diagram this would represent a flow across a horizontal segment.

Problem 3

Disregard the observations made in answer to the previous problem and treat the female proportions single in Table 13.1 as equivalent to single survivors in a nuptiality table. Obtain (1) the series of first marriages and (2) the probabilities of marrying for ages up to 40.

Answer

It is required to construct a gross nuptiality table from the series of proportions in Table 13.1. The procedure is well known and the results are shown in Table 13.2. Since the results for males will be needed later, Table 13.2 has been constructed for each sex separately.

A special notation will be used in this section. All functions are written with a prime (S', M', n') in order to distinguish the raw data from the graduated figures, which will be introduced and discussed later. Age will be denoted by a and not by x, to show that it is measured in completed

Table 13.2 *Gross nuptiality table*

Males				Females		
Single survivors S'_a	First marriages M'_a	Probability of marriage n'_a	Age a	Single Survivors S'_a	First marriages M'_a	Probability of marriage n'_a
			14	10 000	13	0·001
			15	9 987	555	0·006
10 000	3		16	9 932	195	0·020
9 997	48	0·005	17	9 737	457	0·047
9 949	155	0·015	18	9 280	862	0·093
9 794	356	0·036	19	8 418	1114	0·132
9 438	282	0·030	20	7 304	1254	0·172
9 156	1175	0·128	21	6 050	1143	0·189
7 981	1277	0·160	22	4 907	888	0·181
6 704	1375	0·205	23	4 019	816	0·203
5 329	928	0·174	24	3 203	542	0·169
4 401	725	0·165	25	2 661	437	0·164
3 676	490	0·133	26	2 224	283	0·127
3 186	381	0·120	27	1 941	186	0·096
2 805	309	0·110	28	1 755	170	0·097
2 496	280	0·112	29	1 585	120	0·076
2 216	271	0·122	30	1 465	115	0·078
1 945	198	0·102	31	1 350	95	0·070
1 747	181	0·104	32	1 255	74	0·059
1 566	128	0·082	33	1 181	68	0·058
1 438	53	0·037	34	1 113	27	0·024
1 385	32	0·023	35	1 086	18	0·017
1 353	18	0·013	36	1 068	37	0·035
1 335	16	0·012	37	1 031	16	0·016
1 319	43	0·033	38	1 015	26	0·026
1 276	44	0·034	39	989	23	0·026
1 232			40	966		

years. The probabilities are similar to ageing factors (ratios of successive l_x values), which are sometimes used in mortality studies.

Note the irregularities in the number of marriages and in the probabilities of marriage after ages 25 and 30. These are due to the relatively small numbers obtained by differencing the data for different cohorts.

Problem 4

Plot the probabilities obtained in the previous answer. Graduate the series, by taking 0·196 as the probability of marriage between birthday 23 and 24 and assuming that this declines to 0·010 just before age 50. For what part of the series is the graduation most liable to error? Interpolate to obtain annual values for n_x, and also calculate the probability of marrying between birthday 15 and 50.

Answer

The probabilities n'_a obtained in Table 13.2 are plotted in Figs. 13.1 and 13.2. The diagram for males will be used later.

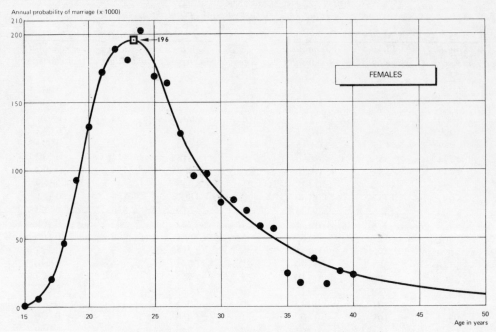

Fig. 13.1   *Annual probabilities of marriage (females)*

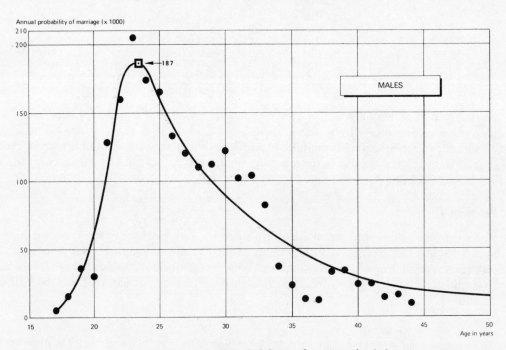

Fig. 13.2   *Annual probabilities of marriage (males)*

In the diagram for females the series appears fairly regular, especially the first eight points. Given that $n_{23} = 0{\cdot}196$ and $n_x = 0{\cdot}010$ when x is near 50, a skew curve can easily be traced. This will graduate the data and smooth out irregularities. The graduation is less satisfactory for males, for the raw data are less regular.

It is particularly difficult to determine the maximum of the curve, even though a value near the maximum is given in the problem (this value has been taken from a current nuptiality table). Normally a graduation should pass between known points and utilize all the information given by the configuration of such points, whilst being as smooth as possible. These principles are generally observed in quantitative demography, but they are insufficient to determine the shape of the curve near its maximum. The position of the maximum will depend on some four or five given points, all of which are subject to random variations. Thus there may be considerable uncertainty about the exact value of the maximum, particularly as the ordinates are large. Finally, the location of the maximum (the value of the abscissa) and its size (the value of the ordinate) have little meaning in themselves. Note that the age at which the maximum is attained is the same for both sexes (23 years), although external information suggests that the maximum may be reached a little later for males than for females (24 or 25 years).

The graduation leads to two estimated series:

1 The 'prospective probabilities of marriage'. These can be used to obtain a nuptiality table in a form particularly useful for projecting first marriages. These will be written n_a and will be analogous to the coefficients n'_a, used in Table 13.2.
2 Probabilities of marrying between birthday x and $x+1$. These will be written n_x, and the value of n_x for $x = 27$ will lie between the values of n_a for $a = 26$ and $a = 27$.

The results are shown in Table 13.3. Probabilities of the n_x type are only given for females. In all subsequent problems ignore first marriages taking place after the age of 50.

Problem 5

Compute the nuptiality table corresponding to the series of n_x and obtain the mean and median age at first marriage.

Answer

Nuptiality tables have been constructed in Table 13.3 by using the three series of probabilities. To be consistent it is necessary that the attrition factors of the table using the n_a ratios should lie between the corresponding probabilities of the table using the n_x ratios, and that the former should approximate to the arithmetic mean of the latter. The method of construction that has been used ensures that this relation holds true for the probabilities, but it does not hold for the 'single survivors' in the latter half of the table. This slight discrepancy is due to the inaccuracy of the method of graphic interpolation and has no practical significance.

It would be possible to calculate the mean age at first marriage from the series of first marriages by using a working mean. However, the method that will be shown here operates on the 'single survivors' column, and uses a formula analogous to that used in calculating the expectation of life at birth in a life table.

Table 13.3 Nuptiality tables for France, obtained from data relating to the population by sex, age and marital status on 1 January 1955

Age a	Females						Males		
	S_a	M_a	n_a	S_x	M_x	n_x	S_a	M_a	n_a
14	10 000	10	0·001						
15	9 990	60	0·006	10 000	30	0·003			
16	9 930	199	0·020	9 970	120	0·012			
17	9 731	457	0·047	9 850	305	0·031	10 000	50	0·005
18	9 274	816	0·088	9 545	640	0·067	9 950	149	0·015
19	8 458	1116	0·132	8 905	971	0·109	9 801	314	0·032
20	7 342	1263	0·172	7 934	1214	0·153	9 487	569	0·060
21	6 079	1149	0·189	6 720	1216	0·181	8 918	963	0·108
22	4 930	961	0·195	5 504	1062	0·193	7 955	1297	0·163
23	3 969	766	0·193	4 442	871	0·196	6 658	1245	0·187
24	3 203	577	0·180	3 571	671	0·188	5 413	991	0·183
25	2 626	404	0·154	2 900	484	0·167	4 422	708	0·160
26	2 222	282	0·127	2 416	338	0·140	3 714	527	0·142
27	1 940	210	0·108	2 078	241	0·116	3 187	398	0·125
28	1 730	163	0·094	1 837	184	0·100	2 789	310	0·111
29	1 567	128	0·082	1 653	145	0·088	2 479	250	0·101
30	1 439	104	0·072	1 508	116	0·077	2 229	201	0·090
31	1 335	87	0·065	1 392	95	0·068	2 028	162	0·080
32	1 248	71	0·057	1 297	79	0·061	1 866	134	0·072
33	1 177	60	0·051	1 218	65	0·053	1 732	113	0·065
34	1 117	50	0·045	1 153	55	0·048	1 619	96	0·059
35	1 067	42	0·039	1 098	46	0·042	1 523	81	0·053
36	1 025	35	0·034	1 052	38	0·036	1 442	68	0·047
37	990	29	0·029	1 014	32	0·032	1 374	58	0·042
38	961	25	0·026	982	27	0·027	1 316	49	0·037
39	936	22	0·024	955	24	0·025	1 267	42	0·033
40	914	19	0·021	931	20	0·021	1 225	37	0·030
41	895	17	0·019	911	18	0·020	1 188	32	0·027
42	878	15	0·017	893	16	0·018	1 156	29	0·025
43	863	13	0·015	877	14	0·016	1 127	26	0·023
44	850	12	0·014	863	13	0·015	1 101	23	0·021
45	838	11	0·013	850	11	0·013	1 078	20	0·019
46	827	10	0·012	839	10	0·012	1 058	19	0·018
47	817	9	0·011	829	9	0·011	1 039	18	0·017
48	808	8	0·010	820	8	0·010	1 021	16	0·016
49	800	7	0·009	812	7	0·009	1 005	15	0·015
50	793			805			990		

Let T stand for the total number of years of single life between ages 15 and 50, for 10 000 women aged 15. Then,

$$T = S_{16} + S_{17} + \ldots + S_{50} + \tfrac{1}{2}(S_{15} + S_{50}).$$

The corresponding value for women who marry before the age of 50 is

$$T' = T - 35S_{50},$$

and the mean age at marriage of such women will be

$$m = 15 + \frac{T'}{S_{15} - S_{50}}.$$

If only values of the S function are to be used:

$$m = 15 \cdot 5 + \frac{S_{16} + S_{17} + \dots + S_{50} - 35 S_{50}}{S_{15} - S_{50}},$$

which yields

$$m = 23 \cdot 14.$$

The median age at marriage m' is defined as the age of the 4597th ($= (10\,000 - 805)/2$) woman who marries and it is required to find m', so that

$$S_{m'} = 10\,000 - 4597 = 5403.$$

Since $S_{22} = 5504$, $S_{23} = 4442$, $22 < m' < 23$, and, by linear interpolation,

$$m' = 22 \cdot 10.$$

These values are not very different from those found for recent French female birth cohorts for which such computations are possible. Although the method is not quite accurate theoretically and cannot be applied in all cases, it yields satisfactory results in this particular application.

Problem 6

Consider the French female birth cohort of 1820 for which Delaporte has computed a generation life table. Apply the female nuptiality table obtained in answer to the previous problem to this cohort and estimate the proportion of women who never marry among women reaching their 15th birthday, and among 10 000 new-born girls. What is the age distribution of first marriages for this cohort? Compare it with the corresponding age distribution in the nuptiality table and comment.

Answer

The answer requires the combination of a life table and a gross nuptiality table into a net nuptiality table, yielding the total number of marriages and of single deaths. The situation differs from the present, as women in the 1820 cohort married rather later than women do today (the average age at marriage was between two and three years higher). The cohort is used because statistics are easily available for it; the didactic value of the example is not affected.

Write M'_x and d'_x for marriages and deaths between ages x and $x+1$ (unprimed symbols will stand for analogous values in the gross nuptiality table and the life table respectively). As was shown in Chapter 11:

$$M'_x = M_x \tfrac{1}{2}(l_x + l_{x+1})$$
$$d'_x = d_x \tfrac{1}{2}(S_x + S_{x+1})$$

where l_{15} and S_{15} are both equal to unity. At present, however, the values of $S_a = \frac{1}{2}(S_x + S_{x+1})$ are available, the equation holding for $a = x$. These formulae assume the absence of any differential mortality between single and married, as well as independence between mortality and nuptiality. The necessary calculations are shown in Table 13.4. l_x has been obtained by writing $l_{15} = 1$ instead of 0·6683 as in Delaporte's table.

Table 13.4 *Marriages and deaths amongst spinsters*

Age x	l_x	$\frac{1}{2}(l_x + l_{x+1})$	M_x	M'_x	S_a	d_x	d'_x
15	10 000	9965	30	29·9	9990	70	69·9
16	9930	9893	120	118·7	9930	74	73·5
17	9856	9815	305	299·4	9731	81	78·8
18	9775	9735	640	623·0	9274	80	74·2
19	9695	9653	971	937·3	8458	84	71·0
20	9611	9569	1214	1161·7	7342	84	61·7
21	9527	9484	1216	1153·3	6079	86	52·3
22	9441	9398	1062	998·1	4930	86	42·4
23	9355	9312	871	811·1	3969	85	33·7
24	9270	9227	671	619·1	3203	86	27·5
25	9184	9142	484	442·5	2626	84	22·1
26	9100	9058	338	306·2	2222	84	18·7
27	9016	8973	241	216·2	1940	86	16·7
28	8930	8888	184	163·5	1730	84	14·5
29	8846	8803	145	127·6	1567	85	13·3
30	8761	8719	116	101·1	1439	83	11·9
31	8678	8635	95	82·0	1335	86	11·5
32	8592	8550	79	67·5	1248	84	10·5
33	8508	8466	65	55·0	1177	84	9·9
34	8424	8382	55	46·1	1117	84	9·4
35	8340	8298	46	38·2	1067	83	8·9
36	8257	8215	38	31·2	1025	83	8·5
37	8174	8131	32	26·0	990	86	8·5
38	8088	8046	27	21·7	961	84	8·1
39	8004	7962	24	19·1	936	84	7·9
40	7920	7877	20	15·8	914	85	7·8
41	7835	7793	18	14·0	895	83	7·4
42	7752	7709	16	12·3	878	86	7·6
43	7666	7623	14	10·7	863	85	7·3
44	7581	7537	13	9·8	850	88	7·5
45	7493	7449	11	8·2	838	87	7·3
46	7406	7361	10	7·4	827	90	7·4
47	7316	7270	9	6·5	817	91	7·4
48	7225	7177	8	5·7	808	95	7·7
49	7130	7082	7	5·0	800	96	7·7
50	7034						
				8590·9			840·5

The group of never-married women consists of:

1 Those who die as spinsters before age 50. Table 13.4 gives this number as 840.
2 Those surviving to age 50, who have not married by that age. There are $805 \times 0·7034 = 566$

such women, 805 being the number of single survivors in the gross nuptiality table and 0·7034 the probability of survival from birthday 15 to birthday 50 in the cohort considered. Thus, for every 10 000 girls at birthday 15 there will be 840 + 566 = 1406 who will never marry.

Only 6683 out of every 10 000 new-born girls will survive to birthday 15, and therefore 3317 will not marry because they will have died before reaching marriageable age. 14·06% of the 6683 or 940 will not marry, so that 3317 + 940 = 4257 out of every 10 000 new-born girls will remain unmarried.

In order to compare the age distributions of the marriages M_x and M'_x, these will have to be reduced to percentages. It will be found that there is a relatively larger number of marriages at younger ages in the actual population than there is in the nuptiality table, and the mean age at first marriages will be lower than m.

In Table 13.5 marriages are shown below and above the age of 22. The differences are relatively small, because the effect of mortality is less important at the younger ages.

Table 13.5 *Distribution of first marriages by age*

Age	Marriages in the population	The nuptiality table
Before 22	61·9%	60·4%
After 22	38·1%	39·6%
	100·0%	100·0%

It is now possible to decompose the figures in the same manner as was done in Table 11.3 (p. 103). Using the numbers in italics in that table as base data, the other figures may be derived from them. The number of women marrying for the first time before birthday 50 is 8594 and not 8591 as in Table 13.4. This slight inconsistency is due to the use of S_a rather than S_x in the computations.

Table 13.6 *Marriages and deaths of spinsters before birthday 50 per 10 000 reaching birthday 15*

	Married before birthday 50	Not married by birthday 50	Total
Died before birthday 50	2126	840	2 966
Survived to birthday 50	6468	566	7 034
Total	8594	1406	10 000

Problem 7

French nuptiality has not changed greatly over time, so that the nuptiality table that has been calculated may be taken as characterizing present conditions. Applying the same methods as in previous problems to French male birth cohorts, it is assumed for purposes of graphic graduation that the probability of marrying at age 23 is 0·184 and falls to 0·015 at age 50.

Show how some of the data previously calculated may be used to obtain projections of the number of marriages in the future. Perform such a calculation for the period 1960–76, using the population projections published in *Études Statistiques*, No. 2, April–June 1960 (see Statistical Appendix).

For each sex, calculate the number of first marriages by single years of age to birthday 29 (it will be necessary to divide the age group 25–29 into single years). Also compute the number by five-year age groups to birthday 49. Add the number of marriages for each sex and compare the numbers, using a graph. Relate these to marriages observed since 1 January 1950 and comment.

Answer

The required male nuptiality table has already been computed in previous answers. Projections are most easily carried by ageing different cohorts between successive new year's days. Consider women aged a last birthday on 1 January of a given year. The ageing factors to be used for nuptiality purposes are the S_a series.

Since a projection of first marriages is required, the method will be illustrated by considering women aged a last birthday on 1 January of a given year. The functions in a nuptiality table relating to a series of one-year age groups will be used.

Writing L_a for the total number aged a last birthday on 1 January, and assuming that $S_{14} = 1$, the number of spinsters at that date will be $S_a l_a$, where S_a is the single survivorship function in the gross nuptiality table, which is assumed to be constant over time.

As was shown in **Chapter 11** the number of first marriages will be given by $l_a S_a n_a (1 - \frac{1}{2} q_a)$, where n_a and q_a are the probabilities of marrying and of dying respectively. The mortality of single women could have been used if it had been thought desirable. But $S_a n_a = M_a$, where M_a will be the numbers in Table 13.3 divided by 10 000. This follows as S_{14} is taken as 1.

Thus the number of first marriages in a given year for the cohort aged a last birthday will be given by $L_a M_a (1 - \frac{1}{2} q_a)$. The computations become much simpler if the expression in parentheses could be neglected. This would overestimate the number of marriages by $L_a M_a \frac{1}{2} q_a$, and the error in the total number of marriages would be $\frac{1}{2} M q$, where M is the total number of marriages and q the probability of dying within one year at the mean age at marriage. This value is less than 0·001 for women and 0·002 for men, according to the French

Table 13.7   *First marriages of women aged under 50, France, 1967*

Age a	L_a (000)	M_a ($S_{14} = 1000$)	$L_a M_a$	Age a	L_a (000)	M_a ($S_{14} = 1000$)	$L_a M_a$
14	387·1	10	387	25	242·7*	404	9 805*
15	386·9	60	2 321	26	256·7*	282	7 239*
16	403·9	199	8 038	27	283·6*	210	5 956*
17	409·4	457	18 710	28	285·3*	163	4 650*
18	406·3	816	33 154	29	287·4*	128	3 679*
19	405·4	1116	45 243	25–29(T)	1355·7*		31 329*
20	390·9	1263	49 371	0·995T	1348·8		31 172
21	294·2	1149	33 804	30–34	1505·6	74·4	11 202
22	287·3	961	27 610	35–39	1571·6	30·6	4 809
23	286·2	766	21 923	40–44	1576·4	15·6	2 459
24	264·4	577	15 256	45–49	1211·7	9·0	1 091
				14–49			306 550

* Data relate to five years earlier.

life table of 1952–6. Thus the error in the total number of marriages will be less than 0·5 per 1000 for marriages of females and less than 1 per 1000 for those of males. Calculations using the formula L_aM_a thus yield satisfactory results, and this formula has been used in Table 13.7 for women aged under 50 in 1967.

Some of the figures in this table need explaining:

1 Because information for the population aged 25–30 by individual years of age was not available, the computations have been based on the numbers in each cohort five years earlier – i.e. when the women were five years younger. The total number was 1 355 700 instead of 1 348 000 on 1 January 1967, or 5 per 1000 in excess. The figure for marriages is therefore multiplied by 0·995 to allow for this.

2 For the quinquennial age groups (30–50) the M-values used are the arithmetic means of the five values of M for individual years of age. Thus, for the age group 30–34:

Age a	M_a
30	104
31	87
32	71
33	60
34	50
Mean	74·4

The same result would have been obtained if the mean population had been multiplied by the sum of the five M-values.

The results are shown in Table 13.8. The figures based on projections begin at 1961. For 1959 and 1960 the method discussed has been applied to an *estimated* sex-age distribution of the population. This has also been done for 1958 (*P*) and the result compared with the number actually observed (*O*). For earlier years (from 1950) only observed figures are shown, so that 1958 is the link-year.

The observed figures show considerable annual fluctuations, but the trend of spinster marriages closely parallels that of men (although it tends to run about 1% in excess of the male figure). The projected figures show a regular trend, but the two series diverge.

Table 13.8 First marriages by sex in France: recent data and projections (in 000s)

Year	Males	Females	Year	Males	Females
1950	287·7	290·8	1963	264·4	258·6
1951	278·2	281·3	1964	261·2	265·2
1952	273·0	276·3	1965	262·1	276·2
1953	270·4	273·5	1966	266·9	290·6
1954	276·9	279·9	1967	275·4	306·6
1955	276·2	279·2	1968	288·1	320·8
1956	257·8	260·1	1969	304·1	332·1
1957	274·8	277·6	1970	319·2	339·9
1958 {O	276·4	279·1	1971	331·0	344·6
1958 {P	284·9	267·5	1972	338·7	346·9
1959	283·3	263·8	1973	342·9	347·7
1960	281·6	261·0	1974	344·6	348·0
1961	275·9	257·2	1975	345·4	348·5
1962	270·1	256·1	1976	346·1	349·2

The two figures for 1958 do not agree; even the relative position of the two sexes is different. This is not due to faults in the basic population data, but to defects in the M_a series, which for various reasons is badly adapted for the calculations (annual fluctuations, approximations, etc.). However, the most noticeable phenomenon is the reversal in the relative position of the sexes; a slight but constant excess of female marriages before and up to 1958 is suddenly replaced by an increased excess of male marriages.

This is caused by an imbalance between the numbers of men and women at the principal ages at marriage: the ratio of men aged 22–27 per 100 women aged 19–24 is given below (actual data up to 1 January 1960, projections thereafter):

1956	1957	1958	1959	1960	1961	1962	1963	1964
107	110	113	112	114	115	115	111	106.

This is a consequence of the fall in births before and during the Second World War. The values of M_a that have been used assume that there is approximate equilibrium, as is normally the case (between 100 and 105 men for every 100 women). It follows that in periods of male excess the use of these numbers overestimates male and underestimates female marriages.

Because men tend to marry women younger than themselves, the number of women reaching the ages where nuptiality is high will increase before the number of men does. They will be the survivors of the large birth cohorts of the immediate post-war years. For a transitional period, therefore, there will be a majority of women. The ratios shown in the preceding paragraph continue as follows:

1965	1966	1967	1968	1969	1970	1971	1972	1973	1974	1975	1976
103	95	87	81	83	86	89	94	100	105	106	105

These ratios are based on projections that assume zero migration. They are not, therefore, exactly comparable with the preceding ratios, which include foreigners. Many of these, particularly Algerian Muslims, hardly enter the French marriage market. The figures in the first series must therefore be reduced by a few percentage points to make them comparable with the second.

This new situation will again lead to inconsistent projections: female marriages will be overestimated and male marriages underestimated.

Fig. 13.3 shows the divergence between the two series graphically for the whole period of the calculations. Just before 1976, however, a normal situation is reached again (the sex ratio of the marriageable population returns to near 1·05, so that female marriages slightly exceed those of males, as was the case before 1958).

In theory this divergence is not sufficient to suggest that the results are inconsistent. There is no necessity for the number of first marriages of men and women to be equal (they are hardly ever identical in fact). It is remarriages that make the total number of men and women marrying equal.

However, there are reasons why so great a divergence as the projections show is impossible. In 1958 when the sex ratio was abnormally high (113 men per 100 women) marriages in which one of the partners married for the first time were divided between men and women in the same ratio as in preceding years. The nuptiality rates for each sex are unlikely to remain constant under these conditions, but will change in order to compensate for the disequilibrium. If they were to remain constant, then the proportion never married at age 50 in different cohorts would remain the same, and the proportion of remarriages would change. In the past, however,

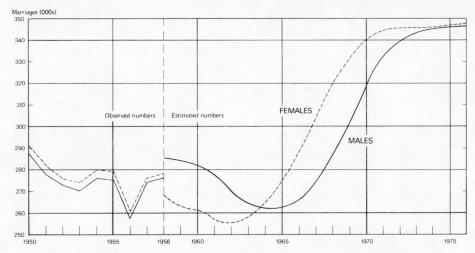

Fig. 13.3   *First marriages for each sex in France, observed and estimated numbers*

cohorts which had experienced such differences in sex structure showed varying proportions of never-married. This shows that first-marriage rate did not remain unaffected by these variations. Moreover, the timing of marriages was frequently affected in order to compensate for the abnormal sex ratios.

All these considerations will render the study of French nuptiality in the future an extremely interesting topic.

V
DISUNIONS AND REMARRIAGES

14

The statistical study of divorce

Statistical studies of divorce often lack a sound theoretical foundation. A variety of indices have come to be used which have been constructed by analogy with indices of mortality. In this chapter the study of divorce will be related to the event that must naturally precede it – marriage. This very general principle will be applied even to current measures of divorce, but the difficulty of applying these methods will be stressed.

Data

The distribution of divorces by duration of marriage in a western European country has not varied much over time. The distribution is as follows:

(Duration of marriage (calculated as difference between calendar years) = *D*.
Number of divorces per 1000 = *N*.)

D	N	D	N	D	N	D	N	D	N	D	N
0	0	6	63	12	48	18	28	24	13	30	7
1	14	7	64	13	45	19	25	25	12	31	5
2	28	8	62	14	41	20	23	26	11	32	4
3	43	9	59	15	38	21	20	27	10	33	3
4	53	10	54	16	34	22	17	28	9	34	1
5	60	11	51	17	31	23	15	29	8	35	1

Problem 1

Compute the mean and median length of marriages that are dissolved by divorce.

Answer

Since the durations of marriage at divorce are given by individual years, the mean length of a marriage dissolved by divorce at duration x will also be x years. This is shown graphically in

Fig. 14.1 by comparing the total number of divorces at duration 2, with the differences in calendar years (parallelogram AA′B′B). A special problem would arise for divorces shown to take place at duration 0. Fortunately there are no divorces at that duration and the problem need not detain us.

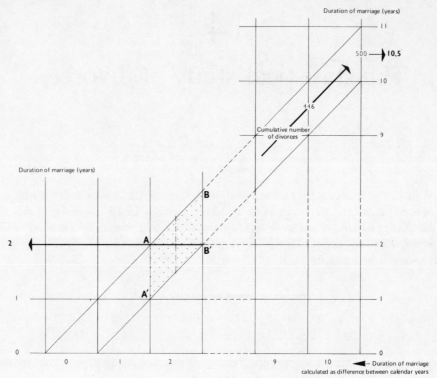

Fig. 14.1 *Divorce and the duration of marriage*

If n_x be the number of divorces at duration x, the mean length of broken marriages is given by the formula

$$\bar{x} = \frac{\Sigma n_x x}{\Sigma n_x} = \frac{1}{1000}\Sigma n_x x.$$

In computations of this type it is normal to choose a working mean near the required average and to write ξ for the difference between x and the working mean. In this chapter the working mean will be taken as 12, so that $x = 12 + \xi$. Then,

$$\Sigma n_x x = \Sigma n_x(12 + \xi) = 12\Sigma n_x + \Sigma n_x \xi,$$

so that

$$\bar{x} = 12 + \bar{\xi}.$$

It is much quicker to work with the variable ξ than with x, and the computation is shown in detail in Table 14.1, whence $\bar{x} = 12 - 68/1000 = 11{\cdot}932$, or $11{\cdot}9$ years approximately. The median duration is that corresponding to the 500th divorce. By cumulating the durations from

Table 14.1 *Calculation of mean duration of broken marriages*

Duration x	Frequency $n_x = n_\xi$	Difference from working mean (ξ)	$n_\xi\xi$	Duration x	Frequency $n_x = n_\xi$	Difference from working mean (ξ)	$n_\xi\xi$
0	0	−12	00	19	25	7	175
1	14	−11	−154	20	23	8	184
2	28	−10	−280	21	20	9	180
3	43	−9	−387	22	17	10	170
4	53	−8	−424	23	15	11	165
5	60	−7	−420	24	13	12	156
6	63	−6	−378	25	12	13	156
7	74	−5	−320	26	11	14	154
8	62	−4	−248	27	10	15	150
9	59	−3	−177	28	9	16	144
10	54	−2	−108	29	8	17	136
11	51	−1	−51	30	7	18	126
12	48	0	−2947	31	5	19	95
13	45	1	45	32	4	20	80
14	41	2	82	33	3	21	63
15	38	3	114	34	1	22	22
16	34	4	136	35	1	23	23
17	31	5	155				2879
18	28	6	168				−68

0 onwards, 500 divorces are obtained by year 10. Thus the 500th divorce takes place at exact duration 10·5 (Fig. 14.1), which will be the median duration of broken marriages.

Problem 2

In 1938, 28 600 divorces were registered. Assume that each marriage cohort has a constant proportion, p, of marriages ending in divorce. Estimate the value of p from the distribution of divorces by duration of marriage given above and the statistics of marriages given in the table below:

Number of marriages (in 000s)

1885	293·6	1895	294·8	1905	316·2	1915	86·0	1925	352·8	1936	279·9	1947	427·1
1886	293·7	1896	302·1	1906	320·2	1916	125·0	1926	345·4	1937	274·5	1948	370·8
1887	287·2	1897	303·6	1907	327·7	1917	180·0	1927	336·4	1938	273·9	1949	341·1
1888	287·2	1898	299·7	1908	328·9	1918	202·7	1928	338·8	1939	258·4	1950	331·1
1889	283·3	1899	308·8	1909	320·9	1919	552·7	1929	334·3	1940	177·0	1951	319·7
1890	280·1	1900	312·1	1910	320·6	1920	622·7	1930	342·1	1941	226·0	1952	313·9
1891	296·4	1901	316·5	1911	321·1	1921	455·5	1931	326·7	1942	267·0	1953	308·4
1892	301·3	1902	307·7	1912	325·3	1922	384·6	1932	315·0	1943	219·0	1954	314·5
1893	298·6	1903	308·5	1913	312·0	1923	355·1	1933	315·7	1944	205·0	1955	312·8
1894	298·3	1904	312·1	1914	205·0	1924	355·4	1934	298·5	1945	393·0	1956	293·5
								1935	284·9	1946	516·9	1957	310·5

Answer

A general result must first be established. Denoting the year studied by 0 and preceding years by 1, 2, 3, …, write $M_0, M_1, M_2, M_3, \ldots$ for the marriages taking place in these years and $\alpha_0, \alpha_1, \alpha_2,$

α_3, ... for the proportion of divorces by duration, so that $\sum \alpha_i = 1$. Fig. 14.2 illustrates this notation and will help in understanding the reasoning.

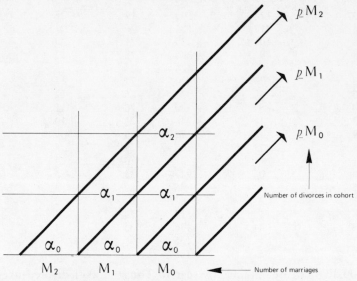

Fig. 14.2   *Marriages and divorces in different cohorts*

It is assumed that the proportion of marriages dissolved by divorce in each cohort is the same (p). Of the M_0 marriages in year 0, pM_0 will end in divorce and $p\alpha_0 M_0$ will so end in year 0. Similarly $\alpha_1 p M_1$ of the marriages in year 1 will end by divorce in year 0. Then, if D_0 is the total number of divorces in year 0:

$$D_0 = p \sum \alpha_i M_i,$$

whence we obtain

$$p = D_0 / \sum \alpha_i M_i.$$

p may therefore be obtained by dividing the number of divorces in a given year by a weighted mean of marriages of that and preceding years. The calculation of the weighted mean is shown in Table 14.2, where $\sum \alpha_i M_i$ is calculated for the years 1938 to 1920 (this value will be useful later). For 1938 $\sum \alpha_i M_i = 331\,700$, so that $p = 28\,600/331\,700 = 0.086$.

Thus, on the assumption that the proportion of divorces in different marriage cohorts does not change, a figure of 28 600 divorces in 1938 implies a rate of 86 divorces per 1000 marriages in each cohort.

The distribution of divorces by duration of marriage is assumed to take account of the other attrition processes diminishing the number of marriages (widowhood and migration). The assumption that the distribution of divorces by duration of marriage remains unchanged when the fall in mortality has reduced the incidence of widowhood implies that this fall has been compensated for by changes in migration and in the probability of divorce in particular years, so that the distribution as a whole remains unchanged.

Table 14.2 *Computation of a weighted mean of marriages*

Year	Marriages (000s)	α_i	$\alpha_i M_i$	α_i	$\alpha_i M_i$	Year	Marriages (000s)	α_i	$\alpha_i M_i$	α_i	$\alpha_i M_i$
						1909	320·9	8	2·6	51	16·4
1938	273·9	0				1908	328·9	7	2·3	48	15·8
1937	274·5	14	3·8			1907	327·7	5	1·6	45	14·7
1936	279·9	28	7·8			1906	320·2	4	1·3	41	13·1
1935	284·9	43	12·3			1905	316·2	3	0·9	38	12·0
1934	298·5	53	15·8			1904	312·1	1	0·3	34	10·6
1933	315·7	60	18·9			1903	308·5	1	0·3	31	9·6
1932	315·0	63	19·8			1902	307·7		331·7	28	8·6
1931	326·7	64	20·9			1901	316·5			25	7·9
1930	342·1	62	21·2			1900	312·1			23	7·2
1929	334·3	59	19·7			1899	308·8			20	6·2
1928	338·8	54	18·3			1898	299·7			17	5·1
1927	336·4	51	17·2			1897	303·6			15	4·6
1926	345·4	48	16·6			1896	302·1			13	3·9
1925	352·8	45	15·9			1895	294·8			12	3·5
1924	355·4	41	14·6			1894	298·3			11	3·3
1923	355·1	38	13·5			1893	298·6			10	3·0
1922	384·6	34	13·1			1892	301·3			9	2·7
1921	455·5	31	14·1			1891	296·4			8	2·4
1920	622·7	28	17·4	0		1890	280·1			7	2·0
1919	552·7	25	13·8	14	7·7	1889	283·3			5	1·4
1918	202·0	23	4·6	28	5·7	1888	287·2			4	1·1
1917	180·0	20	3·6	43	7·7	1887	287·2			3	0·9
1916	125·0	17	2·1	53	6·6	1886	293·7			1	0·3
1915	86·0	15	1·3	60	5·2	1885	193·6			1	0·2
1914	205·0	13	2·7	63	12·9						278·7
1913	312·0	12	3·7	64	20·0						
1912	325·3	11	3·6	62	20·2						
1911	321·1	10	3·2	59	18·9						
1910	320·6	9	2·9	54	17·3						

α_i is the distribution of the number of divorces by duration of marriage, i, per 1000 divorces.
M_i is the number of marriages of duration i.

Problem 3

p, the total proportion of marriages in a cohort that are broken by divorce, will vary for different marriage cohorts. The method of computation illustrated in the previous problem yields a *current* index of divorce for year k, say $p_{(k)}$. Interpret this index. What is the value of $p_{(1920)}$, given that the number of divorces in 1920 was 37 000? Compare with $p_{(1938)}$ and comment.

Answer

Normally the proportion of marriages broken by divorce will vary in different marriage cohorts, even if other attrition factors (migration, widowhood) influencing the number of divorces remain constant. In most Western countries the proportion of marriages ending in divorce has tended to increase recently.

If it were assumed that the distribution of divorces by duration of marriage had not changed significantly in different marriage cohorts, it would be possible to allocate to each marriage cohort i a proportion p_i of marriages that end in divorce. But the distribution of divorces by duration of marriage does not change, and the proportion for duration j would be given by α_j as previously.

Under these assumptions divorces in year 0 will be given by

$$D_0 = \sum \alpha_i p_i M_i$$

and the ratio that has previously been calculated, $D_0/(\sum \alpha_i M_i)$, will now become $\sum \alpha_i p_i M_i / \sum \alpha_i M_i$. This ratio is a weighted average of the p_i values, each value being weighted by $\alpha_i M_i / \sum \alpha_i M_i$. In other words, the value $p_{(0)}$,[1] which applies to year 0, will be a weighted mean of the final frequency of divorces in the thirty-six marriage cohorts contributing to the divorces of that year; the current frequency will therefore lie between the maximum and the minimum value of the frequencies for the cohorts composing the population. It will further be assumed that the proportions p_i vary linearly with i. This is acceptable, provided that p_i changes only slowly. In this case it is possible to write $p_{i+1} = p_i + a$, where a is the increment in the frequency of divorce from one cohort to the next. Thus, if $p_i = 0.081$ and $p_{i+1} = 0.079$ (i.e. the frequency of divorces increases for more recent cohorts), a will be negative: $a = -0.002$. This assumption makes it possible to express every p_i in terms of p_0, for $p_i = p_0 + ia$, so that

$$\sum \alpha_i p_i M_i = \sum (p_0 + ia) a_i M_i = p_0 \sum a_i M_i + a \sum i a_i M_i$$

and the current index may be written

$$p_{(0)} = p_0 + a \sum a_i i M_i / \sum a_i M_i.$$

If the variation in M_i is small, the factor multiplying a is nearly

$$\bar{i} = \sum i a_i / \sum a_i$$

where $\bar{i}$ is the mean duration of marriages broken by divorce in each cohort. By hypothesis this will be constant, because the distribution of marriages by duration does not change. The formula obtained is thus

$$p_{(0)} = p_0 + \bar{i} a.$$

The current index of divorce $p_{(0)}$ may therefore be regarded as equivalent to the cohort index for the cohort for which the duration of marriage at year 0 is the same as the mean length of marriages broken by divorce. With the given values of d_i this mean is 11.9 years. Provided that the assumption is satisfied the current index $p_{(k)}$ will be equivalent to the index for the cohort of marriages taking place twelve years ago.

$p_{(1938)}$ was found to be 0.086. Similarly $p_{(1920)} = 37\,000/278\,800 = 0.133$ (278 800 was the weighted mean of marriages relating to 1920 computed in Table 14.2). Hence $p_{(1938)} < p_{(1920)}$, so that in this population the frequency of divorce is declining. As $p_{(1938)} = p_{1926}$ and

---

[1] Suffixes in parentheses will be used for current frequencies to distinguish them from cohort frequencies with the same suffix.

$p_{(1920)} = p_{1908}$, it follows that $p_{1926} < p_{1908}$. This somewhat paradoxical conclusion leads to a re-examination of the assumptions.

It has been shown that if the current index of divorce is to be interpreted as a weighted mean of cohort indices, the distribution of divorces by duration of marriage in different cohorts must remain invariant. But this distribution may change, both because of changes in secular trends and also, as is shown in Chapter 19, and particularly in Fig. 19.1, because short-term, almost random, fluctuations may exercise a considerable influence on the distribution of broken marriages by duration.

Both World Wars have led to such changes and the figures have been affected by them, as is clear from the statistics of annual marriages. The number of marriages between 1914 and 1918 was very low, and there was a compensating increase between 1919 and 1922. In 1920 a large number of divorces were granted, probably as an aftermath of the war. These marriages were broken because of special circumstances, and are additional to the rising trend of divorce. It can be shown that the sum of the divorces of the war and the post-war period is in excess of the number that would have been expected if pre-war trends had continued. Therefore, in the calculation of $p_{(1920)}$ weights for duration of marriage from different cohorts will be used, the sum of which will exceed unity. In these circumstances the current index will no longer be a weighted mean of cohort indices, and may even exceed the largest value of the index for one of the constituent cohorts. It follows that it would not be justifiable to regard the current index as applying to any particular cohort.

It would also be unjustified to regard annual fluctuations in the current index as reflecting corresponding fluctuations in cohort indices, for changes in the distribution of divorces by duration of marriage may completely change the significance attributed to the current index.

Problem 4

Recompute $p_{(1920)}$ and $p_{(1938)}$ by relating the number of divorces in those years to an appropriate arithmetic average of marriages over a ten-year period. Compare your answers with those obtained in Problems 2 and 3 and comment.

Answer

The index $p_{(k)}$ was obtained by dividing the number of divorces in year k to a related number of marriages. This 'related' number must be a function of all marriages that may end in divorce in year k. But many marriage cohorts will only contribute a relatively small number of divorces in year k, and it seems reasonable to include in the index only those marriages that make an appreciable contribution to the divorces of that year. If only ten marriage cohorts are to be retained in the denominator, this would suggest using durations 4 to 13. A simple arithmetic mean of the number of marriages is equivalent to weighting them all equally, though in the first calculation the weights varied between 0·045 and 0·065 and the ten cohorts together were given a weight of 0·559. The two procedures are compared in Table 14.3.

Clearly, the simplified method yields satisfactory results, particularly for 1938. The results are less good for 1920, because of the irregular variations in the number of marriages in the immediately preceding period. This suggests that a simplified method of calculating $p_{(k)}$ may be used, provided that the annual number of marriages in the preceding period had not varied

Table 14.3   *Value of $p_{(k)}$ obtained by two different methods*

| | 1920 | | 1938 | |
	Weighted mean	Unweighted mean Ten cohorts	Weighted mean	Unweighted mean Ten cohorts
Marriages	278 700	267 300	331 700	330 600
Divorces	37 000	37 000	28 600	28 600
$p_{(k)}$	0·133	0·138	0·0862	0·0865

greatly. Where this condition is not fulfilled the more exact method will, in theory, give better results. However, even in such cases the difference between the two methods is small, and in view of the difficulties in interpreting the current index the simplified method appears preferable.

Problem 5

It is estimated that approximately 33 000 divorces were granted in 1957. Compute the proportion of marriages ending in divorce in 1957 (current index) by using the arithmetic mean suggested in Problem 4. Comment.

Answer

1957 is sufficiently far removed from the Second World War to allow the use of the simplified method. The calculations give $p_{1957} = 33\,000/352\,700 = 0.094$. This proportion may be regarded as applying to the 1945 marriage cohort ($= 1957 - 12$). However, as these marriages took place immediately after the war it is possible that the distribution of divorces by duration of marriage in this cohort could present some unusual features.

If 0·094 were simply regarded as a proportion applying to the year 1957, it could be compared with the figure of 0·086 for 1938 to obtain an indication of the rising trend of divorce: a slight increase over a period of twenty years. This would suggest that the proportion of marriages ending in divorce might become stabilized in the future.

15

Widow remarriage in India

The circumstances in which demographic data are collected may make for difficulties of interpretation. The statistics discussed in this chapter relate to information about the past, which may be obtained either at a census or a special survey and which refers either to the whole or part of a population. The histories of remarriages take place at different dates, but all observations terminate at the time of the census, and this makes for difficulties in analysis. It will be shown, however, that some lines of approach make it possible to carry a rigorous analysis quite a long way, even though they do not lead to definite conclusions.

Data

In an inquiry held in six Indian districts in 1954–5 information was obtained for certain age groups on the percentage of widows who had remarried. The data were classified by age at widowhood and the results are given below:

Age at Survey	*Percentage remarrying* Age at time of widowhood					
	Under 13	*13–22*	*23–32*	*33–42*	*43 and over*	*All*
13–22	83·3	47·3				56·8
23–32	93·0	57·3	8·4			47·4
33–42	90·1	69·2	15·0	2·5		31·9
43 and over	86·1	61·8	16·1	2·0	0·0	18·5
All	87·4	60·5	14·2	2·1	0·0	25·6

Problem 1

Comment on this table. Consider the data in the bottom row first, then those in the final column, and lastly the data in the body of the table.

Answer

Before commenting on the table, some general remarks will be useful.

In the statistical study of remarriage in a cohort of widows two different factors are considered: the final frequency of remarriage, and the distribution of second marriages in time. The statistics given in the table can only show those second marriages that have already taken place at different durations of widowhood. For the data in the body of the table the duration of widowhood is the difference between the age of the woman at the time of the survey and her age when she was widowed. Therefore, throughout the table, other things being equal, the frequency of remarriage will increase with increasing duration of widowhood. In particular the nearer age at survey is to age at widowhood, the smaller will be the percentage of women who have remarried.

There are two separate factors influencing the probability of remarriage:

1 Age at widowhood influences the chance of remarriage, the youngest widows having the highest chances. A French study confirms this hypothesis.[1]
2 The frequency of remarriage is also likely to vary between different cohorts, and it is necessary to analyse the data for women widowed at the same age in different cohorts.

Looking at the marginal distributions in the first place, the bottom line of the table shows that the chance of remarriage falls as age at widowhood rises. This is in agreement with the considerations mentioned previously. However, women who are widowed at relatively late ages will generally belong to earlier cohorts, and their chances of remarriage may well be different. Hence it would not be right to regard the percentages in the bottom line as indicating the variation in the probability of remarriage with age at widowhood.

The right-hand column shows a fall in the percentage remarrying as age increases, i.e. for earlier cohorts. But again this series of percentages does not provide a pure measure of the cohort effect; the youngest women, i.e. those who belong to the most recent cohorts, will also be those who were widowed at very young ages. They would therefore be expected to have a higher chance of remarrying than their sisters who were widowed later in life. Therefore any cohort effect would be exaggerated by the figures given in the right-hand column.

This exaggeration of the cohort effect will be less pronounced for the data in the body of the table. But it will not be possible to separate the effect of age at widowhood from that of cohort, because the percentages observed in the different subgroups relate to different periods of observation.

On every line the frequency of remarriage falls with increasing age at widowhood; the fall is pronounced and clearly shows the influence of this variable on the chance of remarriage. But the nearer age at widowhood is to present age, the shorter has been the exposure to the risk of remarriage and therefore the smaller the chance that the final frequency of remarriage has been achieved at the time of the survey. The data do not yield an estimate of the final frequency of remarriage.

The same reasoning applies to the study of the relationship between frequency of remarriage and age, which is equivalent to the study of the trend by cohort. As the cohort effect seems to be much less important than the effect of age at widowhood, and, as it operates in the opposite

[1] 'Le remariage des veufs et des veuves', *Population*, 11, 1, 1956.

direction, the study of the figures in the table is of limited value. The cohort effect only becomes apparent in the first column, and in the last three lines of the column at that. It is in this column that any cohort effect would be expected to become apparent, for the widows have all been widowed for at least ten years. Thus, whilst the data leave little doubt that age at widowhood is an important factor influencing the chances of remarriage, it is much more difficult to demonstrate that remarriage has become more frequent in recent generations.

There is one possible way of extending the study. The percentage of women remarried at a particular age and in a given cohort is an approximation to the percentage remarried at a specific duration of widowhood (which may be obtained by subtracting age at survey from age at widowhood). By assuming that the distribution of remarriages by duration of widowhood is the same for all groups (as was the case in France), and by choosing a realistic distribution, an estimate of the final percentage remarrying, the most important statistic required, might be obtained.

16

The remarriage of widowers

In the study of the frequency of the remarriages of widowers, methods very similar to those described in Chapter 12 will be used. These will illustrate the importance of a procedure that has already been employed for other purposes (e.g. in Chapter 14).

The formulae demonstrated are widely applicable and always yield fruitful results. They illustrate general principles which beginners often find difficult to understand because they are normally only illustrated with reference to very trivial problems.

At the beginning only the simplest of data will be used to show the kind of conclusion that it is possible to draw.

Data

In a French eighteenth-century parish, 500 men were widowed for the first time between the ages of 40 and 49. The distribution of their remarriages and deaths by age and marital status is given in the table below:

Time elapsing since end of marriage (complete years)	Remarriages	Deaths		
		Total	Widowers	Remarried men
0	150	10	10	0
1	80	10	8	2
2	40	10	8	2
3	20	10	6	4
4	10	10	6	4

Men who died after having become widowers for the second time have been included among the deaths of remarried men.

Problem 1

Find the distribution of this group of widowers by marital status at different anniversaries of the end of their marriages.

Answer

To compute the number of widowers remaining at successive anniversaries of the end of their marriages, it is necessary to subtract the losses caused by remarriage and deaths of widowers from the initial figure of 500.

Thus, at duration 0 there are 150 remarriages and 10 deaths of widowers. The original figure of 500 will therefore be reduced by $160 (= 150 + 10)$ to 340 men who remain widowers one year after the deaths of their wives. Similarly, the 80 remarriages and 8 deaths of widowers at duration 1 must be subtracted from the figure of 340 to arrive at 252 men remaining widowers on the second anniversary of the deaths of their wives, and so on.

The total number of men who have remarried at different durations after having become widowers (which will include those who have become widowers for the second time) is obtained by cumulating the number of remarriages and subtracting from these the deaths of remarried men. The following results are obtained:

At anniversary 1: $150 - 0 = 150$ remarried men
At anniversary 2: $150 + 80 - 2 = 228$ remarried men
At anniversary 3: $228 + 40 - 2 = 266$ remarried men, ... etc.

The consistency of these calculations may be checked by adding the total number in both categories at each anniversary. This will give the total number of survivors, irrespective of marital status, i.e. 500 less the cumulated deaths, as follows:

At Duration 1: $500 - 10 = 490$
At Duration 2: $490 - 10 = 480$
At Duration 3: $480 - 10 = 470$, etc.

Finally, Table 16.1 may be obtained.

Table 16.1 *Distribution of men by marital status, after having become widowers between the ages of 40 and 49, by duration since end of marriage*

Time elapsed since end of marriage (complete years)	Widowers	Remarried	Total
0	500	0	500
1	340	150	490
2	252	228	480
3	204	266	470
4	178	282	460
5	162	288	450

Problem 2

Compute the probability of remarrying within one year of each anniversary of the end of marriage. Clearly state the assumptions made in this calculation.

Answer

Let n' be the probability of remarrying between successive anniversaries of the end of the first marriage. If there are W widowers at the first anniversary, then in the absence of mortality there would be Wn' remarriages. However, there will also be, say, d deaths between these two anniversaries.

To calculate the total number of remarriages, assume that deceased widowers had the same chance of remarrying as did widowers who survived, i.e. that there is independence between the mortality and nuptiality rates of widowers. On this assumption, it is possible to estimate the additional number of remarriages that would have taken place if there had been no mortality. These would have come to dn' if deaths had taken place immediately after the first anniversary and to 0 if they had taken place immediately before the second. The number of additional remarriages that have been prevented by deaths will be taken as the arithmetic mean between these two quantities.

The total number of remarriages would therefore come to $r = Wn' - \frac{1}{2}dn'$. From this equation n' may be obtained in terms of the known quantities, namely

$$n' = r/(W - \tfrac{1}{2}d).$$

This formula is analogous to that established when the nuptiality and mortality of bachelors was studied. In that case, too, it was assumed that the two attrition factors (marriage and death) had effects that were independent of one another.

Note that this assumption is unlikely to be realistic in the present case. It is reasonable to suppose that those men who were oldest when their wives died and who therefore had the lowest chance of surviving will also experience the lowest probability of remarriage. The calculations are shown in Table 16.2.

Table 16.2 *Probability of remarrying within one year* (n'), *at different anniversaries of the end of first marriage*

Anniversary	r	W	d	$W - \frac{1}{2}d$	n'
0	150	500	10	495	0·303
1	80	340	8	336	0·238
2	40	252	8	248	0·161
3	20	204	6	201	0·100
4	10	178	6	175	0·057

Problem 3

Calculate the nuptiality table for this group of widowers, using the answers obtained in Problem 2, and comment on the results.

Answer

The values of n' used in the calculation of the nuptiality table of widowers are applied in exactly the same way as are $_n q_x$ values in the construction of life tables, or probabilities of marriage of bachelors in the case of ordinary nuptiality tables.

The data required in the problem are shown in Table 16.3. The table ends on the fifth anniversary of the termination of first marriages. The notation is the same as in Table 16.2 with the subscript x added to indicate the anniversary referred to. Note that this subscript refers to the duration since the end of the first marriage, and not to age as is more usually the case. In the present problem the cohorts are defined by the time that has elapsed since the men first became widowers. Cohorts are normally defined as groups of persons to whom a particular vital event happened at a particular time – for instance, a cohort of women who have had their third child in a given year may be studied in order to obtain fourth-order birth rates. Sometimes it is desirable to take account of age. In the problem under consideration, for instance, the chances of remarriage are likely to differ for men widowed at different ages, and it would be valuable to divide the group of widowers into subgroups containing those who were widowed at the same age. But this would introduce complexities into the calculation, and the subdivision is therefore often omitted.

Table 16.3 *Nuptiality table of widowers*

Duration of widowerhood	W_x	n'_x	r_x
0	1000	0·303	303
1	697	0·238	166
2	531	0·161	85
3	446	0·100	45
4	401	0·057	23
5	378		
			$\overline{622}$

This omission is not important, for the interesting explanatory variable in this case is the length of time that has elapsed since the end of the first marriage, and not the age of the individual widower at the time of remarriage.

Table 16.3 is incomplete, because it only deals with the first five years after the men became widowers. It is therefore only possible to give a partial answer to the following questions:

1 What proportion of men, who became widowers between the ages of 40 and 49 ultimately remarry?
2 How are these remarriages distributed by length of widowerhood?

The proportion of remarriages is high; in the absence of mortality 62·2% of the men will have remarried by the time five years have elapsed since the deaths of their wives. The final proportion remarrying could be obtained by extrapolating the curve n'_x. But the tail of the n'_x distribution is unlikely to have an important effect, for it may be noted that the probability of remarriage is highest soon after the man is widowed and declines rapidly with the passing of time from the end of the first marriage. It is noteworthy that no fewer than 30% of widowers remarry within a year of losing their wives.

Problem 4

Use the results obtained in the answer to Problem 1 to construct a series comparable to one of the nuptiality table functions that has been constructed and comment.

Answer

Table 16.1 obtained in answer to Problem 1 will be reconstructed as follows:

Let W_x be the number of surviving widowers in the absence of mortality.

Let l'_x be the life table survivorship function for widowers.

Let l_x be the life table survivorship function for the whole population.

Take $W_0 = 1$ and $l_0 = l'_0 = 500$. The suffix 0 refers to the time when the first marriage ended.

Assuming that there is no relationship between the chances of dying and the chances of remarriage, the number of widowers surviving to anniversary x, if account were taken of mortality, would be $W_x l'_x$. The total number of survivors at anniversary x would be l_x.

The ratios $W_x l'_x / l_x$ will give a series of values which will differ from those of the series W_x to the extent that l'_x differs from l_x. In other words, the nearer the mortality of widowers is to the mortality of the group as a whole, the closer will the ratio be to the series W_x. The results of the two calculations are given in Table 16.4.

Table 16.4 *W_x and proportion of widowers surviving at different anniversaries*

Duration of widowerhood	W_x (from Table 16.3)	Proportion of widowers (from Table 16.1)
1	0·697	0·694
2	0·531	0·525
3	0·446	0·434
4	0·401	0·387
5	0·378	0·360

The values shown in the last column are always below those in the preceding one. The total proportion remarrying would come to 0.64% ($= 1 - 0.360$). If it is assumed that the values given in Table 16.3 are the correct ones, it is possible to deduce that $l'_x < l_x$ throughout – in other words, that the mortality of widowers is always higher than that of men who have remarried.

From the proportions given in Table 16.4 it is possible to calculate the probability of remarriage for widowers in the same way as in Chapter 12 the probability of marriage for bachelors was calculated from the series of single survivors. The result obtained in Chapter 12 holds true in the present calculation: the probabilities obtained will approximate to the probabilities obtained by the other method to the extent that there are no mortality differences between widowers and remarried men at the ages for which the calculations are carried out. If there were an excess mortality of widowers the probabilities of remarriage obtained in this way would be higher than the true values.

Note that even if the proportions given in Table 16.4 are all lower than W_x, it does not necessarily follow that the probabilities of remarriage obtained from them would all be higher than n'_x. This would only be the case under much more restrictive assumptions regarding the mortality differences between widowers and remarried men. In the present problem, however, the result will hold.

Problem 5

Compute the number of remarriages between successive anniversaries of the date of the end of the first marriage and express these per 1000 survivors. What is the significance of this ratio and the sum of all the ratios?

Answer

The calculations are shown in Table 16.5.

Table 16.5 *Number of remarriages per 1000 survivors at various durations*

| Duration | Total cohort | | Remarriages | |
	At exact duration	At mid-point	Number	Ratio per 1000 survivors
0	500	495	150	303
1	490	485	80	165
2	480	475	40	84
3	470	465	20	43
4	460	455	10	22
5	450			
				617

Using the notation of the answer to the previous problem, consider remarriages taking place between anniversary x and $x+1$. At anniversary x, there are $W_x l'_x$ surviving widowers and there will therefore be $W_x l'_x n'_x (1 - \frac{1}{2}q'_x)$ remarriages, where n'_x is the probability of a widower remarrying and q'_x that of a widower dying. The formula may be obtained by the same reasoning that has been used in other chapters of this book, and also in the answer to Problem 2 in this chapter.

The number in the cohort at midpoint between anniversary x and $x+1$ will be approximately

$$\tfrac{1}{2}(l_x + l_{x+1}) = l_{x+1/2}.$$

The required rates can therefore be written:

$$W_x l'_x n'_x (1 - \tfrac{1}{2}q'_x)/l_{x+1/2}.$$

But as

$$W_x n'_x = r_x$$

and

$$l'_x(1 - \tfrac{1}{2}q'_x) = l_{x+1/2},$$

the ratio of remarriages to 1000 survivors will be

$$r_x l'_{x+1/2}/l'_{x+1/2}$$

and this will not be equivalent to the remarriages in the nuptiality table of widowers unless

$l_{x+1/2} = l'_{x+1/2}$, i.e. unless there were no difference in the mortality rates of widowers and remarried men.

If there were an excess mortality among widowers, as was found to be the case in the answer to Problem 4, the rates calculated here will be lower than the remarriages in the nuptiality tables. It can easily be confirmed, by comparing the last columns of Tables 16.3 and 16.5, that this is the case; only the first number is the same in both these columns.

As has been shown the sum of the ratios will give the frequency of remarriages during the first five years after the end of the first marriage on the assumption of zero mortality. The excess mortality of widowers in this case leads to an underestimate of this frequency, whereas the procedure employed in the answer to Problem 4 led to an overestimate. The three different values were:

617 remarriages per 1000 widowers obtained from remarriage rates.
622 remarriages per 1000 widowers obtained from probabilities of remarriage.
640 remarriages per 1000 widowers obtained from the proportions of widowers.

Problem 6

In present-day France 45% of widowers widowed between the ages of 40 and 49 remarry in the absence of mortality. The distribution of these remarriages by the time elapsed since the end of the first marriage is as follows:

Time elapsed	Number	Time elapsed	Number	Time elapsed	Number
0	135	5	53	10	18
1	255	6	42	11	15
2	160	7	32	12+	70
3	105	8	26		
4	67	9	22		1000

Compare these data with those for the eighteenth century.

Answer

It is not possible to make an exact comparison because one of the two series is incomplete. But there can be no doubt that the two distributions are very different.

The frequency of remarriage is much lower in **modern times**: 45% against over 62·2%; and the length of time elapsing between the end of first marriage and remarriage is longer. Only 13·5% remarry in the year of their wife's death, against 30·3% who did so during the eighteenth century. In those days these marriages accounted for at least 40% of all second marriages, if it is assumed that the final frequency of remarriage was at least 75%.

VI
FERTILITY

17

The fertility of marriages

Fertility is frequently studied for a particular marriage cohort, and this is the best method of looking at the subject. Such cohorts (and cohorts in general) may be studied in two ways – retrospectively, from answers given by surviving members of the cohort about past events, or currently, from events registered as they occur. The census provides an example of the first type of observation, while the second is based on vital registration statistics.

In this chapter the reader will be shown both these methods and will be able to assess the results to which they lead. Moreover, the material used provides an interesting example of the variation in fertility within a population.

Data

In a European country, which was a belligerent in the last World War, censuses were taken at the end of 1920, 1930, 1946 and 1950. Married women were asked to state the dates of their marriage and the numbers of their live born children. Table 17.1 was constructed from these data.

Problem 1

What can be deduced from a study of this table?

Answer

Table 17.1 takes account only of continuing marriages – i.e. those between persons who remain married and resident in the country at the time of the relevant census.

This number of continuing marriages depends on previous dissolutions of marriage (through divorce or widowhood) and on migration. In the long run the first of these, particularly widowhood, is the major factor, and cancels out the effects of any net immigration among the cohorts under review. Table 17.1 shows how the size of a cohort declines with the passage of time. For instance, the figures for those married for two years by the end of 1920 (roughly the 1918 marriage cohort) are as follows:

End of 1920 (duration   2 years): 16 404
End of 1930 (duration 12 years): 15 554
End of 1946 (duration 28 years): 12 162

Table 17.1

Marriage duration (years)	1920 census		1930 census		1946 census		1950 census	
	Marriages	*Births*	*Marriages*	*Births*	*Marriages*	*Births*	*Marriages*	*Births*
0	11 116	5 029	15 172	4 236	25 663	6 051	23 757	5 287
1	12 601	10 450	16 212	10 290	24 390	15 404	26 697	15 771
2	16 404	18 521	15 869	14 809	22 359	20 252	29 013	24 076
3	15 543	22 909	15 154	18 107	23 030	25 414	29 394	30 967
4	14 536	25 815	14 404	20 205	23 278	29 845	29 056	36 058
5	13 254	27 179	14 955	24 216	24 346	35 156	24 324	35 310
6	13 087	30 411	14 836	27 248	26 030	41 042	21 876	35 566
7	12 161	30 905	14 705	29 986	23 369	39 755	22 155	39 000
8	12 122	33 590	14 814	33 630	21 696	39 060	22 643	42 437
9	11 437	34 748	15 163	37 437	20 770	39 322	23 819	47 398
10	11 460	36 996	15 955	41 833	19 842	38 528	25 602	52 503
11	10 453	36 555	12 915	35 757	17 504	36 142	22 944	48 930
12	10 695	39 465	15 554	45 649	16 258	34 625	21 147	46 478
13	10 415	40 449	13 988	44 418	15 047	33 150	20 559	45 798
14	9 718	39 722	13 254	43 868	14 860	33 661	19 171	43 297
15	9 659	41 369	12 089	41 938	14 289	33 313	17 268	40 248
16	8 945	40 428	11 949	43 606	15 380	36 325	15 824	37 450
17	8 875	40 988	11 118	42 016	14 222	34 610	14 649	35 312
18	9 106	43 796	11 081	43 001	13 407	33 750	14 420	35 170
19	8 883	43 737	10 454	42 659	12 428	32 430	13 963	34 637
20	9 885	50 532	10 387	43 285	12 212	32 475	15 020	37 421
21	8 801	45 715	9 353	41 054	12 199	33 470	13 735	34 828
22	8 874	46 726	9 487	42 277	12 168	34 190	12 867	33 478
23	8 111	43 168	9 215	42 149	12 000	35 052	12 097	32 322
24	7 895	43 054	8 669	40 338	11 928	36 352	11 760	31 811
25	7 789	43 456	8 602	40 694	12 324	38 750	11 939	32 961
26	6 925	38 770	7 909	38 325	12 557	41 193	11 757	33 587
27	6 764	38 138	7 665	37 466	10 269	34 057	11 401	33 580
28	6 328	35 786	7 531	37 638	12 162	41 709	11 285	34 762
29	6 054	34 535	7 549	38 355	10 658	38 624	11 533	36 637
30	6 640	37 917	8 339	42 503	10 114	38 006	11 964	39 396

Note that the durations in Table 17.1 were computed by subtracting the year of marriage from that of the census. The justification of this method will become apparent in the answer to Problem 3.

The exceptions to the decline in the numbers remaining married at successive durations within a single cohort are of particular interest. They are of two kinds. The first relates to the size of groups at marriage duration 0 at the different censuses. If these are taken as the original sizes of the marriage cohorts of the census year, and the numbers in subsequent censuses are observed, we arrive at the following figures:

Cohort 1920	*Cohort 1930*	*Cohort 1946*
Duration 0: 11 116	Duration 0: 15 172	Duration 0: 25 663
Duration 10: 15 955	Duration 16: 15 380	Duration 4: 29 056
Duration 26: 12 557	Duration 20: 15 020	
Duration 30: 11 964		

There is invariably an increase in cohort size at the second census; and in two cases this increase is considerable. The only explanation is that the censuses (especially those of 1920 and 1946) were taken some time before the end of the calendar year, so that only a proportion of marriages in that year had taken place by census date.

The second exception concerns duration 1 in 1920 (i.e. the 1919 cohort); 12 601 marriages are recorded as continuing at that date, and by 1930 numbers in this cohort (now at duration 11 years) had increased to 12 915. Unless there are doubts about the accuracy of the data, this increase must be regarded as an indication of a net immigration of married couples between 1920 and 1930. This immigration more than compensated for the attrition caused by dissolutions of marriages during the period between the two censuses.

It will be useful to compare the number of marriages relating to the same cohort and recorded at different censuses. A study of changes in these numbers can suggest interesting lines of thought, and enable the quality of the enumeration to be assessed.

It is also worth noting one further point. The different duration groups in the table are not equally representative of the original cohort, particularly in relation to their ages at marriage. At longer durations couples marrying at a lower age will be over-represented, because the data refer to survivors who are therefore, on average, likely to be the younger members of the original group; and as their marriages by definition are of equal durations, they are likely to have married at younger ages. The force of this observation will become apparent when the fertility of these cohorts comes to be considered. At present, it is clear that within one cohort, at longer durations of marriage, the couples' ages at marriage are likely to have been lower. They have also proved to be more fertile, partly because couples who married young tended to come from particular social groups, and partly because they were exposed to the risk of conception for longer periods. Selection of this kind will thus lead to an overestimation of cohort fertility.

Problem 2

Assemble the data relating to the marriage cohorts of 1890, 1895, 1900, 1905, 1910, 1915, 1920, 1925, 1930, 1935, 1940 and 1945, and use them to estimate the fertility of these cohorts. Plot these data, and comment.

Answer

Table 17.2 has been constructed to show the relationship between marriage cohorts, duration of marriage and census dates (assumed to be 31 December). It is sufficient, then, to assemble the data for each cohort and to calculate the fertility accordingly (Table 17.3).

Table 17.2   *Relation between census years (to 31 December), cohort dates and marriage durations, in complete years*

	Census			
Cohort	1920	1930	1946	1950
1890	30 years			
1895	25			
1900	20	30 years		
1905	15	25		
1910	10	20		
1915	5	15		
1920	0	10	26 years	30 years
1925		5	21	25
1930		0	16	20
1935			11	15
1940			6	10
1945			1	5

Table 17.3   *Fertility, by marriage duration, in different cohorts of continuing marriages*

Marriage duration (years)	Continuing marriages	Total of live births	Average number of live births	Marriage duration (years)	Continuing marriages	Total of live births	Average number of live births
1890 Cohort				*1925 Cohort*			
30	6 640	37 917	5·71	5	14 955	24 216	1·62
1895 Cohort				21	12 199	33 470	2·74
25	7 789	43 456	5·58	25	11 939	32 961	2·76
1900 Cohort				*1930 Cohort*			
20	9 885	50 352	5·09	0	15 172	4 236	0·28
30	8 339	42 503	5·10	16	15 380	36 325	2·36
1905 Cohort				20	15 020	37 421	2·49
15	9 659	41 369	4·28	*1935 Cohort*			
25	8 602	40 694	4·73	11	17 504	36 142	2·06
1910 Cohort				15	17 268	40 248	2·33
10	11 460	36 996	3·23	*1940 Cohort*			
20	10 387	43 285	4·17	6	26 030	41 042	1·58
1915 Cohort				10	25 602	52 503	2·05
5	13 254	27 179	2·05	*1945 Cohort*			
15	12 089	41 938	3·47	1	24 390	15 404	0·63
1920 Cohort				5	24 324	35 310	1·45
0	11 116	5 029	0·45				
10	15 955	41 833	2·62				
26	12 557	41 193	3·28				
30	11 964	39 396	3·29				

For each of the twelve cohorts, only a limited amount of data (mean number of children born at up to four different durations of marriage) is available; the data for the 1920 cohort are the most complete.

Table 17.3 is represented graphically in Fig. 17.1.

Although the number of points is limited, the differences in fertility among the various cohorts stand out very clearly.

There is a steady decline between 1890 and 1930. The completed fertility for the 1890 cohort is nearly equivalent to that obtained under a regime of 'natural fertility' (about six children), whereas that of the 1920 cohort was just over three children; and the figure is unlikely to reach that level for the 1925 and 1930 cohorts. For cohorts married after 1930, however, there is a continuous rise. The data are sketchy, but the figures for each successive cohort are higher than those for the preceding.

This experience is typical of the fertility data for many European countries. A decline during the first half of the nineteenth century and the early years of the twentieth is followed by a return to higher fertility; the lowest fertility rate is exhibited by women born between about 1900 and 1910 (i.e. roughly the marriage cohorts of 1920 to 1925).

Problem 3

Table 17.4 shows the annual statistics of marriages taking place during each year between 1931 and 1950. Relate these figures to data already discussed, and comment.

Table 17.4

Year	Marriages	Year	Marriages
1931	17 666	1941	26 459
1932	17 612	1942	25 814
1933	17 995	1943	24 021
1934	19 235	1944	21 990
1935	20 511	1945	23 504
1936	22 375	1946	29 688
1937	23 959	1947	29 923
1938	24 335	1948	29 558
1939	26 095	1949	27 469
1940	27 983	1950	27 222

Answer

This calculation will help to elucidate further the remarks made in Problem 1. The initial sizes of the marriage cohorts between 1931 and 1950 will be compared with the census figures at the close of 1946 and 1950 (see Table 17.5).

The census totals are generally lower than the corresponding initial cohort sizes; the later the census (in relation to the date of the cohort) the more marked does the difference become. The 1944 and 1945 cohorts are an exception; the census figures for these years exceed initial cohort size, and this situation (especially for 1945) is borne out by the 1950 census figure. Several

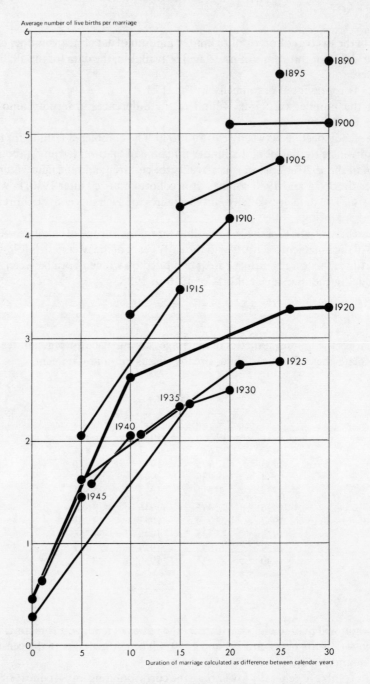

Average number of live births per marriage

Duration of marriage calculated as difference between calendar years

Fig. 17.1   *Fertility, by marriage duration, in different cohorts of continuing marriages*

Table 17.5 *Figures for marriages in different cohorts*

Cohort	Initial size	Census figure at end of 1946	at end of 1950
1931	17 666	14 289	13 963
1932	17 612	14 860	14 420
1933	17 995	15 047	14 629
1934	19 235	16 258	15 824
1935	20 511	17 504	17 268
1936	22 375	19 842	19 171
1937	23 959	20 770	20 559
1938	24 335	21 696	21 147
1939	26 095	23 369	22 944
1940	27 983	26 030	25 602
1941	26 459	24 346	23 819
1942	25 814	23 278	22 643
1943	24 021	23 030	22 155
1944	21 990	22 359	21 876
1945	23 504	24 390	24 324
1946	29 688	25 663	29 056
1947	29 923		29 394
1948	29 558		29 013
1949	27 469		26 697
1950	27 222		23 757

explanations may be put forward for this – deficiencies in registration (particularly in the transmission of marriage certificates to the centre) during the difficult, immediate post-war years, or an influx of couples who had married outside the country while the armed forces had been stationed abroad, immediately after the end of the war, or a combination of both these factors.

On the other hand, the census shows marriages at duration 0 in 1946 as markedly fewer in numbers (25 663) than those registered during that year (29 688). The same is also true of 1950; and it is worth noting that the 1950 census figure for duration 4, taken as applying to the 1946 cohort, is reasonably close to the number of marriages registered for that cohort. This confirms the deduction in Problem 1 from an examination of the figures given in Table 17.1 alone – namely, that the census must have been taken some time before the end of the calendar year. Moreover, the previous hypothesis, that the durations given in Table 17.1 must have been obtained by taking the differences between the year of observation and the year of marriage, is confirmed.

Problem 4

In Table 17.6 annual statistics of legitimate births by duration (in individual years) of the parents' marriage are shown. Relate this information to the findings in Problem 3 and use the results to illustrate the pattern of fertility in the marriage cohorts studied in Problem 2.

Table 17.6

Births by marriage duration (years)

Year of observation	0	1	2	3	4	5	6	7	8	9	10	11	12	13	14	15	16	17	18	19
1931	4117																			
1932	4244	6298																		
1933	4005	5879	3881																	
1934	4112	6038	3969	3268																
1935	4197	6275	3865	3170	2803															
1936	4336	6801	4077	3315	2850	2500														
1937	4695	7181	4412	3488	3109	2621	2261													
1938	4680	7809	5005	3853	3173	2597	2284	2038												
1939	4886	7980	5245	4067	3386	2831	2271	1977	1692											
1940	5146	8407	5321	4233	3550	2914	2439	1895	1732	1432										
1941	4981	8686	5316	3858	3272	2680	2177	1700	1437	1289	1145									
1942	5583	9376	6114	4723	3972	3268	2643	2096	1828	1559	1387	1215								
1943	5868	9909	6653	5211	4409	3631	2928	2308	1993	1689	1487	1290	990							
1944	5990	10242	7303	5884	5041	4164	3350	2626	2258	1900	1666	1434	1093	923						
1945	5300	8742	5334	4938	4652	4684	3941	3276	2808	2338	2005	1613	1250	1116	915					
1946	6102	9963	5757	5277	5201	5093	5357	4231	3566	3116	2664	2019	1586	1295	1143	956				
1947	6340	11669	6131	4586	4690	4236	4166	4024	3220	2809	2457	1925	1548	1304	970	868	673			
1948	6027	11370	7079	5046	4272	3863	3686	3470	3342	2705	2219	1882	1561	1204	1007	802	662	519		
1949	5537	10836	6952	5759	4620	3753	3358	2980	2847	2707	2121	1794	1468	1211	999	780	618	464	388	
1950	5442	10494	6806	5804	5278	4114	3202	2759	2582	2440	2254	1798	1470	1150	1021	754	588	437	388	276

Table 17.7 Net fertility (in live births) of different marriage cohorts

Marriage duration	1935 cohort (20 511 marriages) Births	Births per 1000 marriages (1)	(2)	1940 cohort (27 983 marriages) Births	Births per 1000 marriages (1)	(2)	1945 cohort (23 504 marriages) Births	Births per 1000 marriages (1)	(2)	1950 cohort (27 222 marriages) Births	Births per 1000 marriages (1)	(2)
0	4197	205	205	5146	184	184	5300	225	225	5442	200	200
1	6801	332	537	8686	310	494	9963	424	649			
2	4412	215	752	6114	218	712	6131	261	910			
3	3853	188	940	5211	186	898	5046	215	1125			
4	3386	165	1105	5041	180	1078	4620	197	1322			
5	2914	142	1247	4684	167	1245	4114	175	1497			
6	2177	106	1353	5357	191	1436						
7	2096	102	1455	4024	144	1580						
8	1993	97	1552	3342	119	1699						
9	1900	93	1645	2707	97	1796						
10	2005	98	1743	2254	81	1877						
11	2019	98	1841									
12	1548	75	1916									
13	1204	59	1975									
14	999	49	2024									
15	754	37	2061									

(1) Births at different durations.
(2) Cumulative births.

Answer

Table 17.6 shows births from 1931 onwards; and for that year only duration 0, which relates to the 1931 marriage cohort, is considered. For later years only births in successive years for the cohorts 1931 to 1950 inclusive are given. Reading Table 17.6 diagonally, births at different durations for the cohorts 1935, 1940, 1945 and 1950 may be extracted. These cohorts have already been considered in Problem 2. The numbers of births are shown in Table 17.7, together with rates per 1000 original marriages in the cohort (the table gives births at different durations, as well as cumulative numbers).

Comments on these results will be given when they are compared with similar findings obtained earlier.

Problem 5

Compare the results obtained in Problems 2 and 4, and comment.

Answer

Fig. 17.2 shows two different measures of births per marriage for each of the marriage cohorts 1935, 1940 and 1945. We will begin by analysing the results of the calculations in the previous problem. These give net fertility figures (in the sense that one speaks of *net* as opposed to *gross* reproduction), for they are derived from the cumulative totals of rates related to the *initial* size of the cohort. They are therefore not an index of pure fertility. However, comparisons between such fertility figures for different cohorts at equal durations are justified, for they do in fact represent fertility differences with some degree of accuracy.

When fertility is studied in relation to continuing marriages it appears to show a continuous rise from the oldest cohort (1935) to the most recent (1945). This may be due to the comparative lack of data; but the true picture is more complex. At shorter durations, the fertility of the 1940 cohort is below that of the previous (1935) cohort; it is only from marriage duration 6 onwards that it exceeds that of 1935, and the excess increases with duration. The change from the fifth to the sixth year is very marked, and clearly corresponds to an important increase in 1946 (1940 + 6 = 1946). These are births that would have taken place earlier but for the Second World War. If there had been no war the short fall of the 1940 cohort at early durations might have been reduced, or even avoided altogether. A similar though less marked jump may be seen in the passage from the tenth to the eleventh year in the 1935 cohort, and the explanation is probably the same (recovery in 1946: 1935 + 11 = 1946). These recoveries may, of course, be examined in greater detail by using duration-specific fertility rates that correspond exactly to each of the calendar years studied (see column (1) in Table 17.7). To take an example – the rates for durations 10–11 in the marriage cohort of 1935 are higher than adjacent values on either side; and the same is true of duration 6 for cohort 1940.

It now only remains to compare the graphs obtained from the data in Problem 4 with those for the same cohorts derived in Problem 2 (Fig. 17.2).

For the cohorts of 1935 and 1940, the two curves are clearly separate, diverging steadily as duration of marriage increases. This is to be expected; for the births are related to the initial size of the cohort, and the resultant cumulative fertility figures are affected by the dissolution of

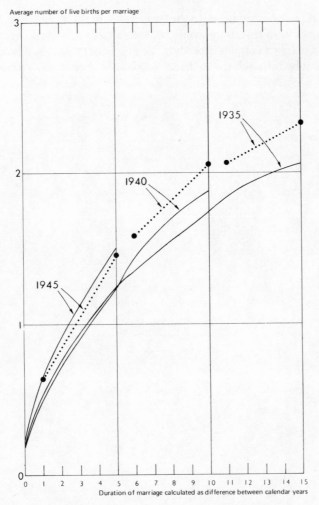

Fig. 17.2 *Fertility of different marriage cohorts (dotted lines = in relation to continuing marriages; continuous lines – in relation to initial size of cohort)*

unions (underestimation of fertility, at least where these losses are not matched by net immigration). If, on the other hand, births had been related to continuing marriages, only fertility was bound to be overestimated because of progressive selection of couples married at younger ages. This point has already been made in Problem 1. This last factor, however, is of little importance for the early durations of marriage considered here; the divergence between the two curves essentially reflects that between *gross* fertility and *net* fertility.

In the case of the 1945 cohort, the curve representing the cumulative fertility rates (i.e. those related to the initial size of the cohort) lies uppermost. This anomaly may be linked to the fact noted in Problem 3 – that the number of marriages registered in 1945 was lower than the number of that year's marriages still continuing in 1946 and 1950 (see Table 17.5). This fact explains the special relationship between the two curves, at least in a purely arithmetical sense. If the relevant figures were true, they would indicate that in this particular cohort there was a net immigration of married couples exceeding the number of losses by dissolution. And in such a case, measurement by rates related to the initial size of cohort usually leads to an overestimation of fertility.

18

The fertility of American women

It is possible to make a very detailed study of fertility movements in a modern population if a very long and continuous series of suitable data is available. Besides the intrinsic interest of the results obtained, the data provide occasion for a study of methodological considerations on the relationships between cohort and period analyses of fertility. Statistical examination based on exact data of this kind, rather than a theoretical approach, shows up the almost 'accidental' nature of some of the results obtained by period analysis, compared with the clarity and reliability of the cohort method. Period analysis is necessary for the study of very recent phenomena, and in particular for revealing significant changes in trend. Without seeking to dismiss this type of analysis as completely unprofitable in the study of fertility, the discussion will show that only very limited conclusions can reasonably be drawn from period data.

Data

The data in Table 1 of the Statistical Appendix will be used to study the fertility of white native-born women in the United States. These data come from nationwide investigations carried out at the relevant dates.

Problem 1

Modify the data in Table 1 of the Appendix so as to bring out the fertility history of the five birth cohorts observed; and trace the progeny of these cohorts without reference to birth order.

A cohort will be defined as consisting of all women of a given age. This definition is slightly different from that normally used. It is important to make this point clear before selecting groups of individual and separate calendar years, which will be used to define the cohorts.

Table 18.1 *Live births, by birth order, per 1000 women in different birth cohorts*

Age groups (years)	Birth order								
	1	2	3	4	5	6	7	8 and over	All orders
1871–5 cohort									
35–39	812	632	486	367	270	192	125	167	3051
40–44	828	662	521	399	300	231	171	312	3424
45–49	830	666	726	405	308	239	181	360	3515
50–54	830	666	526	405	308	240	181	365	3521
1876–80 cohort									
30–34	759	545	380	256	163	95	48	36	2282
35–39	809	630	464	335	235	162	103	135	2873
40–44	824	654	494	367	265	199	144	260	3207
45–49	826	657	498	372	273	207	153	307	3293
50–54	826	657	498	372	273	207	153	312	3298
1881–5 cohort									
25–29	632	394	228	119	52	19	6	33	1453
30–34	757	544	362	230	136	76	40	30	2175
35–39	802	615	438	305	204	140	90	112	2706
40–44	816	636	467	337	238	174	123	218	3009
45–49	817	639	471	342	244	182	131	258	3084
50–54	817	639	471	342	244	182	132	261	3088
1886–90 cohort									
20–24	349	151	50	14	3				567
25–29	629	389	220	109	46	17	5	2	1417
30–34	747	533	340	209	118	68	35	26	2076
35–39	791	597	414	280	184	125	79	98	2568
40–44	803	616	440	309	213	154	106	186	2827
45–49	805	618	443	313	218	159	113	217	2886
50–54	805	618	443	313	218	160	113	221	2891
1891–5 cohort									
15–19	44	6							50
20–24	349	146	48	12	2				557
25–29	619	372	194	91	37	15	5	2	1335
30–34	742	521	326	198	113	62	31	23	2016
35–39	780	581	393	260	168	111	69	86	2448
40–44	791	597	414	283	191	133	91	156	2656
45–49	792	599	417	286	195	138	96	180	2703
50–54	792	599	417	286	195	138	96	182	2705
1896–1900 cohort									
15–19	43	5							48
20–24	339	138	44	10	2				533
25–29	618	373	191	91	37	14	5	2	1331
30–34	724	510	310	183	105	57	29	20	1938
35–39	760	563	366	234	149	97	60	71	2300
40–44	770	579	384	254	168	115	76	125	2471
45–49	772	581	387	257	172	119	81	143	2512
50–54	772	581	387	257	172	119	81	144	2513

1901–5 cohort

15–19	38	5							43
20–24	358	144	44	11	2	1			560
25–29	604	357	178	83	34	13	4	2	1275
30–34	704	478	277	159	88	48	23	17	1794
35–39	745	533	327	201	123	78	47	58	2112
40–44	761	554	348	219	140	93	60	100	2275
45–49	764	557	352	223	143	96	63	114	2312
50–54	764	557	352	224	144	96	63	115	2315

1906–10 cohort

15–19	45	5							50
20–24	340	133	40	10	2	1			526
25–29	567	320	151	69	28	10	3	2	1150
30–34	689	445	238	129	69	37	18	14	1639
35–39	748	524	299	172	100	61	36	46	1986
40–44	770	557	331	196	118	75	47	79	2173
45–49	773	561	335	200	122	78	50	89	2208

1911–15 cohort

15–19	43	5							48
20–24	300	112	32	8	2				454
25–29	555	293	127	55	22	8	3	1	1064
30–34	715	462	230	115	59	30	15	12	1638
35–39	782	567	316	168	91	53	30	38	2045
40–44	799	597	350	196	111	66	40	64	2223

1916–20 cohort

15–19	36	4							40
20–24	308	108	29	7	1				453
25–29	621	337	140	57	22	8	3	1	1189
30–34	789	554	274	126	60	29	14	11	1857
35–39	839	653	376	195	99	53	29	35	2279

1921–5 cohort

15–19	39	5							44
20–24	348	125	36	9	2				520
25–29	715	415	163	60	22	8	3	1	1387
30–34	845	648	346	158	69	32	15	12	2125

1926–30 cohort

15–19	39	5	1						45
20–24	427	159	39	9	2				636
25–29	757	519	233	87	30	10	3	2	1641

1931–5 cohort

15–19	57	9	1				67
20–24	479	222	67	17	4	1	790

1936–40 cohort

15–19	65	11	1	77

Answer

Fig. 18.1 illustrates the relationship between age groups and birth-year groups, exemplified by the group aged 35–39 years on 1 January 1910.

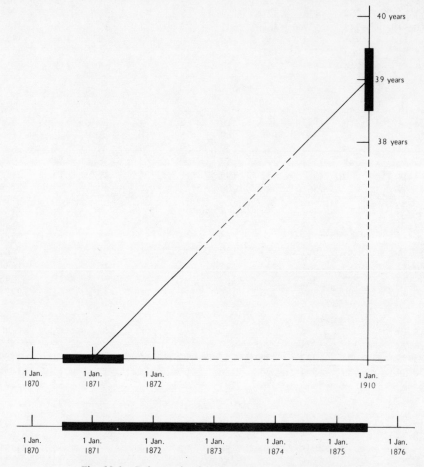

Fig. 18.1   *Relationship between age and date of birth*

The group of those aged 39 on 1 January 1910 consists of women born during the twelve months centred on 1 January 1871 – i.e. between mid-1870 and mid-1871. The group aged 35–39 on 1 January 1910 therefore comprises those born between mid-1870 and mid-1875. They may therefore be defined as constituting either the cohort of 1870–4 or that of 1871–5. The latter alternative has been chosen here, and this choice has determined the remainder. The group of those aged 30–34 on 1 January 1910, for instance, is assigned to birth-years 1876–80, and the 25–29 age group to 1881–5, etc. Note, too, that the group aged 35–39 on 1 January 1910 has become the 40–44 group on 1 January 1915, the 45–49 group on 1 January 1920, etc.

Data from the table given in the Statistical Appendix have been modified to produce Table

18.1. This shows live births, by parity, per 1000 women; the births are arranged by cohorts (in the sense defined above). Births of all parities are added in the final column, to illustrate the pattern of total fertility. In this way all or part of the fertility history of cohorts from 1871–5 to 1936–40 can be obtained. Information is complete only for the cohorts from 1891–5 to 1901–5; it may be regarded as practically complete, however, for the 1906–10 cohort because the data are available to the date when the women in this cohort were aged 45–49. For the earlier cohorts the information is available at the end of their reproductive lives and for the period since 1910 only. For the 1911–15 and subsequent cohorts the series end on 1 January 1955 and cover only the beginnings of the reproductive span.

Note that the total number of live births at different ages, per 1000 women in a cohort, is related to the number of *survivors* at the dates of the successive censuses. It follows that the results are only comparable if mortality and fertility are independent. It will be assumed that there is such independence, or at least that the effect of 'selection' by mortality is negligible.

Problem 2

Draw one graph to illustrate the pattern of fertility in different cohorts (without reference to birth order), and show how this pattern fits into the time scale. Comment.

Answer

The graph in Fig. 18.2 gives the particulars required. The ordinate gives the total number of births, the abscissa the year of observation. Points on the same vertical line thus correspond to total births per 1000 women attained by different age groups at a particular date (see Table 1 in the Appendix); data relating to the same cohort are joined by continuous lines (see Table 18.1). To avoid too much detail, the graph ends at ages 45–49; the additional fertility for the age group 50–54 adds no significantly new information. Dotted lines link total births at the same ages attained by different cohorts (omitting the 40–44 age group for the sake of clarity, and the 15–19 age group as being of limited interest.

The dotted lines place different cohorts in relation to one another. In each case, the line first falls and then rises; in general, the higher the age group, the greater is the variation. This wave pattern may be understood by remembering that cohorts may vary, either (1) in the final number of births (total fertility), or (2) in the distribution of births by age (or birth timing).

The highest dotted line shows a regular decline in the total of births from the 1871–5 cohort (3515 children per 1000 women) to the 1906–10 cohort (2208 children). These are the cohorts whose fertility can be traced until the women are 45–49 years old. In these cohorts, the decline in fertility is accompanied (as is usual) by slight modifications in the timing of births, leading to a concentration at younger ages. It is for this reason that, although the declining trend for the 45–49 group is repeated in almost all other age groups, it becomes progressively less marked at younger ages. But the trend in these fertility patterns is disturbed by some irregularities. Temporary disturbances, in particular those connected with the First World War and the economic crisis of the 1930s, are responsible for these irregularities. For instance, a slight postponement of births is apparent at ages 20–24 in the 1896–1900 cohort, and at ages 25–29 in the 1891–6 cohort. These movements, recorded in 1920, were clearly a consequence of the war.

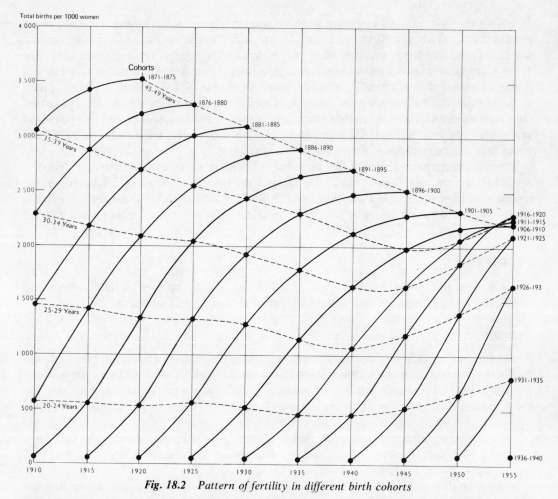

Fig. 18.2   *Pattern of fertility in different birth cohorts*

On the other hand, by 1935 and 1940 fertility for the youngest group at present under consideration, the 1906–10 cohort, was lower in relation to its ultimate completed fertility, at least when compared with that of the 1901–5 cohort at corresponding durations. This postponement was due to the economic crisis which affected this cohort at the period when fertility would have been at the peak. But the figures used here represent total past fertility and do not show up temporary fluctuations with any degree of accuracy. The latter will become apparent by studying period fertility rates obtained by differencing the figures in the last column of Table 18.1.

The 1906–10 cohort marks a turning point. Although it is not yet possible to know the completed fertility of later cohorts, it is certain to be greater than for the 1906–10 cohort; indeed, women belonging to the later cohort have already exceeded this figure before reaching the age of 45–49. In fact, it is clear from Fig. 18.2 that, using a self-explanatory symbolism,

$$T(1906\text{--}10)_{45-49 \text{ years}} < T(1911\text{--}15)_{40-44 \text{ years}} < T(1916\text{--}20)_{35-39 \text{ years}}.$$

The situation is more complex in the cohorts born after 1906–10. On one hand completed fertility for these cohorts increases regularly, at least for the three or four five-year cohorts following that of 1906–10. On the other hand, an obvious change has taken place in birth timing. If this were not the case, it would have to be assumed that the 1926–30 cohort, for instance, whose members had had more children at ages 25–29 than did the women of the 1851–5 cohorts at the same age, would also show a markedly higher completed fertility. A simple proportionate increase would yield a completed fertility of 3489 children for the 1926–30 cohort, representing a very considerable increase of 58% on that of 1906–10; and the 1931–5 cohort, compared with that of 1886–90, would achieve a still higher total (4028 children), an increase of 82%!

It is worth stressing that the conditions of the problem restrict the discussion to the data shown in Fig. 18.2. A more systematic treatment of the numerical data would have led to a clarification of some of the points, and an opportunity to do this will arise at a later stage.

Problem 3

Where possible, calculate the female gross and net generation reproduction rates.

In the absence of the necessary generation life tables, assume that the numbers of survivors to birthday 20, as shown in current life tables for white women in the USA, give a good approximation to the survival rates relating to the same date as the tables.

Discuss this approximation briefly.

Current tables are available only for certain years (these tables, moreover, cover only those states where death registration was adequate at the time; this fact will be ignored here, although it may lead to inaccuracy). It will be convenient to interpolate where necessary; and for this purpose the figure relating to 1850, which cannot easily be obtained, will be useful. In that year $l_{20} \doteq 67613$, where $l_0 = 100\,000$.

Answer

The gross reproduction rate (R) is the number of daughters born per woman, if there were no mortality at all, before the end of the reproductive period. It is obtained for the cohorts in Table 18.1 by multiplying the total number of births at ages 50–54 by the proportion of females at birth (0·488), and dividing the result by 1000. For the 1871–5 cohort, for example,

$$R = \frac{3521 \times 0\cdot488}{1000} = 1\cdot72.$$

Strictly speaking, calculations should not be continued beyond the 1901–5 cohort, since this is the last cohort for which fertility at age 50–54 is known. It is, however, possible to make estimates for the three following cohorts by extrapolation from the last available figures. The following additions to these totals have been made:

175 live births between 35–39 years and 40–44 years
37 live births between 40–44 years and 45–49 years
2 live births between 45–49 years and 50–54 years

– these being the mean figures for the last twenty cohorts for which information is available.

Table 18.2 shows the different values of R obtained in this way.

Table 18.2   *Gross reproduction rate (R) and net reproduction rate (R$_0$) in different birth cohorts*

Birth cohorts	Completed fertility	R $\left(\dfrac{d \times 0.488}{1000}\right)$	Probability of survival to age 27**	R_0
1871–1875	3521	1·72	0·722	1·24
1876–1880	3298	1·61	0·733	1·18
1881–1885	3088	1·51	0·744	1·12
1886–1890	2891	1·41	0·755	1·06
1891–1895	2705	1·32	0·766	1·01
1896–1900	2513	1·23	0·779	0·96
1901–1905	2315	1·13	0·793	0·90
1906–1910	2210*	1·08	0·809	0·87
1911–1915	2262*	1·10	0·828	0·91
1916–1920	2493*	1·22	0·850	1·04

* Extrapolations.
** These probabilities are taken to equal the probabilities of survival to age 20 in appropriate current life tables.

Proceeding now to a calculation of the net reproduction rate (R_0) for the same cohort, the following formula may be used:

$$R_0 = R l_{\bar{x}}$$

$\bar{x}$ being the mean age of mothers at confinement. For the sake of simplicity, this may be assumed as 27 years. Generation life tables do not, however exist; only current life tables are available, for the whole or part of the USA, and for the years listed below (the survival probabilities for women at age 20 ($_{20}p_0$) in these tables are shown in the last column; these figures will be used at a later stage).

Tables	Mean year	$_{20}p_0$
1850	1850	0·676
1900–1902	1901	0·790
1909–1911	1910	0·818
1919–1921	1920	0·873
1929–1931	1930	0·909
1939–1941	1940	0·940

By plotting these values on a graph (see Fig. 18.3) the values of $_{20}p_0$ corresponding to the mean dates of birth of the relevant cohorts may be obtained by interpolation. Fig. 18.1 shows the mean date of birth for the '1871–5' group as 1 January 1873; the mean dates of birth for the other groups follow at five-year intervals. These are the interpolated values shown in Table 18.2, where they represent probabilities of survival to age 27 in different cohorts.

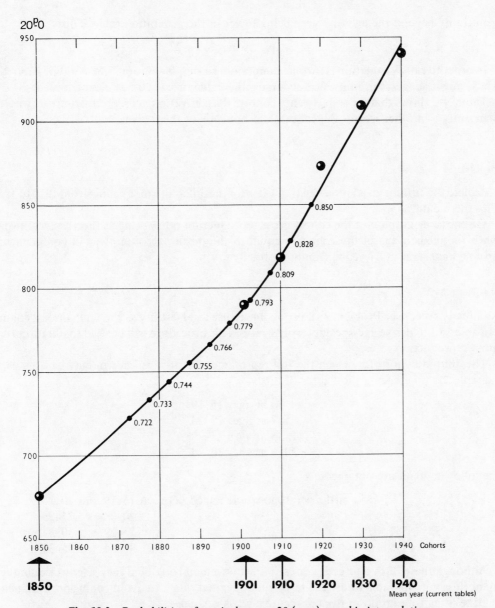

Fig. 18.3 *Probabilities of survival at age 20 ($_{20}p_0$), graphic interpolation*

The substitution of the current probabilities of survival to age 20 for the probabilities of survival to age 27 in cohorts with the same birth date needs justification. If p' be written for the probability of survival in a cohort, and if $_{27}p'_0$ were compared with $_{27}p_0$, taken from the current table relating to the birth-year of the cohort, it is clear that in conditions of falling mortality,

$$_{27}p'_0 > {}_{27}p_0$$

– mortality beyond the age of 1 year being lower in the generation table. Thus

$$_{27}p'_0 = {}_xp_0 \quad \text{where} \quad x < 27. \tag{1}$$

In order to satisfy Equation (1), whilst maintaining a simple solution, and avoiding subtleties which might suggest an unjustified accuracy, the value of $x = 20$ has been adopted.

Table 18.2 shows that for some twenty cohorts the generation net reproduction rate was less than unity – in other words, the cohorts did not replace themselves.

Problem 4

Calculate the current gross reproduction rates for the different quinquennia from 1910 to 1955. Plot these data.

On the same graph plot the cohort gross reproduction rates, using as the abscissa the date when the median age of the cohort is equal to the mean age of mothers at confinement – assumed constant at 27 years. Comment briefly.

Answer

As already noted (see Problem 2), it is possible to use total fertility as shown in the last column of Table 18.1 to derive age-specific fertility rates. This procedure will be used to obtain current gross reproduction rates.

The 1891–5 cohort, for which the full reproductive history is known, may be used as an example. By differencing the figures of births

50 at ages 15–19
557 at ages 20–24
1335 at ages 25–29
2016 at ages 30–34

the following data are obtained:

50 births per 1000 women aged between 15–19 and 20–24

557–	50 = 507	20–24	25–29
1335–	557 = 778	25–29	30–34
2016–1335 = 681		30–34	35–39

Although these birth figures are rates, it must be remembered that they refer to a quinquennium (it is not advisable to use the term 'quinquennial rates', to avoid confusion with *annual* rates relating to a group of five consecutive years of age).

Fig. 18.4 shows the rates calculated in this way for the period 1925–9. Eight cohorts are concerned. The cumulative total of live births is 2617. This may be regarded as a completed fertility figure, but is used here as a current index, and it yields the gross reproduction rate when multiplied by the proportion of female births and divided by 1000.

$$R_{1925-9} = \frac{2617 \times 0.488}{1000} = 1.28.$$

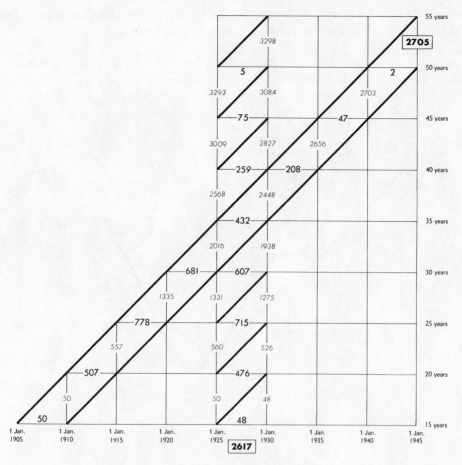

Fig. 18.4 *Total fertility and age-specific rates*

In order to extend the series, births occurring in 1910–14 and 1915–19 respectively have been estimated from the cohorts born before 1871, and figures of 100 births and 6 births respectively per 1000 women have been adopted.

The figures shown in Table 18.3 have been obtained in this way.

Table 18.3 *Gross current reproduction rate (R)*

Period	R	Period	R
1910–1914	1·56	1935–1939	1·02
1915–1919	1·43	1940–1944	1·16
1920–1924	1·43	1945–1949	1·38
1925–1929	1·28	1950–1954	1·55
1930–1934	1·08		

In Fig. 18.5 these rates are compared with generation gross reproduction rates. The rate for the 1931–5 cohort, which will be considered later, is also shown.

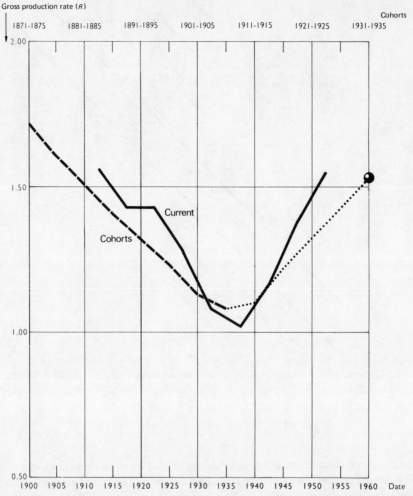

Fig. 18.5   *Generation gross reproduction rate and current gross reproduction rate*

A cohort is specified here by the date when the median age of its members is 27 years – in other words, when members of the cohort played a predominant part in current fertility statistics (from this point of view, the age of maximum fertility might have been preferred as an index; this would be slightly lower than the mean age at confinement).

The two series show a similar trend, but fluctuations in current rates are more marked than those in the generation rates, which are very regular. The reason is that each current rate is affected not only by the basic fertility characteristics of the thirty-five or so cohorts that contribute births during the period studied, but also by irregular movements which may affect the fertility history of these cohorts. Such fluctuations may be linked with historical events – slumps, wars, the return to normal conditions, etc. – in other words, by events that affect a significant number of cohorts for a certain period of time. The current rate registers the impact made by exceptional circumstances upon each cohort at different ages; it records the history of a synthetic cohort, which would throughout its lifetime have been subjected to exceptional conditions.

This is the explanation for the peak in 1920–4 (post-war recovery), the trough in 1930–9 (economic crisis), and the more recent rise, which most probably has not yet ended and which markedly anticipates the main trend of the generation rates. In the last case, although the rapid rise in the current rate reflects the increase in fertility among the younger generations, it may also be due in part to the recovery from the pre-war economic depression and wartime conditions, and to the growing tendency for American women to have their children at younger ages.

The current fertility index – in this case the gross reproduction rate – therefore reflects exceptional and temporary conditions, in addition to basic trends in the population studied. This point will be elaborated in the next problem, in which first births will be used as an example.

Problem 5

Attention will now be concentrated on first births. With the available data it is possible to calculate period age-specific first birth rates for the quinquennia between 1910 and 1955. By summing the rates for a given period (p), an index i_p may be obtained, which can be compared with the total number of first births for the different cohorts.

Calculate i_p for each of the quinquennia from 1910 to 1955. Compare the results with the total of first births in the various cohorts, using the same type of graph as suggested in Problem 4 (for convenience, the mean age of mothers at the birth of their first child is taken to be 22 years, though the mean age at first marriage suggests that it is normally over 23 years).

Answer

In this section live first births are studied by the same method that was used for births of all orders in Problem 4. The rates used here are first birth rates. The closeness of the analogy makes it possible to be brief.

Certain simple extrapolations can be made, to extend the period of observation (Problem 7 will involve some bolder extrapolation). These are as follows:

1 A figure of two first births per 1000 women in 1910–14 is assigned to the cohorts born before 1871.
2 The final figure of 802 first births is arrived at by adding, to the 799 first births registered on 1 January 1955 for the 1911–15 cohort, three first births taking place after that date.

The average age of mothers at their first confinement is taken as 22 years. This fixes 1 January 1895 as the date when the median age of the oldest group (the 1871–5 cohort) was 22; the dates for the other cohorts follow from this, spaced out at successive five-year intervals.

Table 18.4 and Fig. 18.6 show the final total of first births for the different cohorts as well as the values of i_p.

Table 18.4 *Total number of first births; cohort and period (i_p) totals*

Cohort	Date when median age = 22 years*	Total first births	i_p
1871–1875	1.1.1895	830	
1876–1880	1.1.1900	826	
1881–1885	1.1.1905	817	
1886–1890	1.1.1910	805	
			821
1891–1895	1.1.1915	792	
			784
1896–1900	1.1.1920	772	
			827
1901–1905	1.1.1925	764	
			741
1906–1910	1.1.1930	773	
			669
1911–1915	1.1.1935	802	
			740
	1.1.1940		
			898
	1.1.1945		
			1072
	1.1.1950		
			1017
	1.1.1955		

* These dates also specify the periods to which the values of i_p relate.

The results of certain extrapolations that are discussed in later problems have been used to complete Fig. 18.6, which will be considered in greater detail once these results have been established.

Problem 6

The following data on the nuptiality of recent birth cohorts of white women in the USA are taken from N. B. Ryder, *Measures of Recent Nuptiality in the Western World* (International Congress on Population, New York, 1961):

Birth cohorts	1906–10	1911–15	1916–20	1921–5	1926–30
Percentage single at age 50	7·4	6·2	5·0	4·0	3·8
Average age at first marriage (years)	22·79	22·83	22·61	22·01	21·42

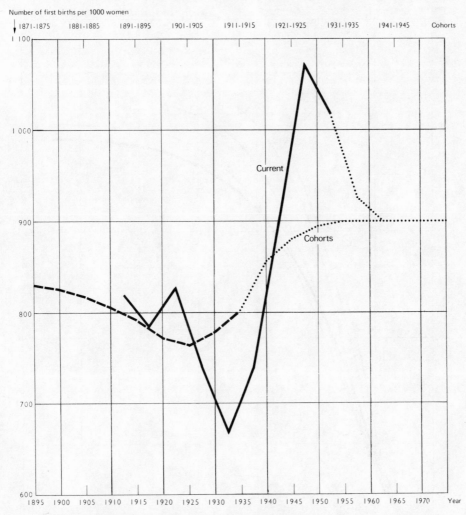

Number of first births per 1000 women

Fig. 18.6   *Final first-birth totals, values for cohorts and as current index* (i_p)

Compare these data with those relating to the dates of first births in the same cohorts. Can you offer any explanation for the changes in the fertility of recent cohorts?

Answer

We are concerned here exclusively with measures of general fertility. When appreciable variations in these measures occur, the first task is to examine whether they can be explained by significant changes in nuptiality.

The analysis is confined to first births. The situation of the cohorts from 1905 onwards is shown in Table 18.5 and plotted in Fig. 18.7 (the numbers italicized in the table and the dotted lines on the graph are obtained from later estimates and are irrelevant to this section).

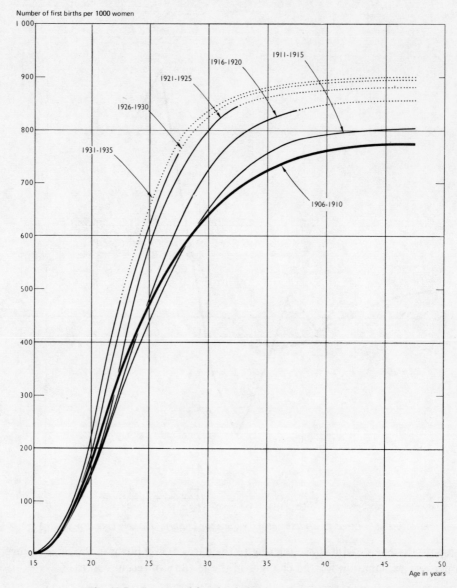

Fig. 18.7 *Pattern of first-birth fertility in certain cohorts*

It must be remembered that members of the 1906–10 cohort had fewer births than any other; and this is virtually true of the total number of *first* births also (in fact, the three adjacent cohorts were very similar in this respect, 1896–1900 with 772, 1901–5 with 764, and 1906–10 with 773 per 1000 women).

The members of four of the five cohorts born after 1906–10 began their reproductive lives with fewer first births than that of 1906–10. At the outset of their reproductive lives they lived through the difficult pre-war and war years. Despite this unpromising start, however, they all caught up with the 1906–10 group and very soon surpassed it (this is also true of the 1931–5 and 1936–9 cohorts which were not affected by unfavourable conditions).

In addition to the rise in the number of first births, the same cohorts exhibit a rise in nuptiality (a declining percentage of single persons aged 50), and a fall in the average age at first marriage. This would tend to increase fertility (basically composed of legitimate children), and to lower the age at which women bear their first child.

Table 18.5 shows that the rise in the percentage of women marrying at least once is less than 4%, whereas the total number of first births to women of the 1921–5 cohort, born by the time they are 32·5 years old on average, already exceeds the *final* figure for the 1906–10 group by close on 10%.

As regards the earlier timing of first births, it is impossible to separate this completely from the general rise in fertility, as long as the final number of first births is not known. Moreover, members of almost all the cohorts, including that of the 1906–10 reference group, faced difficult conditions at the beginning of their reproductive lives. But the two youngest cohorts, which were not subject to these difficulties, show such a marked advance on the older ones for which data are available, and the general trend of development is so obvious, that it may safely be concluded that there has been a change in the timing of first births that owes very little to the comparatively slight change in the age at marriage. It is also worth noting that the first and last cohorts show a remarkable degree of dispersion in the number of first births between the ages of 25 and 30; the gap here is much greater than in the final total of first births, which tends to converge towards a figure of 900 births.

More precise results can only be obtained by undertaking more complex calculations which go beyond the general treatment to which the present analysis is limited.

Problem 7

The recent rise in nuptiality and changes in fertility in the younger cohorts lead to a situation in which only 10% of the women in the 1931–5 cohort will be childless at the age of 50.

On this assumption, use the data already obtained, interpolating where necessary, to estimate the timing pattern of first births in quinquennial cohorts between 1911 and 1935.

Answer

The necessary interpolations can be performed on the data given in Table 18.5, assuming 900 first births per 1000 women reaching the menopause (at ages 45–49) in the 1931–5 cohort. Note that the last line of the table may be obtained by slightly increasing the figures of the line immediately above. Very few first births occur after the age of 44 (according to Table 18.1, the number of these additional first births for the cohorts between 1871 and 1910 varied between 1 and 3 per 1000). First births at ages 40–44 in the 1916–20 cohort have been calculated in a similar way, by adding 15 to the number achieved at age 39 (the range at this age in the 1871–1915 cohorts was between 10 and 22).

Table 18.5   *Estimates of first birth totals (first births per 1000 women; estimated values in italics)*

Age (years)	Cohorts					
	1906–10	1911–15	1916–20	1921–5	1926–30	1931–5
15–19	45	43	36	39	39	*57*
20–24	340	300	308	348	427	*479*
25–29	567	555	621	715	757	*780*
30–34	689	715	789	845	*860*	*865*
35–39	748	782	839	*870*	*885*	*890*
40–44	770	799	854	*878*	*892*	*898*
45–49	773	802	856	*880*	*894*	*900*

Now that these results have been established, the other estimates can be made in two stages:

1 By interpolating the final totals of first births for the 1921–5 and 1926–30 cohorts (see Fig. 18.8A).
2 By interpolating the estimated totals in the intermediate age groups for the 1921–5, 1926–30 and 1931–5 cohorts. Two of these are plotted in Fig. 18.8B.

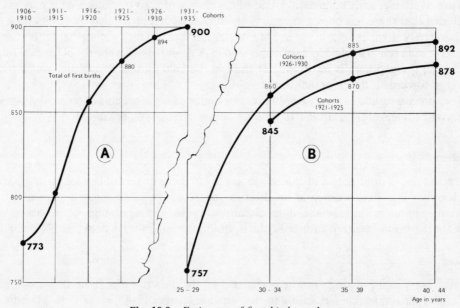

Fig. 18.8   *Estimates of first-birth totals*

These estimates may appear arbitrary, because they are based on only one hard fact, the completed fertility of the 1921–5 cohort. In fact, however, the method is simple, and, since a logical sequence has been followed from the outset, it has the advantage of yielding consistent results. The graphs, too, in this case are subject to only a slight margin of uncertainty. Fig. 18.7, which illustrates the results just obtained, is in fact strikingly regular. Although this does not prove that the estimates are accurate, it at least demonstrates the validity of the procedure within the framework of the accepted hypotheses.

Problem 8

Assume that the reproductive histories of the post-1935 birth cohorts will be substantially similar to that of the 1931–5 cohort. On this basis, calculate the probable value of i_p (see Problem 5) for 1955–80.

Use the data obtained in Problems 7 and 8 to extend the graph drawn in Problem 5.

Answer

Fig. 18.1 shows that members of the 1936–40 cohort had already produced a total of 65 first births per 1000 women at ages 15–19. If it is assumed that the progressive rise in fertility observed in the cohorts before 1935 will be followed by a stabilization for the post-1935 cohorts, it seems logical to retain this rate for the youngest women, although it differs slightly from the stationary reference level. This modification will, however, be applied only to the immediately following age group. First birth rates can thus be assumed stable and to have the values shown in Table 18.6.

Table 18.6   *First birth rates (per 1000 women)*

Age-group (years)	Cumulative rate	First birth rate
15–19	65	65
20–24	479	414
25–29	780	301
30–34	865	85
35–39	890	25
40–44	898	8
45–49	900	2

Table 18.4 and Fig. 18.6 may be completed by entering different first birth rates for successive cohorts, on a Lexis diagram, and adding the vertical columns (this has already been done for the period before 1 January 1955; see also Fig. 18.4, which clearly illustrates the method for births of all orders). The new values obtained are listed below (the cohort rates have already been given in Table 18.5):

Period	i_p (per 1000 women)
1955–1959	926
1960–1964	900
1965–1969	899
1970 and after	900

A comparison of final totals of first births to different cohorts with the current fertility index (i_p) shows the same kind of difference that has been found previously, although their magnitude has increased.

Here, too, the trend in cohort fertility is very regular, while the current index fluctuates. Special circumstances at particular periods have a much more marked effect upon i_p than upon current reproduction rates. For instance, the decline due to the First World War and the recovery that followed it are reflected, the effects of the economic depression are obviously significant, and the recovery during the decade following the Second World War is very noticeable indeed. On the other hand, the Second World War has not affected the current index, which at that period had already reached the level which it was later to recover, when the situation had stabilized once more after the adoption of new fertility norms. This may seem surprising at first; but the explanation may well be that the recovery in births, impeded for a decade by poor economic conditions, had already begun during 1940–4 and had affected first births (besides, the USA was not at war throughout the whole period).

It is worth noting that the i_p index exceeds the 1000 mark for two consecutive five-year periods. This result is arithmetically absurd, but shows that the current method (as well as the procedure employed – the addition of age-specific rates for a given period) compounds developments observed at different ages in *different* cohorts, which would be impossible at *different* ages in the *same* birth cohort. Births taking place to different cohorts are spliced together to make up the index.

To sum up, the striking comparisons of Fig. 18.6 clearly show the instability of current fertility measures. They are of value only when related to a specific period; and it is difficult, indeed impossible, to interpret their meaning whilst the cohorts contributing to these measures have not yet reached the end of their reproductive lives.

Problem 9

Calculate wherever possible the proportion of women in each cohort with at least one live birth, the proportion of women with one birth who have at least two – and so on to the proportion of women with at least six live births who have at least seven (the parity progression ratio).

These ratios will be written a_0, a_1, a_2, a_3, a_4, a_5 and a_6 respectively.

Represent graphically fluctuations in the ratios, incorporating extrapolated values for a_0.

Answer

It is possible to compute a_i for all birth cohorts for which the number of births by order is known up to ages 45–49. The numbers of births beyond this age group are negligible and can affect only very large families (eight or more live births), which are not considered in this exercise. It is thus possible to compute a_i for eight cohorts by relating the total of births of order $(i+1)$ (T_{i+1}) to the births of order i (T_i):

$$a_i = \frac{T_{i+1}}{T_i}$$

Taking the 1871–5 cohort as an example (see Table 18.1, last line of the cohort column), it is clear that

$$a_0 = \frac{830}{1000} = 0\cdot830; \quad a_1 = \frac{666}{830} = 0\cdot802; \quad a_2 = \frac{526}{666} = 0\cdot790;$$

$$a_3 = \frac{405}{526} = 0\cdot770; \quad a_4 = \frac{308}{405} = 0\cdot760; \quad a_5 = \frac{240}{308} = 0\cdot780;$$

$$a_6 = \frac{181}{240} = 0\cdot755.$$

The results for a_4, a_5 and a_6 have been rounded off to multiples of five, because the data do not allow a greater degree of accuracy. These proportions will be called parity progression ratios – although this concept, introduced by L. Henry, is more commonly applied to the births of individual married couples. Table 18.7 shows the results for the eight cohorts, and they are shown on a diagram in Fig. 18.9, where the values of a_6 (whose trend is very similar to that of a_5) have been omitted for the sake of clarity.

Table 18.7 *Parity progression ratios (per 1000, calculated on the total of women in a single cohort)*

Birth cohort	Parity progression ratio						
	a_0	a_1	a_2	a_3	a_4	a_5	a_6
1871–1875	830	802	790	770	760	780	755
1876–1880	826	795	758	748	735	760	740
1881–1885	817	782	731	726	715	745	725
1886–1890	805	768	717	706	695	735	705
1891–1895	792	756	696	686	680	710	695
1896–1900	772	753	666	664	670	690	680
1901–1905	764	729	632	636	645	665	655
1906–1910	773	726	598	596	610	640	640

Practically all the ratios show a consistent decline from the 1871–5 cohort to that of 1906–10 inclusive. The only exception is a_0; this is higher for the 1906–10 cohort than for its predecessor.

Clearly, then, the decline in fertility, which continues up to and including the 1906–10 cohort (see Problems 2 and 3), is apparent in families of all sizes. This decline is least marked in a_0 and a_1 (which also remain at a distinctly higher level than the other ratios); and the trend is similar for a_2, a_3, a_4, a_5 and a_6. At the latest period for which analysis is possible, however, a_2 and a_3 are a good deal lower than a_4 and much below a_5 and a_6.

The estimates for the ratios in the 1931–5 cohort show that a_0 is continuing to rise. This is only to be expected, in view of what is already known of the recovery in fertility in recent cohorts.

The results that have been obtained, particularly in Problem 7, make it abundantly clear that a significant rise in a_0 is certain to take place. In fact, a_0 is another index of the total number of first births per woman, and the graph of a_0 in Fig. 18.9 repeats the curve for that cohort in Fig. 18.6.

Problem 10

More detailed study has made it possible to predict the following values (per 1000) for the 1931–5 cohort:

$$a_1 = 900 \quad a_4 = 500$$

$$a_2 = 750 \quad a_5 = 550$$

$$a_3 = 600 \quad a_6 = 560$$

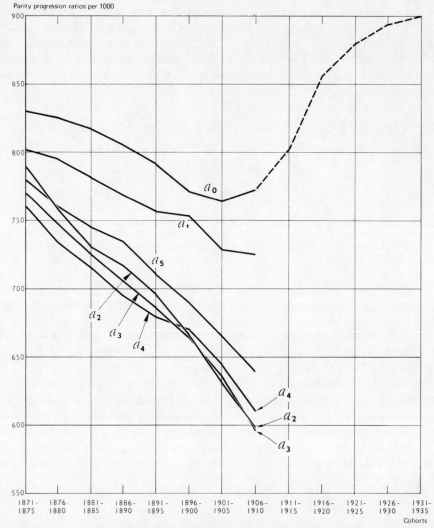

Parity progression ratios per 1000

Fig. 18.9 *Parity progression ratios (for cohorts)*

Calculate the final distribution of women by number of children born implied by these values. Compare the results with the data for the 1871–5 cohort. Represent graphically, and comment.

The comparison should relate to (1) the total of births of the two cohorts, and (2) the net reproduction rate of the two cohorts.

Answer

It is interesting to begin by comparing the most recent observed values for a_i (for the 1906–10 cohort) with those to be expected for the 1931–5 cohort (see Table 18.8).

The general rise in fertility is the result of a decrease in childlessness and an increase in the number of families with one or two children. Fertility in families with three children has remained constant; beyond that number the decline recorded in Fig. 18.9 has been maintained.

Table 18.8 *Parity progression ratios (per 1000)*

	Cohorts	
	1906–10	1931–5
a_0	773	900
a_1	726	900
a_2	598	750
a_3	596	600
a_4	610	500
a_5	640	550
a_6	640	560
a_7		640

A change in behaviour is clearly taking place. More extensive voluntary birth control is producing a noticeable decline in the fertility of families with three or more children; while at the same time an increase in fertility in the group that had previously restricted fertility most will lead to a progressive predominance of medium-sized families. These points become still clearer if one computes the distributions of family sizes corresponding to the two extreme series of parity progression ratios (those of the 1871–5 and the 1931–5 cohorts).

This may be done immediately from the data in Table 18.1 on the 1871–5 group. If 830 out of 1000 women have one child, 666 have two children, 526 have three, etc., then there are:

$$1000 - 830 = 170 \text{ women with no live births}$$
$$830 - 666 = 164 \text{ women with one live birth}$$
$$666 - 526 = 140 \text{ women with two live births, etc.}$$

To find the number of women with seven live births, however, it is necessary to obtain figures for births of the eighth order; this parity is not distinguished from births of higher order (365 births of order 8 or over) in Table 18.1. If it is assumed, however, that $a_7 = 0.75$ (a figure close to that for a_4, a_5 and a_6), then

$$181 \times 0.75 = 136 \text{ births of order 8}$$
and $\qquad 181 - 136 = 45$ women with seven live births.

In the case of the 1931–5 cohort, the distribution of births by order is found by multiplying by successive parity progression ratios as follows:

$$1000 \, a_0 = 900 \text{ first births}$$
$$1000 \, a_0 \, a_1 = 810 \text{ second births}$$
$$1000 \, a_0 \, a_1 \, a_2 = 607 \text{ third births}$$
$$\text{etc.}$$

It is possible to distribute these 1000 women by the number of their live births in the same way.

$$1000 - 900 = 100 \text{ women with no live births}$$
$$900 - 810 = 90 \text{ women with one live birth}$$
$$810 - 607 = 203 \text{ women with two live births}$$
$$\text{etc.}$$

Table 18.9, giving the complete distribution, is thus constructed and forms the basis of Fig. 18.10.

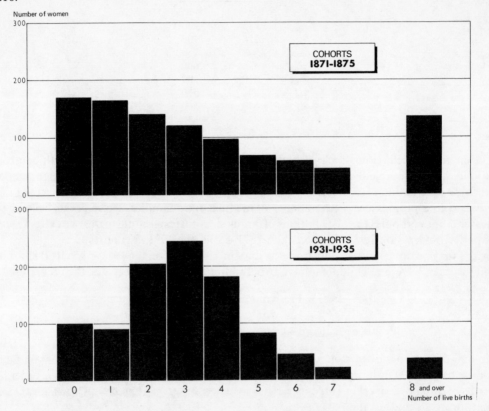

Fig. 18.10   *Distribution of 1000 women by the number of their live births*

Among recent cohorts there has clearly been a concentration on medium family sizes (totals of 63% of women have between two and four births), while very large families are now much less important, probably because of more widespread and more efficient contraception. The proportion of childless women or those with only one child has fallen because fewer couples are now voluntarily childless or subfertile, and also because the number of first marriages has increased.

It should be noted, however, that there is a proportionately smaller number of *surviving* children (because of higher mortality) among the 1871–5 birth cohort than in that of 1931–5. Families thus differ less in the number of live children below a given age than in the number of

Table 18.9 *Distribution of 1000 women by the number of their live births*

		Cohorts	
Women with		1871–5	1931–5
0 live births		170	100
1 „ „		164	90
2 „ „		140	203
3 „ „		121	243
4 „ „		97	182
5 „ „		68	82
6 „ „		59	44
7 „ „		45	20
8 „ „ and over		136	36
Total		1000	1000

live births. This is true of the *larger families*. On the other hand, these differences among the smaller families (no children or only one child) are more pronounced. Higher mortality in the past meant that a considerable proportion of women who had borne two or three children no longer had any surviving children or had only one. This increases the proportion of families with that number of surviving children, particularly in the 1871–5 cohort.

The relationship between fertility and mortality in the 1871–5 and the 1931–5 cohorts may also be studied by computing some of the usual synthetic indices – for example, total fertility or the net reproduction rate.

Total fertility in the 1871–5 group amounted to 3521 live births per 1000 women. The figure for the 1931–5 group may be found by adding together the values a_0, $a_0 a_1$, $a_0 a_1 a_2$, etc.; these give the live births per woman of different parities (a_0 first births, $a_0 a_1$ second births, etc.). One minor difficulty emerges in the case of the last term that it is possible to compute:

$$a_0 a_1 \ldots a_7 = 0.036.$$

This represents not only eighth births but the *proportion of women* having eight or more children. Assuming that the parity progression ratios beyond a_7 remain constant at 2/3, the total number of eighth or subsequent children is

$$0.036\left[1 + \frac{2}{3} + \left(\frac{2}{3}\right)^2 + \ldots\right] = \frac{0.036}{1 - 2/3} = 0.036 \times 3 = 0.108.$$

This yields a final fertility of 3127 live births per 1000 women for the 1931–5 cohort.

As for net reproduction rates, these are found as follows:
for the 1871–5 cohort:

$$3521 \times \frac{0.488}{1000} \times 0.722 = 1.24,$$

for the 1931–5 cohort:

$$3127 \times \frac{0.488}{1000} \times 0.93 = 1.42,$$

where 0·722 and 0·93 respectively represent the probabilities of survival to age 20 at the period when the respective groups were born. As before, these probabilities are substituted for the probabilities of survival to mean age at confinement in the different cohorts. The figure of 0·93 assigned to 1937 has been obtained by taking the mean between 0·909 (the American life table for 1929–31) and 0·940 (the life table for 1939–41).

Table 18.10

	Cohorts	
	1871–5	*1931–5*
Final total of births (number of live births per 1000 women)	3521	3127
Net reproduction rate	1·24	1·42

The decline in mortality has meant that although fertility has decreased by 11%, the net reproduction rate has risen by 15%.

19

Fluctuations in nuptiality and fertility

The example discussed here deals mainly with events that occurred in France during and just after the Second World War. Only a few simple hypotheses are discussed, in order to avoid complex calculations and to bring out as clearly as possible the interaction of the various constituent elements.

One of the objectives is to trace the reproductive histories of birth cohorts, by using data on current nuptiality, and to determine the relative importance of nuptiality and legitimate fertility in influencing the number of births.

Data

The stationary population (with radix 1 000 000) associated with the French life table for 1952–6 will be used. A nuptiality table (see Table 19.1) sets out the annual figures for first marriages in this population.

Problem 1

Using the probabilities of marriage for females (Table 19.1), calculate the annual total of first marriages for women aged under 50. How are these marriages distributed by age of bride? Represent the data graphically. What is the proportion of spinsters aged 20, 25, 35, 40, 45 and 50 among the female population? What is the annual total of first marriages for men under 50? Compare this with the number of first marriages among women.

Answer

It is assumed that the reader will be familiar with the method of computing the stationary population associated with a life table. The results obtained from the French life table for 1952–6 are given in *Études statistiques* No. 1 for January–March 1959. Note, however, that in the present case *two* stationary populations are being computed, associated with life tables for males and females respectively, the sex ratio at birth being 105 to 100.

Table 19.1

Age	Probability of marriage		Age	Probability of marriage	
	Men	Women		Men	Women
15	—	—	35	0·0087	0·0045
16	—	0·0056	36	0·0079	0·0042
17	—	0·0190	37	0·0071	0·0039
18	0·0046	0·0471	38	0·0063	0·0032
19	0·0146	0·0827	39	0·0054	0·0027
20	0·0317	0·1091	40	0·0048	0·0023
21	0·0408	0·1240	41	0·0039	0·0020
22	0·0817	0·1144	42	0·0033	0·0018
23	0·1360	0·0543	43	0·0028	0·0016
24	0·1150	0·0720	44	0·0025	0·0014
25	0·0925	0·0543	45	0·0022	0·0013
26	0·0729	0·0401	46	0·0020	0·0012
27	0·0567	0·0296	47	0·0017	0·0011
28	0·0438	0·0224	48	0·0015	0·0010
29	0·0340	0·0174	49	0·0013	0·0009
30	0·0268	0·0136	50	0·0012	0·0009
31	0·0207	0·0109			
32	0·0160	0·0085			
33	0·0126	0·0069			
34	0·0103	0·0058			

Note: Age attained in calendar year of marriage. Marriage ratios are computed by relating the first marriages in a cohort to the size of that cohort on 1 January.

The probabilities as defined are particularly suitable for computing the numbers of first marriages at different ages (simple multiplication, for instance, gives $6870 \times 0·0056 = 38$). It will be shown that these ratios, which have not been much used, and which have not been rigorously defined, are also suitable for other purposes.

Table 19.2 illustrates the method of calculating the number of first marriages by sex and age.

The proportion of spinsters aged 20 last birthday in the female population is computed as follows:

There are 6850 women aged 20 last birthday, a certain number of whom are married. It is necessary to determine

The survivors among the 38 who married in the calendar year of their 16th birthday (i.e. at average age 16),

The survivors among the 130 who married in the calendar year of their 17th birthday (i.e. at average age 17),

...,

The survivors among the 746 who married in the calendar year of their 20th birthday (i.e. at average age 20).

Let l_x denote the survivors to birthday x and L_x those aged x to $x+1$. Of the 38 women married during the year in which they attained the age of 16, $38L_{20}/l_{16}$ will survive to make up

Table 19.2 *Marriages of single persons, according to sex and age*

Age on 1 Jan.	Women			Men			Age on 1 Jan.	Women			Men		
	Pop.	Probability	1st mar.	Pop.	Probability	1st mar.		Pop.	Probability	1st mar.	Pop.	Probability	1st mar.
15	6870	0·0096	38				35	6726	0·0042	28	6870	0·0079	54
16	6867	0·0190	130				36	6713	0·0039	26	6850	0·0071	49
17	6863	0·0471	323	7112	0·0046	33	37	6699	0·0032	21	6828	0·0063	43
18	6859	0·0827	567	7104	0·0146	104	38	6684	0·0027	18	6805	0·0054	37
19	6854	0·1091	748	7094	0·0317	225	39	6668	0·0023	15	6781	0·0046	31
20	6850	0·1240	849	7084	0·0406	288	40	6651	0·0020	13	6754	0·0039	26
21	6845	0·1144	783	7073	0·0817	578	41	6633	0·0018	12	6726	0·0033	22
22	6839	0·0947	648	7061	0·1360	960	42	6614	0·0016	11	6696	0·0028	19
23	6833	0·0720	492	7050	0·1150	811	43	6594	0·0014	9	6660	0·0025	17
24	6827	0·0543	371	7037	0·0925	651	44	6572	0·0013	9	6623	0·0022	15
25	6820	0·0401	273	7025	0·0729	512	45	6548	0·0012	8	6581	0·0020	13
26	6813	0·0296	202	7012	0·0567	398	46	6522	0·0011	7	6535	0·0017	11
27	6805	0·0224	152	6999	0·0438	307	47	6494	0·0010	6	6485	0·0015	10
28	6797	0·0174	118	6985	0·0340	237	48	6463	0·0009	6	6431	0·0013	8
29	6789	0·0136	92	6971	0·0268	187	49	6430	0·0009	6	6371	0·0012	8
30	6780	0·0109	74	6956	0·0207	144	Total of first marriages		6229				6127
31	6770	0·0085	58	6941	0·0160	111							
32	6760	0·0069	47	6925	0·0126	87							
33	6750	0·0058	39	6908	0·0103	71							
34	6738	0·0045	30	6890	0·0087	60							

the population aged 20–21, provided that there is no differential mortality between the married and the single. In that case, the total number of married women (or those who have been married) among the 6580 aged 20 last birthday is equal to

$$38 \frac{L_{20}}{l_{16}} + 130 \frac{L_{20}}{l_{17}} + 323 \frac{L_{20}}{l_{18}} + 567 \frac{L_{20}}{l_{19}} + 748 \frac{L_{20}}{l_{20}}. \tag{1}$$

Substituting L_x values for those of l_x in the denominators slightly reduces the value of Equation (1), but makes it possible to express the number of married survivors in a much simpler way. Equation (1) becomes, in fact,

$$38 \frac{L_{20}}{l_{15}} + 130 \frac{L_{20}}{l_{16}} + 323 \frac{L_{20}}{l_{17}} + 567 \frac{L_{20}}{l_{18}} + 748 \frac{L_{20}}{l_{19}} = L_{20}\left(\frac{38}{L_{15}} + \frac{130}{L_{16}} + \ldots + \frac{748}{L_{19}}\right).$$

The expression in brackets is *the sum of the ratios between 15 and 19 complete years*. If L_{20} is taken to represent the population aged 20 (last birthday), it is clear that the brackets represent the *proportion* of women already married at age 20. It follows that the sum of the ratios in Table 19.2 up to the ages of 19, 24, 29, ... 49 yields the proportion of women already married at birthday 20, 25, etc., up to 50. The complements to these proportions yield the proportion never married at these ages:

		%
at birthday	20:	73·65
	25:	27·71
	30:	15·40
	35:	11·74
	40:	10·11
	45:	9·30
	50:	8·79

With the life table employed, the relative error introduced by this approximation is negligible – a few units per 10 000. It is worth noting that if central marriage rates (first marriages divided by the *mean* size of the cohort during that particular year) had been used instead of the probabilities of marriage, this method of computation would have given exact results in the absence of differential mortality.

Table 19.2 shows the number of first marriages for men under 50 as 6127, compared with 6229 first marriages for women. This discrepancy is consistent with there being an equal number of men and women marrying, since only first marriages are considered here (and only those taking place under the age of 50), and women are known to marry at a lower age than men.

Problem 2

Because of war, all the female probabilities of marriage (see Table 19.1) have been reduced by 35% overall in year 1, 25% in year 2, and 10% in years 3 and 4. The end of hostilities at the beginning of year 5 leads to a rise during that year of 20% (except among women reaching age 16, where it is 10%), of 40% in year 6 (25% among those aged 16 and 17), and of 10% during year 7 (5% among those aged 16, 17 and 18). In subsequent years, the probabilities revert to their normal values. It is assumed that casualties during the war were light and that the life table remains unchanged.

Trace the changes in the annual number of first marriages of women under 50. Do all marriages postponed because of the war take place ultimately? If not, why not? Plot the distribution of first marriages of women under 50 in *each* of the five birth cohorts attaining ages 16–20 in year 1. Calculate the mean age at marriage and compare it with the mean age if there had been no war. Obtain a measure of the total nuptiality of these cohorts, and compare it with that in the stationary population (using the percentage of spinsters of age 50 in the relevant cohorts).

Answer

As the figures for marriages have been derived from probabilities, every change in these values involves a proportionate change in the number of marriages. Consequently, first marriages among women under 50 (6229 in a normal year) are multiplied by 0·65 in year 1, by 0·75 in year

2, etc., ... by 1·1 in year 7. But note that the results of this multiplication must be adjusted for years 5, 6 and 7, in view of the smaller increase in the probabilities of marriage at lower ages.

The results are given in Table 19.3. Of the 4983 marriages postponed because of the war, only 4307 take place later (i.e. 676 do not); so recovery has not been complete. Several explanations may be put forward for this, based on observations and measurements among populations that have suffered similar disturbances. The first point to note is that the process of ageing among women postponing marriage has a twofold effect – some die and others leave the relevant age group (15–50). A more important factor, however, is that opportunities for marriage were rarer during the war; and as a consequence, even when recovery became possible, some spinsters who would normally have married when younger were no longer inclined to do so and remained single. This is the reason for the arbitrary alterations to the probabilities suggested for years 1 to 7.

Table 19.3 *First marriages of women under age 50*

	Normal year	War years				Recovery years		
		1	2	3	4	5	6	7
Multiplier	1	0·65	0·75	0·90	0·90	1·20	1·40	1·10
Corrected number of marriages	6229	4049	4672	5606	5606	7475 −4	8721 −25	6852 −25
First marriages	6229	4049	4672	5606	5606	7471	8696	6827
Total			19 933				22 994	
First marriages in normal period			24 916				18 687	
Difference			−4 983				+4 307	
Marriages permanently prevented				676				

Members of the cohort attaining ages 15 to 20 during year i will be distinguished by the digit corresponding to the year of marriage: i_{16}, i_{17}, ... i_{20}. The probabilities and the related marriages can be read off diagonally from a table which gives, by single years of age, the probabilities and marriages in different calendar years, beginning with the first year appropriate to marriage: $i-4$ for the i_{20} cohort, $i-3$ for the i_{19} cohort, ... i for the i_{16} cohort. This is done in Table 19.4, which also shows, for comparison, the development of an undisturbed cohort. The wartime probabilities are in italics, and these figures trace the passage of the various cohorts from years i to $i+6$.

Fig. 19.1 illustrates the changes caused by disturbances in the distribution of first marriages in cohorts i_{20} and i_{16}.

In the former, marriages took place as usual up to birthday 19 reached in year $i-1$. The war affected this generation at ages 20–23 when nuptiality is normally at its peak. The age distribution of marriages is therefore completely changed, and the subsequent recovery obviously fails to compensate for the effects of the war. Thus the i_{20} cohort, disturbed during the

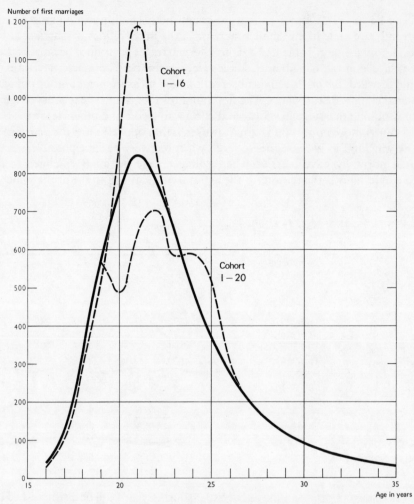

Fig. 19.1   *Distribution of first marriages (women) according to age*

years of maximum nuptiality, is affected by the hostilities to a larger extent than any other cohort.

The i_{16} cohort, whose members began to marry when the war was at its height, is only slightly affected, because its members were very young during the war and had not yet attained the age of maximum nuptiality. When the war ended, this group had reached the age at which most marriages take place, at a moment when nuptiality was generally recovering. There is, therefore, a marked rise in the number of marriages contracted at ages 20, 21 and 22. Members of the cohort were too young to have been greatly affected by the war, and they were affected more than any other group by the upsurge of marriages that followed when hostilities ended, thus more than compensating for the earlier deficiency. Note that the general pattern of the distribution of marriages by age remains the same.

Table 19.4 *First marriages in certain cohorts*

Nuptiality in different cohorts

Mean age*	Normal cohort		1–20		1–19		1–18		1–17		1–16	
	Prob.	Mar.	Prob.	Mar.	Prob.	Mar.	Prob.	Mar.	Prob.	Mar.	Prob.	Mar.
16	0·0056	0·0038	0·0056	0·0038	0·0056	0·0038	0·0056	0·0038	0·0056	0·0038	0·0036	0·0025
17	0·0190	0·0130	0·0190	0·0130	0·0190	0·0130	0·0190	0·0130	0·0123	0·0084	0·0142	0·0097
18	0·0471	0·0323	0·0471	0·0323	0·0471	0·0323	0·0306	0·0210	0·0353	0·0242	0·0424	0·0291
19	0·0827	0·0567	0·0827	0·0567	0·0538	0·0638	0·0620	0·0425	0·0744	0·0510	0·0744	0·0510
20	0·1091	0·0748	0·0709	0·0486	0·0818	0·0561	0·0982	0·0673	0·0982	0·0673	0·1309	0·0898
21	0·1240	0·0849	0·0930	0·0637	0·1116	0·0764	0·1116	0·0764	0·1488	0·1019	0·1736	0·1188
22	0·1144	0·0783	0·1030	0·0705	0·1030	0·0705	0·1373	0·0939	0·1602	0·1096	0·1258	0·0861
23	0·0947	0·0648	0·0852	0·0583	0·1136	0·0778	0·1325	0·0907	0·1042	0·0713	0·0947	0·0648
24	0·0720	0·0492	0·0864	0·0590	0·1008	0·0689	0·0792	0·0541	0·0720	0·0492	0·0720	0·0492
25	0·0543	0·0371	0·0760	0·0519	0·0597	0·0408	0·0543	0·0371	0·0543	0·0371	0·0543	0·0371
26	0·0401	0·0273	0·0441	0·0300	0·0401	0·0273	0·0401	0·0273	0·0401	0·0273	0·0401	0·0273
27–50**	0·1491	0·1007	0·1491	0·1007	0·1491	0·1007	0·1491	0·1007	0·1491	0·1007	0·1491	0·1007
Total	9·121	6·229	8·621	5·885	8·852	6·044	9·195	6·278	9·545	6·518	9·751	6·661
Mean age		23·2		23·5		23·5		23·4		23·3		23·1
Proportion never married at 50 (%)	8·79		13·79		11·48		8·05		4·55		2·49	

* Birthday falling within the year of marriage.
** This line represents the sum of probabilities and marriages corresponding to these ages.

The elementary calculation of the mean ages at first marriage requires no elaboration. The results are recorded in Table 19.4. The changes due to disturbance are not important; a maximum increase of 0·3 years occurs for the i_{20} and i_{19} cohorts, and those belonging to the i_{16} cohort marry earlier (mean age 23·1 years against 23·2).

Disturbance has a much more marked effect upon total nuptiality in the cohorts. The proportion never married at birthday 50 is a good index. The lower this proportion, the higher the nuptiality. As was noted in Problem 1, the proportions required are the complements of the total probability of marrying at least once by birthday 50.

These figures confirm and amplify earlier conclusions. The effects of incomplete recovery are illustrated most clearly in the i_{20} and i_{19} cohorts; in these groups, 13·79% and 11·48% respectively remain unmarried at birthday 50, as against 8·79% in a normal group. By contrast, the three other cohorts (i_{18}, i_{17} and i_{16}) have a higher than normal nuptiality, with 8·05%, 4·55% and 2·49% remaining single at age 50 respectively.

Problem 3

Table 19.5 shows the distribution of legitimate live births by duration of first marriage in a stationary population.

The annual number of illegitimate births and of children born to remarried women may be assumed negligible. Compute the mean number of children per first marriage.

Answer

As the population is stationary, the annual number of births (B) is obtained by dividing the total population by the life expectancy at birth:

$$B = \frac{1\,000\,000}{68\cdot02} = 14\,702.$$

Table 19.5

Duration	Births	Duration	Births
0	55	14	18
1	180	15	15
2	113	16	13
3	97	17	11
4	83	18	9
5	71	19	7
6	64	20	5
7	53	21	4
8	48	22	3
9	40	23	2
10	34	24	1
11	29		
12	24	All	
13	21	durations	1000

Note: Durations are expressed in single years as differences between the year of birth and the year of marriage.

To simplify matters, all births will be considered to be legitimate, and to be the issue of a first marriage (note, in passing, that it would have been possible to consider a distribution of births by duration of marriages covering *all* births following a first marriage; this example would have been more realistic and no less simple).

As this is a case in which current and cohort methods would give the same result, these 14 702 births may be regarded as the total progeny of a cohort of couples married for the first time at ages under 50 (all women beyond that age being assumed sterile). It follows that the mean fertility per marriage is

$$\frac{14\,702}{6229} = 2 \cdot 36 \text{ children.}$$

Problem 4

War conditions cause a decline in the fertility of marriages concluded before the commencement of hostilities. This decline, which applies equally to all marriage durations, is assumed to amount to 15%. At the end of the war, the cohorts involved revert to normal behaviour, with a partial recovery of postponed births spread over years 6, 7 and 8. A 60% recovery takes place, distributed over the three years in the ratio of $1:2:1$.

The fertility of marriages concluded in year 1 and subsequent years is the same as that of the stationary population.

Compute the annual number of births for years 1–15. Compare this series with the number·of births in the stationary population. Represent graphically.

Answer

Consider a base year 0, and preceding years numbered -1, -2, -3, etc., respectively.

If the births are distributed by marriage duration, as assumed in the problem, the births

Table 19.6 *Weighted means of first marriages.*

rs	Numbers of marriages	Coefficients of weight	1	2	3	4	5	6	7	8	9	10	11	12	13	14	15
5	6229																34
4	6229															343	112
3	6229														343	1121	70
2	6229													343	1121	704	60
1	6229												343	1121	704	604	51
0	6229											343	1121	704	604	517	44
9	6229										343	1121	704	604	517	442	39
8	6229									343	1121	704	604	517	442	399	33
7	6827								375	1229	771	662	566	485	437	362	32
6	8696							478	1565	982	843	722	617	556	461	417	34
5	7471						411	1345	844	725	620	530	478	396	359	299	25
4	5606					308	1009	633	544	465	398	359	297	269	224	191	16
3	5606				308	1009	633	544	465	398	359	297	269	224	191	163	13
2	4672			257	841	528	453	388	332	299	248	224	187	159	135	112	9
1	4049	55	223	729	457	393	336	287	259	215	194	162	138	117	97	85	7
0	6229	180	1121	704	604	517	442	399	330	299	249	212	181	149	131	112	9
-1	6229	113	704	604	517	442	399	330	299	249	212	181	149	131	112	93	8
-2	6229	97	604	517	442	399	330	299	249	212	181	149	131	112	93	81	6
-3	6229	83	517	442	399	330	299	249	212	181	149	131	112	93	81	69	5
-4	6229	71	442	399	330	299	249	212	181	149	131	112	93	81	69	57	4
-5	6229	64	399	330	299	249	212	181	149	131	112	93	81	69	57	44	3
-6	6229	53	330	299	249	212	181	149	131	112	93	81	69	57	44	31	2
-7	6229	48	299	249	212	181	149	131	112	93	81	69	57	44	31	25	1
-8	6229	40	249	212	181	149	131	112	93	81	69	57	44	31	25	19	1
-9	6229	34	212	181	149	131	112	93	81	69	57	44	31	25	19	12	
-10	6229	29	181	149	131	112	93	81	69	57	44	31	25	19	12	6	
-11	6229	24	149	131	112	93	81	69	57	44	31	25	19	12	6		
-12	6229	21	131	112	93	81	69	57	44	31	25	19	12	6			
-13	6229	18	112	93	81	69	57	44	31	25	19	12	6				
-14	6229	15	93	81	69	57	44	31	25	19	12	6					
-15	6229	13	81	69	57	44	31	25	19	12	6						
-16	6229	11	69	57	44	31	25	19	12	6							
-17	6229	9	57	44	31	25	19	12	6								
-18	6229	7	44	31	25	19	12	6									
-19	6229	5	31	25	19	12	6										
-20	6229	4	25	19	12	6											
-21	6229	3	19	12	6												
-22	6229	2	12	6													
-23	6229	1	6														
Weighted mean marriages $\bar{M}$			6110	5752	5668	5696	5783	6174	6484	6426	6368	6346	6334	6324	6315	6308	629
which marriages for year 0 $\bar{M}_w$			223	986	1606	2238											
marriages in year or previously $\bar{M}_p$			5887	4766	4062	3458											

during year 0 depend on the marriages in years $0, -1, -2, \ldots, -24$ $(M_0, M_{-1}, M_{-2}, \ldots M_{-24})$. It is now possible to consider more closely the significance of this distribution and the contribution made by different marriage cohorts to the births of that year. On the likely assumption that all cohorts achieve the same total fertility (d), equal to 2·36 live births (see Problem 3), the proportions of the distribution given in the problem $(0·055, 0·180, \ldots 0·001)$ may be replaced by symbols: $\alpha_0, \alpha_1, \ldots \alpha_{24}$ $(\alpha_0 + \alpha_1 + \ldots + \alpha_{24} = 1)$. *The duration-specific legitimate fertility rate for duration 0* is then $\alpha_0 d$, for *duration 1* it is $\alpha_1 d, \ldots$, and for duration 24 it is $\alpha_{24} d$. Moreover, during year 0 marriages concluded in that year produced $\alpha_0 dM_0$ births, marriages at duration 1 produced $\alpha_1 dM_1$ births, ..., and those at duration 24 produced $\alpha_{24} dM_{24}$ births. The total number (B_0) of births during year 0 can thus be evaluated:

$$B_0 = \alpha_0 dM_0 + \alpha_1 dM_{-1} + \ldots + \alpha_{24} dM_{-24}$$
$$= d(\alpha_0 M_{-0} + \alpha_1 M_{-1} + \ldots + \alpha_{24} M_{-24}) \qquad (1)$$
$$= d\Sigma \alpha_s M_{-s}.$$

Provided there is no disturbance, $M_0 = M_1 = \ldots = M_{24} = M$, and Equation (1) becomes

$$dM(\alpha_0 + \alpha_1 + \ldots + \alpha_{24}) = dM = B_0.$$

This result is the same as that established earlier (Problem 3) without the use of symbols, with $M = 6229$ marriages and $B_0 = 14\,702$ births.

When the annual number of marriages varies, the equation becomes

$$d\bar{M} = B_0$$

with

$$\bar{M} = \alpha_0 M_0 + \alpha_1 M_{-1} + \ldots + \alpha_{24} M_{-24}.$$

$\bar{M}$ is thus the weighted mean of the marriages, with $\alpha_0, \alpha_1, \ldots \alpha_{24}$ as weights. Table 19.6 shows values of $\bar{M}$ for each of the years 1–15.

With these general points established, it is possible to return to the problem.

The legitimate fertility rates given in Table 19.7 are those used to compute the annual births during the war years 1, 2, 3 and 4. Only those rates relating to cohorts married during the war are unaltered; all the rest are reduced to 85% of their usual value.

Table 19.7

Marriage duration	Undisturbed year	War years			
		1	2	3	4
0	$\alpha_0 d$	$\alpha_0 d$	$\alpha_0 d$	$\alpha_0 d$	$\alpha_0 d$
1	$\alpha_1 d$	$0·85\alpha_1 d$	$\alpha_1 d$	$\alpha_1 d$	$\alpha_1 d$
2	$\alpha_2 d$	$0·85\alpha_2 d$	$0·85\alpha_2 d$	$\alpha_2 d$	$\alpha_2 d$
3	$\alpha_3 d$	$0·85\alpha_3 d$	$0·85\alpha_3 d$	$0·85\alpha_3 d$	$\alpha_3 d$
4	$\alpha_4 d$	$0·85\alpha_4 d$	$0·85\alpha_4 d$	$0·85\alpha_4 d$	$0·85\alpha_4 d$
.	.	.	.	.	.
.	.	.	.	.	.
.	.	.	.	.	.

Consider the weighted mean $(\bar{M})$ of the marriages for any given year. If the total of war marriages (M_w) is distinguished from that of pre-war marriages (M_p), then the births for that year may be expressed as

$$B = (M_w + 0.85M_p)d.$$

The values of M_w and M_p appear at the foot of Table 19.6. Table 19.8 summarizes the findings for the war period.

Table 19.8

		1	2	3	4
Normal fertility	$\bar{M}$	6110	5752	5668	5696
	$2.36\bar{M}$	14420	13575	13376	13443
	Births (1–4)		54814		
Wartime fertility	M_w	223	986	1606	2238
	$0.85M_p$	5004	4051	3453	2939
	$M_w + 0.85M_p$	5227	5037	5059	5177
	$2.36(M_w + 0.85M_p)$	12336	11888	11939	12218
	Births (1–4)		48381		

Prevented births: $54814 - 48381 = 6433$

The decline in the fertility of these marriages, brought about by war, leads to a shortfall in births of 6433. It is estimated that 60% (3860) of this total was recovered during years 6, 7 and 8, 25% (965) in year 6, 50% (1930) in year 7, and 25% (965) in year 8.

Note that no figure has been given for recovery during year 5, although some recovery appears to have taken place. This year marks a turning point, including as it does both postponed births (which would have been conceived in year 4) as well as births made up (conception early in year 5). For the sake of simplicity, figures of postponed births are given for years 1 to 4 only; in reality, however, temporary fluctuations must have taken place as a result of the changing war situation.

Annual birth figures from year 5 onwards may be computed by using the formula

$$B = \bar{M}d,$$

apart from the recovery years 6, 7, and 8 which have just been mentioned.

Finally, the annual number of births obtained is as follows:

Year	Births	Year	Births
0	14702	8	16130
1	12336	9	15028
2	11887	10	14977
3	11939	11	14948
4	12218	12	14925
5	13648	13	14903
6	15536	14	14887
7	17232	15	14859

However, nuptiality is disturbed as well as fertility, and the effects of this disturbance persist over a much longer period. Indeed, even the figure for births in year 15 (14 859) differs appreciably from that in a stationary population (14 702).

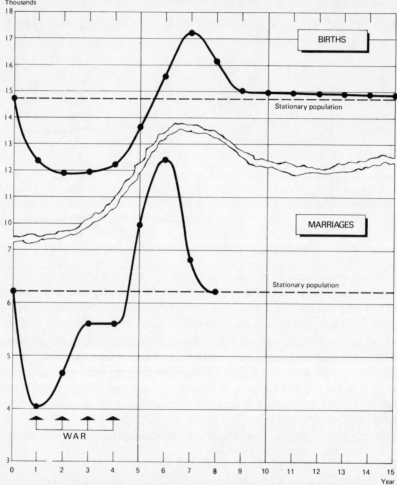

Fig. 19.2 *Development of annual numbers of first marriages (bride's age less than 50) and births*

During the entire period (1–15) there were 215 453 births, compared with 220 530 in a stationary population. Of the 5077 fewer births thus recorded, 2574 (40% of 6433) were postponed and not recovered; 2503 therefore reflect changes in nuptiality.

The depleted birth cohort born during the war reaches marriageable age in year 15. Its imbalance will lead to modifications in nuptiality; the probabilities given in this problem will require revision. These alterations in turn will affect the annual number of births. The figure for births will gradually approach the stationary level and then diverge from it again; this second disturbance will be due to changes in the structure of the female population brought about by the earlier disturbance.

20

Some indices of natality and fertility among a native African population

The data used in this chapter are taken from statistics obtained from a demographic study conducted in Guinea in 1954–5. Comparison of results from different sets of figures reveals contradictions which arise from inaccuracies in the basic data.

It is not easy to arrive at exact conclusions for the population studied, but the value of the problems considered in this chapter lies in comparing some of the very varied concepts employed in the study of fertility, and the establishment of relations between them. An understanding of these would have an influence on the method of collecting statistical data.

Data

In a native African population, where birth control is not practised, it may be assumed that virtually all women marry before they are 20.

In a demographic survey, women were asked to state how many live children they had borne. Results are set out in the table below:

Live births	Woman's age at survey						
	20–24	25–29	30–34	35–39	40–44	45–49	50–54
0	16 736	10 788	5 903	6 036	3599	3188	1811
1	33 485	15 159	6 838	6 618	3559	2925	1843
2	36 211	25 549	9 686	8 693	4862	4451	2516
3	17 565	27 576	12 863	10 721	6096	5737	3109
4	6 155	23 064	14 483	12 649	6895	6505	3567
5	2 024	11 657	14 605	13 622	7339	7190	4116
6	558	5 748	9 624	12 693	7701	6184	3961
7	145	1 780	5 031	8 385	6298	6375	3825
8	15	507	2 858	5 276	5635	5074	2607
9 and over	10	274	1 638	5 031	6522	8214	5138

FERTILITY

Problem 1

Calculate the proportion of childless women in the different age groups. Comment on the results.

Answer

The proportion of women still infertile is obtained by comparing the figures on the first two lines of Table 20.1.

Table 20.1   *Proportions of women still infertile, and mean number of live births attained at different ages*

	20–24	25–29	30–34	35–39	40–44	45–49	50–54
	Woman's age at inquiry date						
1 Total number of women	112 904	122 100	83 525	90 724	58 506	55 841	32 523
2 Number of childless women	16 736	10 768	5 903	6 036	3 599	3 186	1 811
3 % of women still infertile	14·8	8·8	7·1	6·7	6·2	5·7	5·6
4 Total number of live births	197 915	352 996	327 121	409 244	296 438	295 469	173 977
5 Mean number of live births	1·75	2·89	3·92	4·51	5·07	5·29	5·35

The proportion diminishes as age increases. In the present case almost all the women marry before they reach the age of 20. Advance in age is therefore equivalent to an increase in the mean duration of marriages – an increase that reduces the risk of infertility among non-sterile couples. And since birth control is not practised in the population studied, it follows that the proportion of couples still childless at the most advanced age (about 50) corresponds almost exactly to the number of physiologically sterile couples. However, as the survey included all women, those widowed or divorced soon after marriage may have remained childless although fertile; and some women (though only very few) remained unmarried. These factors explain why the proportions of 5·7% and 5·6% at ages 50–54 slightly overestimate the proportion of young sterile couples. A better estimate could have been obtained by limiting the inquiry to women aged 45–54 who were still married. But the difference would, in any case, have been small; and a value of the order of 5% is commonly found for this proportion among young couples in studies of this kind.

It should be noted that in this answer different birth cohorts are compared. The results obtained would therefore apply to a single cohort only if the situation were stationary. Data for testing this hypothesis are not available; but the smooth progression of proportions through successive age groups does not lead us to doubt it, although we might, for instance, if the percentage sterile in one group were lower than in the two adjacent groups.

Problem 2

Calculate the mean number of live births per woman in the different age groups. Represent the results graphically. Assume that no woman under 30 has had more than 9 live children, and that those with more than 9 live children had an average of 9·5 at ages 30–34 and 10 at age 35 or over.

Answer

Table 20.1 provides the necessary data for calculating this figure. It is obtained by dividing the numbers on line 4 by those on line 1. The graph representing the results (Fig. 20.1) indicates the fertility pattern (given by the mean number of live births) as the woman's age increases. The data can only be interpreted in this way, however, if both fertility had remained constant throughout the period, and the replies to the question 'How many children have you had?' were correctly given by all the members of the birth cohort concerned. These issues will be discussed at a later stage (we shall not consider a possible correlation between mortality and fertility, which would operate selectively on the groups of women questioned on their past fertility).

Problem 3

In a further inquiry, women were asked to state the number of live births they had had during the previous twelve months. The following figures (per 1000) were obtained:

	Woman's age at confinement						
	15–19	*20–24*	*25–29*	*30–34*	*35–39*	*40–44*	*45–49*
Number of women	115 333	112 879	122 064	83 502	90 689	58 496	55 815
Number of live births	28 030	38 369	38 700	21 078	15 841	4 068	1 520

Compute the age-specific fertility rates, and the number of live births per woman at age 20, 25, ... 50, which correspond to these figures.

Answer

Women who had indicated the sizes of their families also stated how many children they had borne during the previous twelve months. Those aged 50–54 had no children during that period and were naturally omitted from the inquiry (it should be noted that the totals of women in all the age groups who replied to this second question are slightly smaller than those who replied to the first. The difference is no doubt due both to non-response and to unusable answers).

Dividing the number of declared births by the total number of women in each age group gives the following fertility rates per 1000:

at 15–19: 243   at 35–39: 175
    20–24: 340   40–44: 70
    25–29: 317   45–49: 27
    30–34: 252

If a woman were subjected to these age-specific fertility rates throughout her reproductive life, the number of children she would have had by given ages may be computed. Table 20.2 illustrates this computation. The births are calculated at ages 20, 25, ... 50.

Table 20.2 *Births calculated according to general age-specific fertility rates*

Age (years)	Per 1000 women			Mean figure of live births per woman	
	Rates	Cumulative rates	Cumulative rates × 5	Number	Age (years)
15–19	243	243	1215	1·21	20
20–24	340	583	2915	2·91	25
25–29	317	900	4500	4·50	30
30–34	252	1152	5760	5·76	35
35–39	175	1327	6635	6·63	40
40–44	70	1397	6985	6·98	45
45–49	27	1424	7120	7·12	50

Problem 4

Compare the results obtained in Problem 2 and 3 by means of a graph. Comment.

Answer

The figures calculated in Problems 2 and 3 give the same information, but have been obtained by different methods. A comparison of the results is illuminating.

Fig. 20.1 shows this comparison in the form of a graph. Note that the data for the birth cohorts are plotted against the value of 22·5 years (the mean age of the 20–24 group), 27·5 (that of the 25–29 group), ... etc., whilst the data obtained by cumulating current fertility rates are given at 20, 25, ... years.

At every age, the mean number of births based on current fertility is higher than that obtained from the birth cohorts.

Unless there are doubts about the reliability of the data, it must be concluded that fertility had risen during the last twelve months; the rise may be fortuitous, or it may be due to the continuation of a short- or long-term trend. But as the total number of children born to the older women is already high (over five children per woman aged 40–44), the latter explanation seems *a priori* unlikely.

When examining the quality of the data, either the statements about the *total* number of live born children or those about the live births during the past twelve months may be incorrect.

The total number of live born children may well have been underestimated, especially by older women who were recalling events that had occurred some time ago. Children who had died in infancy are the most likely to have been omitted, either because they were more liable to have been forgotten, or because the respondents misunderstood the question and failed to mention children who had lived only a short time.

These faults of memory or comprehension are much less likely to occur when the question

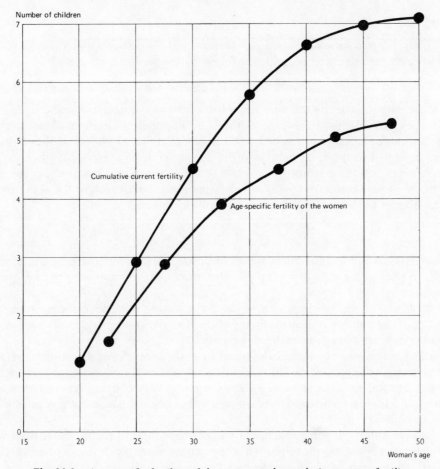

Fig. 20.1 *Age-specific fertility of the women and cumulative current fertility*

refers to events occurring during the past twelve months. But the women may not be conscious of the exact nature of twelve months as a time span. Events occurring during that period may therefore have been omitted (underestimation of the time span), or events happening more than twelve months ago may have been included (overestimation). In the first case, fertility during the twelve months would be underestimated, and in the second it would be overestimated.

In view of the high level of fertility (over seven children per woman), it is tempting to discount the risk of underestimation. The opposite assumption (i.e. a possible overestimation) brings the curve of current cumulative fertility nearer to that of retrospective fertility in the cohorts, and reduces differences for which there seems to be little reason. They become even smaller if, as seems highly probable, women underestimate the number of live children they have borne. The rest of this chapter will be devoted to other aspects of this question.

Problem 5

In the survey, the population included 215 000 boys and 218 000 girls under the age of 5 years. Their mortality rate was studied, with the following results (for both sexes):

$$q_0 = 0.220; \qquad {}_5 q_0 = 0.353.$$

Use these data to estimate the number of live births in the past five years.

The model life tables used are those of the U.N. Population Division *Population Studies* No. 25. Various data have been added to these model tables, in particular the ratios of the numbers aged 0–4 to the total number of births occurring in the previous five years. The proportions used are those relating to the two sets of tables in which q_0 and ${}_5 q_0$ respectively represent the values nearest to those found in the population under review. Thus, two estimates of the number of births in the past five years will be obtained.

Answer

The first step is to find the number of newborn during the past five years, by considering the total of survivors at the date of survey (in other words, those comprising the age group 0–4 (P_{0-4})).

This number cannot be derived *directly*, by a simple arithmetical operation, from a calculation of the number of deaths among them. The data collected are neither sufficiently detailed nor reliable enough to make this possible.

Instead, it is necessary to *deduce* the result from the most probable estimates relating to mortality among young children. The two indices selected for this purpose are the rate of infant mortality (identical with the value of q_0) and the probability of dying between birth and 5th birthday $({}_5 q_0)$. It seems worthwhile enlarging a little upon the particular way in which these results can be used.

The data are admittedly somewhat crude, and are inadequate by themselves to determine the ratio which, when applied to the births of five consecutive years, yields the numbers surviving to form the 0–4 age group. Model life tables will therefore be used. Certain values relating to these tables have been calculated, including the ratio above (cf. *Population Studies* No. 25). The

Table 20.3   *Calculation of births based on survivors in a population*

	Model table in which q_0 is nearest to 0·220 Level: 30; $e_0 = 35$ years q_0 male: 0·225 female: 0·203		Model table in which ${}_5 q_0$ is nearest to 0·353 Level: 25; $e_0 = 32.5$ years ${}_5 q_0$ male: 0·352 female: 0·353	
	Male	*Female*	*Male*	*Female*
P_{0-4}	215 000	218 000	215 000	218 000
Divisors $(P_{N,\,0-4})$	0·7440	0·7627	0·7248	0·7447
Births in the past 5 years	289 000	286 000	297 000	293 000
	575 000		590 000	

particular model tables selected will be those in which the values of q_0 and $_5q_0$ are nearest to those found in the population studied (0·220 and 0·353 respectively). Table 20.3 sets out the results of this comparison.

There is thus a choice of two different model tables (levels 30 and 25); and this shows that values of $q_0 = 0·220$ and $_5q_0 = 0·353$ are not consistent with any of the mortality patterns in the model tables, otherwise the two values would be found in the same model table. In fact a value of $q_0 = 0·220$ corresponds to a model with lower mortality than $_5q_0 = 0·353$ (a life expectancy at birth of 35 years compared with 32·5 years).

This discrepancy may be real – the model tables are statistical artefacts, and the actual values found in a real population may be greater or smaller than in the model table. Or it may be due to faulty assessment – infant mortality may have been underestimated, because the ages of children who died before their 1st birthday have been overestimated. This type of error would seem to be less frequent, however, and less likely, when mortality in the first five years of life is studied.

The stages in the computation are set out in Table 20.3. The numbers of births obtained differ slightly. It will be noted that the sex ratio is abnormal (about 101%). Two explanations (not necessarily incompatible) are possible: excess female mortality among young children (because less care is given to girls, for instance), or underestimation of the male population under five years of age.

The ratios used as divisors $(P_{N, 0-4})$ are computed in the UN study on the assumption that the population is stationary, but this is not the case here. Other things beings equal, however, and in view of the annual rise in total births, the method leads to only a slight overestimation of the total figure of newborn during the five years.

Problem 6

Assume that the population is increasing at an annual rate of 2%, and that the birth rate remains constant. Using the two values obtained in Problem 5, estimate the number of births during the past twelve months.

Three figures for the number of births during this period are now available. Compare these, and use them to throw light on the discussion initiated in Problem 4.

Answer

In estimating the number of births during the past twelve months, taking account of the number during the past five years, it must be borne in mind that births have been increasing at the rate of 2% per year. Writing B for the number of births during the past twelve months, and $\bar{B}$ for the number during the past five years, it is clear that

$$\bar{B} = B\left[1 + \frac{1}{1·02} + \frac{1}{(1·02)^2} + \frac{1}{(1·02)^3} + \frac{1}{(1·02)^4}\right].$$

The expression in parentheses is the sum of the first five terms of a geometric series with $q = 1/1·02$, and this sum can be expressed as

$$\frac{1-q^5}{1-q} = \frac{1-1/(1·02)^5}{1-1/1·02} = \frac{[(1·02)^5 - 1] \times 0·51}{(1·02)^5 \times 0·01}.$$

This gives

$$\bar{B} = 4 \cdot 8B, \text{ so } B = \frac{1}{4 \cdot 8} \bar{B} = 0 \cdot 208 \bar{B}$$

and therefore

$$\text{if } \bar{B} = 575\,000, \; B = 120\,000,$$

$$\text{if } \bar{B} = 590\,000, \; B = 123\,000.$$

When these figures are compared with 147 000 (the total of live births stated as having occurred during the past twelve months), they are found to be deficient by between 17% and 18%.

It is more difficult to compare fertility in the last twelve months estimated in this way with that calculated from the number of births obtained by direct inquiry from women of different ages (see Problem 2), when these were asked to supply details of total numbers of children born. Without going into detail, it may be noted that these totals may be used to estimate age-specific fertility rates, and from these rates an annual figure of births may be obtained which can be compared with other estimates. The figure so obtained is 108 000 births.

So the two estimates obtained from the count of the population aged 0–4 (which are very close to one another) lie between that derived from the total number of births occurring to all women aged 15–55 on one hand, and that obtained from direct inquiry on births occurring during the past twelve months on the other. This result confirms the hypotheses already put forward about these two last measurements of fertility (see the discussion in Problem 3 on the two curves in Fig. 20.1). But although an estimate of the order of 120 000 births a year (in the last twelve months) and a set of age-specific fertility rates that would lie in the middle of the two curves in Fig. 20.1 represent the most plausible results, any findings on this subject must remain estimates rather than certainties.

Problem 7

The proportion of married women in different age groups is as follows:

> at age 15–19: 81%
> 20–24: 96
> 25–29: 96
> 30–34: 96
> 35–39: 95
> 40–44: 91
> 45–49: 83

Ignoring illegitimate births, calculate the age-specific legitimate fertility rate. What is the mean number of children born to a woman who marries at 20 years of age?

Answer

Although comments on the preceding problem have thrown some doubt upon the validity of the age-specific fertility rates calculated above, they will continue to be used in the solution of this problem.

For the sake of clarity, take a given age group – say 25–29. Let W denote the total number of women in this group, of whom W_m are married; let B be the number of live births (all legitimate) occurring to them during the year of observation.

The age-specific fertility rate is then B/W, and the legitimate age-specific fertility rate is B/W_m. Since

$$\frac{B}{W_m} = \frac{B}{W} \times \frac{W}{W_m} = \frac{B}{W} \bigg/ \frac{W_m}{W}$$

it is clear that the legitimate age-specific fertility rate is obtained by dividing the age-specific fertility rate by the proportion of married women in the age group. Note, however, that this rule only holds good if there are no illegitimate births (or if their number is negligible).

Table 20.4 gives the results obtained.

Table 20.4 *Legitimate age-specific fertility rates*

Age groups (years)	*(1)* Age-specific fertility rates	*(2)* Proportions of married women	*(3) = (1)/(2)* Legitimate age-specific fertility rates
15–19	0·243	0·81	0·300
20–24	0·340	0·96	0·354
25–29	0·317	0·96	0·330
30–34	0·252	0·96	0·263
35–39	0·175	0·95	0·184
40–44	0·070	0·91	0·077
45–49	0·027	0·83	0·033

These legitimate age-specific fertility rates may be cumulated in the same way as general fertility rates (see Problem 3), provided that fertility does not depend on age at marriage. The cumulative total of the rates beyond age 20 will in these circumstances represent the mean number of children born to a woman married at age 20 and remaining married till she is 50 years old.

The population studied does not practise voluntary birth control, and the results of numerous investigations lead to the conclusion that the fertility of a married woman depends solely on her age and not on the duration of her marriage. For a woman married at 20 and continuing in that state till she is 50, the mean number of children is therefore

$$5(0·354 + 0·330 + 0·263 + 0·184 + 0·077 + 0·033) = 6·2 \text{ children}.$$

While earlier estimates suggested that this procedure may have overestimated true fertility, natural fertility (in the absence of contraception) seems fairly low. It will be remembered that the number of births recorded for women married at age 20 and remaining married until the age of 50 who do not practise voluntary birth control lies between 5 and 10 live births.

Problem 8

Percentages of married couples (by age of wife) who are sterile are as follows:

<table>
<tr><td>at 15:</td><td>5%</td><td>at 35:</td><td>20%</td></tr>
<tr><td>20:</td><td>5</td><td>40:</td><td>40</td></tr>
<tr><td>25:</td><td>8</td><td>45:</td><td>75</td></tr>
<tr><td>30:</td><td>13</td><td>50:</td><td>100</td></tr>
</table>

Calculate the age-specific fertility rates (up to age 45) for fertile couples. Compute the reciprocals of these rates; interpret and comment.

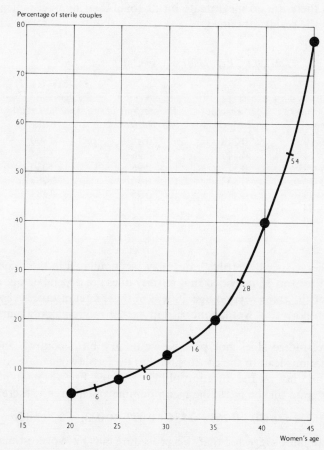

Fig. 20.2 *Graphic interpolation of percentages of sterile couples by age of woman*

Answer

Fertility rates for fertile couples may be calculated by dividing the legitimate fertility rates by the percentage of fertile couples in each age group. This calculation is clearly analogous to that which led from the general age-specific fertility rates to legitimate age-specific fertility rates.

In the present case, it is necessary to interpolate between the percentage figures for women of exact age 15, 20, 25, etc., to obtain percentages for all women in the different age groups. This is done graphically in Fig. 20.2, interpolation between 45 and 50 being too uncertain to be included. The following table gives the results:

Woman's age (years)	Fertility rate of fertile women	Reciprocal fertility rate
15–19	0·316	3·2
20–24	0·377	2·7
25–29	0·367	2·7
30–34	0·313	3·2
35–39	0·256	3·9
40–44	0·167	6·0

The point of interest about these rates is that their reciprocals give the mean intervals between successive births in the age group.

Though this result can be seen to be true intuitively, it is difficult to prove rigorously. It is sufficient to note it and comment briefly on what may be deduced from it.

The mean intervals are lowest (2·7 years) between ages 20 and 30. They then increase, with the woman's age, until they reach the high figure of 6 years between ages 40 and 45. The mean interval is also higher before age 20 than between 20 and 30. In the main, these results are in line with direct measurements of intervals obtained in non-contracepting populations though in the present case the births are relatively more widely spaced.

21

Age, duration of marriage and sterility

There are occasions when statistical data must be analysed in circumstances in which complex calculations are of limited value. This may happen at various stages of the analysis; or may even be due to the nature of the original data. If such is the case, and no other facts are available, only limited conclusions can be drawn.

Census data on the infertility of married women are an example. It is impossible to lay down any precise rules for their analysis. What is essential is to use all the data available, and to reason soundly and accurately from them. This chapter aims simply at illustrating the kind of mental gymnastics of which every demographer must be capable.

The topic treated here has obvious affinities with that discussed in Chapter 15. In each case, some of the precautions that are needed when interpreting the data are made necessary by the way in which they were collected.

Data

At a recent population census attention was focused on women who had married only once and who were still married at the time of the census. These women were classified by age and by duration of marriage at the time of the census. The percentage of women in these cohorts who were childless at census date was calculated (women who had had illegitimate children were excluded). It was assumed that very few of these women had married before age 15.

Problem 1

The percentages childless of those aged 15–49, at different marriage durations, are given below:

Marriage duration (complete years) at census date	Percentage of women still childless
0– 5	10·4
6– 7	9·3
8– 9	8·4
10–14	7·0
15–19	6·6
20–29	5·2
30 and over	4·7

Plot these data, and comment.

Answer

No information is available on the general fertility of the population under review. We do not know whether contraception is generally used. Nor is it known whether the use of birth control was increasing during the period studied.

In any event, the percentages of infertile women at significant marriage durations (15 and over) lie between 5% and 6%, which is close to the proportion normally found to be physiologically sterile among young women. This means that *total* voluntary infertility is relatively unimportant in this population, at least among the older cohorts (the women in the higher marriage duration groups). At the lower durations also (corresponding in general to the youngest women) the proportion of women still childless is quite low (10·4% at durations under 6 years, and 8% to 9% between 6 and 10 years). Voluntary birth control, if practised, clearly has little effect on the general level of *total* infertility; the cohorts differ only slightly in this respect.

It is, of course, possible that voluntary birth control is practised, at least among certain strata of the population; but it is reasonable to assume throughout that the practice of contraception has only a limited effect on first births, and this investigation is concerned essentially with the occurrence of a first birth.

The data are plotted in Fig. 21.1.

Percentages are plotted against median durations within duration groups. In the last group (30 years of marriage or over), which is an open group, the data must relate to women aged 45–49 (apart from exceptional cases of marriage under the age of 15); and such women are unlikely to have been married for much more than 30 years, the maximum being 35 years (see Fig. 21.2). The mean duration is taken as 31 years, on the assumption that the marriages are more or less evenly distributed between the ages of 15 and 20. This approximation is quite acceptable, for the graph would be altered very little by more complex assumptions (which might also be applied to the group with marriage duration 20–29).

At lower marriage durations, some couples capable of having children (i.e. those who are not sterile) have not yet been able to prove their fecundity. This is particularly true of subfertile

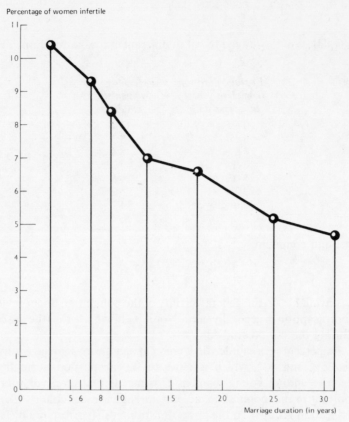

Fig. 21.1

couples (those with a lower than average chance of conceiving within each menstrual cycle). The higher the marriage duration, therefore, the more the percentage of infertile couples is bound to diminish until, at the highest durations, it may be said to be equal to the percentage of couples who are physiologically completely sterile.

At the same time, present observations are concerned with all women married for the first time between the ages of 15 and 50. Hence the lower the marriage duration, the greater, in the corresponding age groups, is the proportion of women who married late. Taking the two extremes as an example, women married for at least 30 years must have married before they were 20 years old, whereas the group of women married for less than six years may include those married at any age under 50 (see Fig. 21.2). Other things being equal, the lower the marriage duration, the greater is the proportion of couples *sterile* because of the wife's age; and this increases the percentages of childless women. In this example, couples presently married for 0–5 years include a higher proportion sterile in this way than did those married for 30 or more years during their first six years of marriage. And the percentage of childless women in the latter group was certainly lower than 10·4% (the figure for the first group).

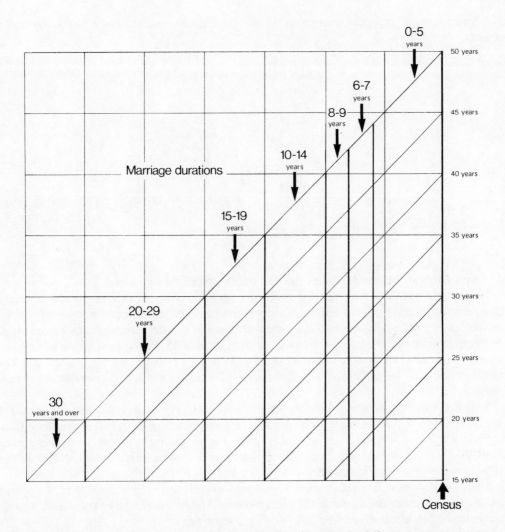

Fig. 21.2 *Marriage durations, at census dates, as distributed among the different female birth cohorts*

To sum up, the more recent the marriage, the greater is the dispersion in age at marriage (with an ever-increasing mean age); and in the data given, as marriage duration increases, this greater dispersion suggests that the fall in the percentages of women who are still infertile is greater than is actually the case.

Problem 2

The percentages of childless women, at all marriage durations, are given below, by age at census:

Woman's age at census	Percentage childless
15–19	24·2
20–24	8·5
25–29	6·8
30–34	6·4
35–39	6·9
40–44	6·9
45–49	7·3

Comment on the above data.

Answer

The data confirm the conclusion at the end of the preceding problem.

The current age of the women (or more precisely, their age at the time of the census) is positively correlated with the length of their marriage; it is therefore to be expected that the percentage of childless women will decrease with age. But this decrease ends at 40 years of age, and is then followed by a slight increase, so that at ages 45–49 the proportion of childless women is as high (7·3%) as it was at about age 25 (8·5% at 20–24 and 6·8% at 25–29). This phenomenon may be explained by reference to the analysis in the last part of the previous problem.

Note that women who are older at the time of the census exhibit a greater dispersion in their age at marriage than do younger women. The Lexis diagram (Fig. 21.2) makes this clear if read horizontally by cohort, and not vertically as in the preceding problem. As this increased dispersion is caused by the presence of older women who have recently married, the percentage of women sterile at marriage increases with the age at census of the groups studied.

After a certain age, this factor cancels and may even reverse the effect due to the greater *average* marriage duration among the older women. And this may well be the reason why the percentage of childless women begins to rise after the age of 35.

The rise is only slight; but it is worth noting one factor which may vitiate the comparisons just made, and which, taken by itself, would have an opposite effect. This is the differential use of birth control by different cohorts (the younger the cohort, the more extensively are these methods used). Though slight, the increase in the proportions childless with age is nonetheless significant, and is not necessarily due to a difference in reproductive behaviour.

Among the younger age groups, as sterility only increases slowly with age at the beginning of a woman's reproductive life, the effects of greater dispersion in age at marriage are outweighed by the longer exposure to risk.

It should be noted, however, that in the youngest group (15–20), all of whom married before they were 20, the situation is different. For the fertility of these women who married at very young ages is lower in the early part of their marriages than among women who married when slightly older (20–25, for instance). Thus, the high percentage of women still infertile in this age group is due partly to the recency of their marriages but also, to a much smaller degree, to the relatively low fertility of the young women forming this group.

Problem 3

The percentages childless in a group of women with marriage durations of 10–15 years are given below, according to their age at the time of the census:

Woman's age at census	Percentage childless
20–24	5·5
25–29	5·1
30–34	5·3
35–39	9·5
40–44	15·1
45–49	25·6

Transform age at census to age at marriage, and comment.

Answer

In the present case, different age groups are considered at the same duration of marriage. This makes it possible to study the relation between age at marriage and infertility. As the marriage duration selected is relatively long, it is reasonable to expect that the proportions of childless couples will approximate to the proportions of physiologically sterile couples among the different age-at-marriage groups. The less birth control is practised among the population, the closer will these two series of proportions be to one another.

Before looking at the different percentages obtained, it should be noted that the youngest group includes only women married before the age of 15 (cf. Fig. 21.2), and who cannot have been married for much more than ten years by the time of the census. Further, the 25–29 group also includes a high proportion of women who married at very young ages (before they were 20), and the mean duration of marriage for them is likely to be lower than for other groups. So the conditions for comparing different birth cohorts are not ideal; the two youngest quinquennial groups are comprised exclusively of women who married very young and were observed at marriage durations several years less than those of the other women.

Table 21.1 shows the relationship between current ages and ages at marriage for the different groups.

Table 21.1 *Relationship between current ages and ages at marriage in women at marriage duration 10–14*

Current age of women	Age at marriage		Percentage childless
	Age interval	Mean age*	
20–24	<15 years	<15 years	5·5
25–29	<20	<20	5·1
30–34	15–25	20	5·3
35–39	20–30	25	9·5
40–44	25–35	30	15·1
45–49	30–40	35	25·6

* See note to Table 21.2.

The first three groups differ very little between one another and nothing can be deduced from the figures, particularly since the two youngest groups are rather unusual. Note, however, that what has been said of women aged 20–24 may explain the rather higher percentage of childless women in this group compared with the two that follow it (a lower mean marriage duration, and lower fertility in the early years of marriage among the very young women who make up the group).

The important point about these youngest women is that the proportion childless after several years of marriage (over 10) is about 5%, and that this is comparable to sterility rates among young women in a non-contracepting population. Moreover, a figure of this order was found in the oldest birth cohort (see Problem 1 : 4·7% among the 'over 30s' (marriage duration) and 5·2% among the '20–29s'). These results combine to confirm the very limited influence of contraception, at least before the first birth, among the women who married at younger ages in the population.

It is interesting to compare the percentages of women childless at other ages with known figures for sterile women at various ages; the relationship between these two series is shown in Table 21.2. Sterility figures are taken from a study by Louis Henry ('La fécondité naturelle: observations, theories, résultats', *Population* No. 4, 1946). They are based upon the mean of five series.

Table 21.2   *Childless and sterile women*

Data from the present study		% of women childless after 10–14 years of marriage	L. Henry's data	
Age at marriage			% of sterile women	
Age interval	Mean age*			Age
15–25	20	5·3	3	20
20–30	25	9·5	6	25
25–35	30	15·1	10	30
30–40	35	25·6	16	35

* These are in fact the medians of the corresponding age intervals in the previous column, the true means being affected by the distribution of marriages by age. They are certainly rather lower than the medians given here, in the case of the 20–30 age group. But the differences are unimportant in a general comparison such as the present one.

The percentages childless, at every age, are distinctly above those of Henry's series. However, Henry's data are obtained by taking the arithmetic mean of five fairly widely dispersed values. It is not, therefore, possible to regard the differences between the series as estimates of the proportion of couples who are voluntarily infertile in the various age-at-marriage groups. At best they give indications; and these clearly suggest that in every age group shown in Table 21.2 there exist some voluntarily childless couples, and relatively more of them in the groups with higher ages at marriage. Two reasons may be suggested for these differences between groups with different ages at marriage:

1 Sterility increases more rapidly with marriage duration among women who marry late. If such women postpone the conception of their first child, they are much less likely to prove fertile than are women who marry young.

2 The woman's age at marriage and the sociocultural background of the newly married couple. Women who marry late often belong to those social groups in which contraception is more widely practised.

VII
THE STUDY OF
A POPULATION
AS A WHOLE

22
Study of a profession

A profession may be regarded as a population, i.e. a group into which individuals enter (in this instance by recruitment), and from which they withdraw (by death or by retirement). Entries and withdrawals correspond to births and deaths in an ordinary population. Indeed, a profession is only one of many possible types of population (such as students, patients, graduates, former pupils etc.).

One profession has already been studied earlier in this book: Chapter 1 dealt with French medical practitioners, and this particular population was studied in relation to the total population of which it formed a part. The point of view in this chapter however, is different; the profession itself is treated as a population; the example given is a very simple application of the concept of a stationary population, designed to throw light on this concept.

Data

The profession in question has an annual entry (on 1 January) of 1000 persons aged 25 last birthday. No member leaves the profession until all retire at exact age 60. It is assumed that mortality within this group is constant over time, and given by the life table below:

Exact age x	Survivors l_x
25	1001
26	999
30	987
35	971
40	951
45	925
50	887
55	833
60	763

The expectation of life at retirement is 15·3 years.

Problem 1

What proportion of those entering the profession attain the age of retirement?

Answer

The life table given relates to a total of 1001 persons at birthday 25 and 999 at birthday 26; it therefore also applies to a group (cohort) of $(1001 + 999)/2 = 1000$ persons aged 25 last birthday. The table shows that 763 of these survive to retire at age 60; so the required proportion is 76·3%.

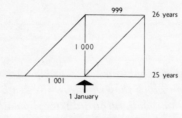

Fig. 22.1

Problem 2

What is the total strength of the profession on 1 January of any one year? How does it vary during the course of a year (between 1 January and 31 December)? Calculate the crude death rate.

Answer

As a population, the profession is very similar to the stationary population P defined as follows:

(a) The constant 'working life' table is made up from mortality between ages 25 and 60, as shown by the life table, and by the withdrawal from the profession of all those surviving to birthday 60 (the second method of leaving the profession). The 'working life' table combines these two forms of 'mortality', if it is borne in mind that the 763 survivors at age 60 are all assumed to disappear immediately at birthday 60.

(b) The constant figure of annual 'births' is supplied by the entry, throughout the year, of 1001 persons on reaching the age of 25.

The distinction between the stationary population and the profession is the intake into the profession of 1001 persons whose 25th birthday fell in the preceding year. If mortality is taken into account this is equivalent to an entry of 1000 persons aged 25 last birthday on 1 January (see Fig. 22.1). On that day the stationary population and the profession will coincide in numbers and structure. This identity justifies the procedure used in calculating the total number in the profession which is shown in Table 22.1 (for the sake of simplicity, the fact that $l_{26} = 999$ has not been made use of in this calculation).

Table 22.1 *Stationary population associated with a life table*

Age x	Survivors l_x	$\frac{1}{2}(l_x + l_{x+5})$	$\frac{5}{2}(l_x + l_{x+5})$
25 years	1001	994	4970
30	987	979	4895
35	971	961	4805
40	951	938	4690
45	925	906	4530
50	887	860	4300
55	833	798	3900
60	763		
			Total: 32180

The 32180 persons on 1 January represent the total number after the intake of 1000 persons on that date; so the total on 31 December is $32180 - 1000 = 31180$.

Assuming that withdrawals through retirement and death are evenly distributed throughout the year, Fig. 22.2 represents the fluctuations in numbers. It may be called a population, stationary on average at $(32180 + 31180)/2 = 31680$ persons.

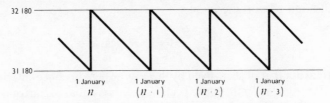

Fig. 22.2 *Evolution of the numbers in the profession*

The annual entry of 1000 persons compensates exactly for those who withdraw by retirement or death; and since the former number 763, there must be $1000 - 763 = 237$ deaths, giving a crude death rate of

$$\frac{237}{31680} = 0 \cdot 00748.$$

Problem 3

Calculate the mean duration of working life and the life expectancy of those entering the profession.

Answer

The analysis in Problem 2 has shown that the profession is equivalent to the stationary population P, reduced (except on 1 January) by the number of those who have attained birthday 25 since the preceding 1 January. This reduction may be made by ignoring the portions of the life line contained within the triangles in Fig. 22.3. This analysis makes calculation easier.

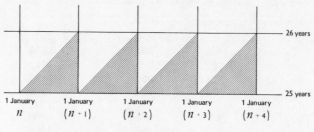

Fig. 22.3

For a group of 1000 persons recruited at age 25 last birthday, the total number of years of working life equals the total number of years lived by a cohort (consisting initially of 1001 persons aged 25 exactly) of the stationary population defined above, *less* the years of life represented by the sections of the life line contained in the triangles in Fig. 22.3 – that is, 500 years.

But the total number of years lived by a cohort of the stationary population is equal to the total number in that population – in this case, 32 180.

So the mean duration of working life is

$$\frac{32\,180 - 500}{1000} = 31\cdot68 \text{ years.}$$

As regards the total number of years lived by these same persons since entering the profession (the sum required for calculating the life expectancy), this is equal to the total number of years of working life *plus* the total number of years lived by the 763 who have retired – that is,

$$e'_{25} = \frac{31\,680 + 763 \times 15\cdot3}{1000} = 43\cdot35 \text{ years.}$$

Note that the mean duration just computed applies to a group of persons with different ages at entry (in this case, between ages 25 and 26 exactly). That is why the expectation of life in this case is written as e'_{25}, lying between e^0_{25} and e^0_{26}.

Problem 4

What is the proportion of retired, per 1000 working members? How would this proportion change if the age of retirement were reduced to 55 years? By how much would the salaries of working members have to be reduced in order to operate a pension scheme, financed exclusively by working members and yielding an income in retirement equal to 50% of average income of those still working?

Answer

Those retired always form a stationary population, and if retirement takes place at 60 they will number 763 $e_{60} = 11\,674$. If the age of retirement were reduced to 55 years, this figure would increase by 3990 (i.e. the number of those aged 55–59 in Table 22.1). This gives a total of

$$11\,674 + 3990 = 15\,664 \text{ retired persons.}$$

The figure of those working in the profession is thus reduced by the same number.

Finally, the proportions of retired, per 1000 working members, can be obtained from the calculations set out in Table 22.2.

Table 22.2 *Retired and working members under different conditions*

Retirement age	Situation on	Retired	Active	$\dfrac{Retired}{Active} \times 1000$
60 years	1 January	11 674	32 180	363
	31 December	11 674	31 180	374
55 years	1 January	15 664	28 190	556
	31 December	15 664	27 190	576

With a fixed retirement age, the number of those retired (per 1000 working members) shows an approximately linear decrease throughout the year. Note that this proportion alters considerably when the retirement age is lowered by five years.

Let A and R denote the total numbers of those working and retired, s the average salary of a working member (excluding any deduction for pension contributions), and k the rate of that deduction. To ensure a pension of $s/2$ to each retired member, the equation determining k must be

$$ksA = \frac{s}{2} R$$

hence

$$k = \frac{1}{2} \frac{R}{A}$$

Thus k equals half the proportions calculated in Table 22.2, roughly 18·45% for retirement at 60 and 28·3% for retirement at 55.

23
Nuptiality, fertility and structure
of a population

The data used in this section have scarcely been rearranged at all; they illustrate some interesting connections between reproduction and population structure.

Since the discussion is mainly confined to the female population, some traditional problems may appear in a new light.

Problem 1

The age structure of a population is set out in Table 23.1. Represent these data by means of an age pyramid. Use appropriate scales, and comment.

Table 23.1

Age (last birthday)	Population per 1000 persons (all ages)	Age (last birthday)	Population per 1000 persons (all ages)
0	33	35–39	62
1– 4	123	40–44	58
5–14	203	45–54	93
15–19	90	55–64	65
20–24	83	65–74	34
25–29	78	75 and over	10
30–34	68	All ages	1000

Answer

As the sexes are not distinguished at this stage, the graph is constructed by recording ages on the vertical axis and population figures on the horizontal (see Fig. 23.1).

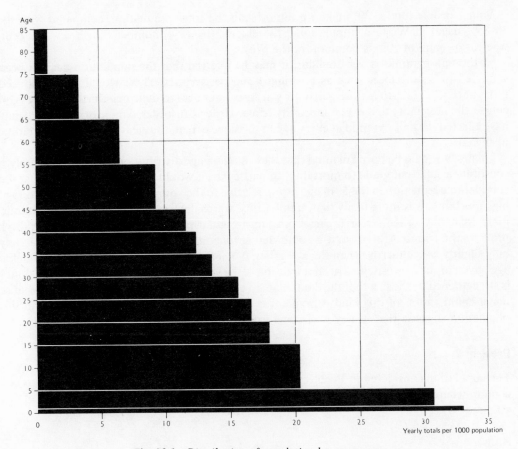

Fig. 23.1   *Distribution of population by age groups*

The total numbers in different age groups in Table 23.1 are best reduced to mean numbers at single years of age. For instance, the 123 persons in the 1–4 age group may be considered as forming four one-year groups with a mean of $123/4 = 30.75$ persons.

Similarly, the 203 persons in the 5–14 age group may be regarded as made up from ten one-year groups with a mean of $203/10 = 20.3$.

The figure for the 90 persons in the 15–19 age group is $90/5 = 18$, etc.

The last (open-ended) group, aged 75 and over, will be regarded as ending at age 85, to avoid unduly distorting the apex of the half-pyramid, so that there will be $10/10 = 1$ person per year of age in the 75–84 age group.

The population selected is obviously young; for it divides into three main age groups as follows:

0–19 years	44·9%
24–64 years	50·7%
65 and over	4·4%.

Young people (under 20) make up almost half the total population, compared with the 30–35% usual in Western populations; the elderly (over 64) number only a few per cent, whereas a figure of 10% is common in the West.

As the half-pyramid is very regular, it may be inferred that the population has not been subjected to disturbances such as prolonged and costly wars. These would have produced pronounced irregularities (due partly to war losses but also to deficits in births). There is, of course, the possibility that excess mortality (caused by civil disorder, famine or epidemics) may have affected the half-pyramid at every age to the same extent, thus leaving the general outline unaltered.

Finally, it should be borne in mind that these data on age distribution do not by themselves constitute a sufficient guide to mortality. In particular, it would be wrong to assume that the considerable reduction in the 5–14 age group relative to the younger groups is an indication of high mortality. It is more likely that high fertility, which determines the shape of the pyramid more than any other factor (apart from any irregularities due to exceptional mortality), provides the reason. Moreover, it is somewhat suspicious that the age group 1–4 is relatively only slightly less numerous than the age group 0–1. This throws doubt on the accuracy of the ages given or the completeness of enumeration of the youngest children; and this second doubt is strengthened by the fact that the data relate to a female population (see Problem 2), because under-enumeration of this kind is frequent in developing countries (the fertility rate in this population suggests that it may well come from such an area).

Problem 2

The population considered in Problem 1 represents the female portion of the population in a country where the sex ratio is said to be 108 men to 100 women. What is your opinion of this estimate?

Answer

The facts that on average 105 boys are born for every 100 girls, and that mortality is higher among males than among females at all ages, makes it obvious that in a *closed* population the sex ratio in the population as a whole must be less than 1·05.

The ratio is generally less than unity. It is easy to show how this comes about in a Western population approaching a stationary condition. For, if life expectancy at birth in a stationary population is 65 years for men and 70 years for women (an excess life expectancy of 5 years, which is closer to the minimum than the maximum of observed values), the proportions will be

$$65 \times 105 = 6825 \text{ for men,}$$

$$70 \times 100 = 7000 \text{ for women,}$$

yielding a sex ratio of 6825/7000 = 0·975.

If the sex ratio were not to fall below unity, life expectancy among men would have to reach at least 7000/105 = 66·7 years. Excess mortality among males would then amount to a difference in life expectancy of 3·3 years. In a country of immigration, where the majority of immigrants are men, this difference may be reversed and the sex ratio for the whole population could exceed unity – without, however, reaching a value as high as 1·08.

Finally, unless the population studied had a most unusual structure and was of limited size, the suggested sex ratio is very probably incorrect, and reflects under-enumeration of girls and women.

Problem 3

The proportions of married women in different age groups of the population in Table 23.1 are set out in Table 23.2. Comment on these data.

Table 23.2

Age (last birthday)	Proportion of married women (%)	Age (last birthday)	Proportion of married women (%)
15–19	30	30–34	92
20–24	80	35–39	90
25–29	93	40–44	83

Answer

The proportion of married women, at any given age, depends on first marriages below that age, and on dissolutions of marriage through widowhood or divorce, modified by any remarriages that may take place.

These factors explain certain features of Table 23.2: the initial rise in the proportions (at lower ages, when most first marriages take place), the maximum (at ages 25–29), and the decline (when dissolutions more than balance late first marriages and remarriages).

An approximate estimate of the effects of first marriages alone may be made, using the data in Table 23.2, and the approximate pattern of such marriages within the population can be outlined.

The proportions of women married at ages 15–19 and 20–24 respectively (30% and 80%) are roughly equal to the proportions first married at those ages (the exact proportions are in fact slightly higher, since some dissolutions will already have occurred, though these will be infrequent at this stage). It may be assumed, therefore, that at least 50% of the women were first married before birthday 20; and as some women do not marry at all, the median age at first marriage is certainly less than 20 years. Spinsters obviously marry fairly early in this population. It should be noted that this kind of reasoning equates what is observed in different quinquennial cohorts with what would happen, over time, in a given single five-year cohort. Such an assumption will be true only if the variables considered have remained constant. This may well be the case for the population in question (except possibly in regard to mortality). The age structure of the population has already shown that fertility is fairly high and that therefore birth control has not been widely practised. In a word, this is a population with a traditional attitude to reproduction.

It is also possible to assess total nuptiality. The maximum proportion shown as married is 93% in the age group 25–29. But not all first marriages have yet taken place at that age, and an appreciable number of dissolutions may have occurred among unions more than half of which have lasted for some ten years. Thus 93% may be taken as an approximation to the proportion of women who will marry at least once. The true proportion may equal or even exceed 95%. There is obviously a very high propensity to marry among women in this population.

Problem 4

Table 23.3 shows legitimate fertility rates by age in the population.

Table 23.3

Age (last birthday)	Legitimate fertility rate (per 1000)	Age (last birthday)	Legitimate fertility rate (per 1000)
15–19	303	30–34	306
20–24	365	35–39	263
25–29	334	40–44	114

Fertility of women aged 45 or over may be neglected.

How far is it possible to use the data in Table 23.3 to calculate the mean number of children born to a woman married at a given age and remaining married until at least the age of 45? Calculate this index for a woman who marries on her 24th birthday.

Answer

This problem is worth studying because there is likely to be a relationship between the fertility of a married woman and the duration of her marriage. In other words, it does not follow that the age-specific rates in Table 23.3 apply irrespective of the age of the women when they married.

Marriage usually marks the beginning of a period when a woman's reproductivity is at a maximum, with the consequence that:

1 The percentage of women who are temporarily or permanently sterile may increase as a result of repeated confinements and their sequelae.
2 Fertility may be controlled, when the couple have reached or exceeded the size of family they want or are prepared to have.

When voluntary birth control is not practised in a population (as seems to be the case here), only the first of these factors needs to be taken into account. Studies of non-contracepting populations have not generally shown any differences in the age-specific fertility of women married at different ages. It may thus be assumed that the rates here are independent of age at marriage, and can therefore be used to calculate the completed fertility of unbroken unions where the woman marries at age 24, or, indeed, any other age.

The necessary calculation can be made by following a woman through her life from 24 to 45 years, and assigning to her at each age a mean number of births equal to the appropriate rate in Table 23.3. The result is as shown at top of page 229.

Age (last birthday)	Births
24	0·365
25–29	5 × 0·334
30–34	5 × 0·306
35–39	5 × 0·263
40–44	5 × 0·114

or, more simply,

$$0·365 + 5(0·334 + 0·306 + 0·263 + 0·114) = 0·365 + 5 × 1·017 = 5·45 \text{ children.}$$

This is the usual method of calculation; but it is open to criticism in regard to the first year of marriage. In principle, few births occur during the first nine months (except those of children conceived before marriage); a large number then follow during the last three months of that year, since almost all the women were at risk of a conception resulting in a birth during this period (at the time of marriage only a few women will not be at risk because of pregnancy or temporary post-partum sterility). But though there may be theoretical objections to applying to these newly married women age-specific fertility rates relating mainly to women who had married earlier, in practice the results obtained by this method are not far from the truth. In any case, errors in the estimated number of births in the first year of marriage would have at most a negligible effect on completed fertility.

Problem 5

Calculate the crude birth rate for a country whose population is described by the data in Problems 1 and 2, and in which 5% of all births are illegitimate. Estimate the birth rate of the female population. Can you connect this rate with any of the results already obtained? Give your conclusions.

Answer

Legitimate births (see Table 23.4) have first to be calculated, by multiplying the female population by the percentage of married women, and applying legitimate fertility rates to this number. The total number of legitimate births has to be increased by 5% to allow for illegitimate births:

$$96·2 × 1·05 = 101·0.$$

These 101 births are related to a population of 2080 persons (1000 women and the corresponding 1080 men):

$$b = \frac{101·0}{2080} = 0·0486$$

Table 23.4 *Calculation of legitimate births*

Age group (years)	Female population	Married women %	Married women Number	Legitimate fertility rate (%)	Births
15–19	90	30	27	303	8·2
20–24	83	80	66	365	24·1
25–29	78	93	73	334	24·4
30–34	68	92	63	306	19·3
35–39	62	90	56	263	14·7
40–44	58	83	48	114	5·5
Per 1000 women of all ages.					96·2

This rate is computed using what is probably much too high a sex ratio, and is thus open to criticism. But it is necessary to consider how the legitimate fertility rates were obtained. If the numbers of women (the denominator) are too low and the births (the numerator) are correctly recorded, the rates will be too high. This compensates (to some unknown extent) for the underestimation of the birth rate caused by an overestimate of the total population (denominator). This is only one of many possibilities, however; and in view of the scanty data available, it would be useless to discuss them. It is sufficient to note that the very high value of the rate seems to exclude the possibility of any appreciable overestimation of age-specific fertility rates.

The birth rate for the female population (b_f) is found by relating female births to the female population:

$$b_f = \frac{101·0 \times 0·488}{1000} = 0·0493.$$

It is worth comparing this rate with the ratio of the age group 0–1 to the total female population (see Table 23.1 above) – namely 33%. Unless considerable fluctuations in the number of births have taken place, this ratio should be equal to the birth rate reduced by some two-thirds of the infant mortality rate (those born during a given year will have been exposed to two-thirds of the infant mortality by the end of that year, when they will constitute age group 0–1). Taking a very high rate of infant mortality – 0·25 – the newborn of a year lose 17% of their number by the following 1 January. They would thus be 83% of their initial strength. A ratio of 33% thus corresponds to a birth rate of the order of 33/0·83 = ~39·8 or 0·0398.

The calculation is not exact, because the total population has also varied, though very slightly.

This is very different from the value of b_f; the fundamental reason for this discrepancy could well be under-enumeration of very young children at the time of survey; this possibility has already been referred to in earlier discussions.

24

An example of a stationary population

A stationary population has already served as an excellent basis for the study of fluctuations in nuptiality and fertility (see Chapter 19). A similar model, supplemented by certain assumptions, will now be used to link various phenomena arising in the lifetime of a population. Since it is impossible to study a population in all its complexity by means of a very simple example, only certain problems already considered elsewhere have been selected for discussion in this new context.

Data

An annual total of 100 000 girls are born in a closed female population with unchanging mortality. Table 24.1 sets out the age structure on a certain date (*D*), by marital status (divorces and remarriages may be ignored; figures in 000s).

Table 24.1

Ages (last birthday)	Single survivors	Married women	Widows
0– 4	362·1	—	—
5– 9	310·3	—	—
10–14	225·5	68·5	1·5
15–19	76·1	197·4	8·3
20–24	16·7	227·2	21·6
25–29	5·6	203·8	35·3
30–34	3·1	172·4	49·1
35–39	2·4	140·5	61·0
40–44	2·2	110·3	70·8
45–49	2·0	82·7	78·0
50–54	1·7	58·3	81·3
55–59	1·4	37·5	79·8
60–64	1·1	21·2	72·4
65–59	0·9	9·9	59·0
70–74	0·5	3·4	41·3
75 and over	0·3	0·5	19·3

Problem 1

What is the average life span in this population?

Answer

A population in which the annual number of births does not vary and in which the life table is constant, is stationary. The relationship between total numbers (T), life expectancy at birth (e_0), and the annual total number of births (B) in such a population is:

$$T = Be_0.$$

In this case, T (the sum of the figures given in the table) and B have the following values (in 000s):

$$T = 3024 \cdot 2 \qquad B = 100$$

so

$$e_0 = \frac{3024 \cdot 2}{100} = 30 \cdot 24 \text{ years.}$$

Problem 2

Do you detect any difference in mortality between single and married women? Give reasons for your answer.

Answer

As there are no direct data available on mortality among single and married women, this question seems, at first, obscure. It may, however, be answered by recalling a result that has been used previously (and proved) in this book – that, if the proportion single in a closed cohort varies with age, the following two factors must be involved:

1 The occurrence of first marriages.
2 A possible difference in mortality between single and married persons.

The smaller the importance of the first factor, the greater the information on differential mortality provided by a study of changes in the proportion single by age. Given a closed cohort in which there are no first marriages, if the proportion of single persons increases (or decreases) with age, there must be excess mortality (or lower mortality) among single persons compared with the married. Conversely, if this proportion is constant, mortality must be equal in the two subpopulations.

This reasoning will now be applied to the present example.

In this case, the data do not relate to a single birth cohort, but to different cohorts forming the various age groups of which the population is composed at a given moment. From a given age (say, 50 years) onwards, first marriages can be ignored. This is true of all cohorts; but it does not imply that the (final) proportion of single survivors aged 50 and over is the same in every cohort (this last statement will be used later to qualify the conclusions reached).

The proportions of single survivors in the different age groups within the population can now be calculated (Table 24.2).

Table 24.2 *Proportions of single survivors in different age groups*

Age (years)	Single survivors (000s)	Total population (000s)	Percentage of single survivors
10–14	225·1	295·5	76·3
15–19	76·1	281·8	27·0
20–24	16·7	265·5	6·3
25–29	5·6	244·7	2·3
30–34	3·1	224·6	1·4
35–39	2·4	203·9	1·2
40–44	2·2	183·3	1·2
45–49	2·0	162·7	1·2
50–54	1·7	141·3	1·2
55–59	1·4	118·7	1·2
60–64	1·1	94·7	1·2
65–69	0·9	69·7	1·3
70–74	0·5	45·2	1·1
75 and over	0·3	20·2	1·5

It is clear that from age 35 onwards the proportion of single survivors remains relatively constant (except for differences at ages 65 and over, and for these age groups the calculations are based on such small numbers that these differences may be ignored).

Note, incidentally, that these calculations suggest that nuptiality within this population is very high and concentrated at young ages.

The constancy in the proportion of single survivors (aged 35 and over) suggests that there is no differential mortality between single and married women. In theory, this conclusion could be refuted if there were differences in the gross nuptiality of different cohorts, which would exactly cancel the effects of differential mortality between the married and the single. This theoretical possibility is mentioned merely to set our conscience at rest, but it is extremely unlikely to hold in practice, since it is highly impracticable that the effects would cancel out exactly.

It may be assumed, then, that there is no differential mortality between single and married women, even outside the age groups to which our conclusions apply (i.e. ages under 35, when first marriages are still taking place and so the proportion of single women is not yet constant).

Problem 3

Assume that the pattern of nuptiality is the same for all the birth cohorts. Taking in particular a group (G) of women aged 20–24 at a given date (D), calculate the number of these women single at time D, (1) who die before the group attains age 25–29, and (2) who marry between D and $D + 5$ and are still alive at $D + 5$.

Answer

It is assumed that nuptiality is not subject to change, that the population is stationary, and that there is no differential mortality between single and married women. In these conditions, Table 24.2 may be taken to illustrate the history of a group of five female birth cohorts – say, group G – subject to the combined influence of the given mortality and nuptiality.

After five years, the 16 700 single survivors in group G at date D (forming the group aged 20–24 at that date) have been reduced to 5600 (forming the group aged 25–29 at date D). This gives the equation

$$16\,700 - d - m = 5600,$$

where d = deaths occurring between D and $D+5$ (including those of women dying after marriage), and m = women married between D and $D+5$, and surviving to $D+5$ (this is contingent upon the definition of d).

These are the two values that have to be computed.

Given the absence of differential mortality between single and married women, d may be found by multiplying the figure of 16 700 by the ageing factor, which may be obtained by comparing the totals at ages 20–24 and 25–29. This ratio can be expressed as:

$$\frac{265 \cdot 5 - 244 \cdot 7}{265 \cdot 5} = \frac{20 \cdot 8}{265 \cdot 5} = 0 \cdot 0783.$$

Thus

$$d = 16\,700 \times 0 \cdot 0783 = 1300 \text{ (to the nearest 100)},$$

and m is found by subtraction:

$$m = 16\,700 - 5600 - d = 9800.$$

Problem 4

All births in this population are legitimate; legitimate births to women under age 15 are ignored, as are births to women who have been widowed.

It is assumed that a woman's fertility does not depend on her age at marriage, and that, in the absence of mortality, 100 births to women married before their 15th birthday are distributed by age of mother as follows:

  4 between 15 and 20 years
25 between 20 and 25 years
26 between 25 and 30 years
23 between 30 and 35 years
18 between 35 and 40 years
  4 between 40 and 45 years

Calculate the legitimate fertility rate at ages 20–24 and the mean total fertility per woman married at 20 and remaining married at age 50.

Compute approximate gross and net reproduction rates.
Calculate the gross reproduction rate again, by the customary method.

Answer

The data on fertility will make it possible to connect certain characteristic values with one another.

Let δ represent the number of births to a woman married at 15 and remaining married until she is at least 45 years old. Given the distribution of births, this woman will reproduce an average of

0·04 δ children between ages 15 and 20
0·25 δ children between ages 20 and 25
0·26 δ children between ages 25 and 30

...

0·04 δ children between ages 40 and 44.

These birth figures relate to five-year intervals; dividing them by five therefore gives the annual legitimate fertility rates for all the married women (since a woman's fertility does not depend upon her age at marriage) and for the different quinquennia. Thus the legitimate fertility rate

at ages 15–19 equals 0·008 δ
20–24   0·050 δ
25–29   0·052 δ

...

40–44   0·008 δ.

It is now possible to compute the annual number of births in this population in two different ways, one of them involving the unknown quantity δ. An equation can thus be formulated to determine the value of δ.

Table 24.3 *Computation of annual births*

Age (years)	Married women	Legitimate fertility rate	Live births
15–19	197 400	0·008 δ	1 579·2 δ
20–24	227 200	0·050 δ	11 360·0 δ
25–29	203 800	0·052 δ	10 597·6 δ
30–34	172 400	0·046 δ	7 930·4 δ
35–39	140 500	0·036 δ	5 058·0 δ
40–44	110 300	0·008 δ	882·4 δ
Total number of live births:			37 407·6 δ.

A preliminary calculation using the legitimate fertility rates obtained above is set out in Table 24.3 and gives a total of 37 407·6 δ annual births. It is known, moreover, that the number of male births corresponding to 100 000 female births is 105 000; the total is thus 205 000 births.

This gives the equation

$$37\,407{\cdot}6\ \delta = 205\,000$$

$$\delta = \frac{205\,000}{37\,407{\cdot}6} = 5{\cdot}48 \text{ children.}$$

We may now calculate all the required quantities.
The legitimate fertility rate at ages 20–24 is

$$0{\cdot}050\ \delta = 0{\cdot}050 \times 5{\cdot}48 = 0{\cdot}274.$$

The total number of children born to a woman, married at age 20 and remaining married to her 45th birthday, will be 96% of the number born to a woman married at age 15. The required value is thus

$$0{\cdot}96\ \delta = 0{\cdot}96 \times 5{\cdot}48 = 5{\cdot}26 \text{ children.}$$

As the female population is stationary, the female net reproduction rate for the whole population must equal unity. So it is possible to use the simplified formula

$$R_0 = Rl_a,$$

which links gross reproduction rate (R) and net reproduction rate (R_0), so that the former can be calculated from the latter. It will be remembered that l_a stands for the probability of surviving to the mean age of mothers at confinement (a). In practice, a always lies between ages 25 and 30. Taking it as 27·5, l_a can be determined by the approximate equation

$$l_a = \frac{l_{25} + l_{30}}{2l_0}.$$

If $l_0 = 100\,000$ (the annual number of births in the female population), $(l_{25} + l_{30})/2$ is equal to one-fifth of the population comprising the group aged 25–29 (this is the usual method of calculating a stationary population from the life table that defines it).
Finally,

$$R = \frac{R_0}{l_a}\ \frac{100}{244{\cdot}7/5}\ \frac{500}{244{\cdot}7} = 2{\cdot}04.$$

The usual method of calculating R involves a long detour by way of the general fertility rate.
The rates are not given here; they have to be deduced from legitimate fertility rates and from the proportion of married women in the different birth cohorts (the method is valid because there are no illegitimate births). If B denotes births in a given birth cohort, P_m the married female population, ϕ and ϕ_l the general and the legitimate fertility rates,

$$\phi = \frac{B}{P} = \frac{B}{P_m} \times \frac{P_m}{P} = \phi_l \times \frac{P_m}{P}.$$

The results of this calculation are set out in Table 24.4. Note that it is unnecessary to compute all the rates in detail; it is sufficient (and simpler) to retain the symbol δ, which can be replaced in the final result by the value to which it corresponds.

The result obtained is

$$R = \frac{5 \times 156 \cdot 6 \; \delta}{1000} \times 0.488 = 2.09,$$

which is fairly close to the value of 2·04 obtained earlier.

Table 24.4   *Calculation of gross reproduction rate*

Age (years)	Total population* P	Married population* P_m	P_m/P	Fertility rate Legitimate	General
15–19	281·8	197·4	0·700	8 δ	5·6 δ
20–24	265·5	227·2	0·856	50 δ	42·8 δ
25–29	244·7	203·8	0·833	52 δ	43·3 δ
30–34	224·6	172·4	0·768	46 δ	35·3 δ
35–39	203·9	140·5	0·689	36 δ	24·8 δ
40–44	183·3	110·3	0·602	8 δ	4·8 δ
					156·6 δ

* In thousands.

Problem 5

Outline briefly the main features of the population studied.

Answer

It has already been noted that this female population must be stationary, since both the annual number of births and the life table are constant. Moreover, in the present case the first-marriage rate and the legitimate fertility rate are also constant – though this need not necessarily be true of every stationary population.

Mortality is very high, life expectancy at birth being no more than 30 years. Fertility is also high, as is shown by the two indices obtained in the previous section – namely, the number of children born to a woman married at age 20 and remaining married until at least the age of 45 (5·26 children), and the legitimate fertility rate at age 20–24 (0·274). These results suggest that the practice of birth control is not yet widespread in the population, but the figures are nonetheless low (in other non-contracepting populations the total number of children per woman may be as high as 10 and the legitimate fertility rate usually exceeds 0·4.) In this case the birth rate (which is equal to the mortality rate) stands at the relatively modest figure of 0·036 (the reciprocal of life expectancy at birth).[1]

We have seen, however, that fertility is governed by the fact that nuptiality is extremely high (with zero mortality, 99% of the women in a cohort marry at least once), and that they marry very early (almost 75% before age 20 and practically all before age 30).

[1] The low figure for the legitimate fertility rate at ages 15–19 is worth noting; this may be due to the fact that the table used here was constructed from Indian data; though early marriage is the custom there, marriages are not generally consummated until a somewhat older age.

VIII
SPECIAL TYPES OF
ANALYSIS

25

The ageing of a population:
some comparisons

The study of the ageing of populations is a classic problem in demographic analysis. Even leading experts have been misled by appearances; so an example may profitably be used to review the whole subject.

Even with this preliminary warning, however, the last part of this section may at first sight seem to contradict the true explanation.

Problem 1

Certain data on the age structure of the population of France have been brought together in the Table 25.1. Comment on the table. What explanation can you offer for the differences in age structure between the four populations?

Table 25.1 *Distribution of the French population by major age groups*

Age groups	1851 census (both sexes)	Estimated figures for 1 January 1959		
		Men	Women	Both sexes
0–19	38·5	33·4	30·3	31·8
20–59	51·3	53·3	50·0	51·6
60 and over	10·2	13·3	19·7	16·6

Answer

The age distribution of the total population (both sexes) in 1851 will be compared with that of 1959, as will the two age distributions obtained for 1959 for each sex.

The data for both sexes in 1851 and 1959 may be set out as in Table 25.2.

The major changes in the age distribution between these two dates consist of an increase in the proportion of older persons, and an almost compensating decrease in that of persons under the age of 20. The proportion of the central group (20–59) has therefore remained roughly constant.

This process illustrates the ageing of a population, defined as an increase in the proportion of older persons (over 60, over 65, etc.). This increase, which naturally involves a reduction in the *total* of all other age groups, generally takes the form shown in the table – a decline in the proportion of young persons, while the proportion in the central age groups remains approximately constant. It would therefore seem that a number of 'young' are simply replaced by a corresponding number of 'elderly' – in so far as these population groups are represented by the age groups in the table.

Table 25.2   *Distribution of the French population by major age groups*

	1851 census	1 January 1959 Estimate
0–19 years	38·5	31·8
20–59 years	51·3	51·6
60 years and over	10·2	16·6
All ages	100·0	100·0

In the present instance, the change has occurred in a period when both births and deaths were decreasing in number. In such cases it is tempting to seek an explanation in the changes that have taken place in the size of successive *birth cohorts* during the period studied (a declining mortality rate increases the proportion of survivors beyond a certain age – say, 60 years – and the result is a relative (or even an absolute) increase in the number of older persons within the population. Alternatively, the ageing process may be thought of as being due to increasing expectations of life, as the proportion of old people in the stationary population increases as expectation of life goes up. In either case, ageing is attributed to the decline in mortality.

This explanation is mistaken, for it ignores the effect of changes in births. For instance, since in any stationary population births are always balanced by deaths, if in a succession of such populations deaths decrease, so, necessarily, must births; and the problem remains. Moreover, at a time when both deaths and births are decreasing simultaneously, an actual population cannot exhibit the properties of a stationary population.

The only possible way of distinguishing between the effects of changes in deaths and births on age structure is to apply different rates of mortality and fertility to populations with the same age distribution. Provided the rates are reasonably realistic, it has been shown that it is fertility changes that are mainly responsible for changes in age structure, and that mortality only plays a minor part, at least in the type of situation usual in recent times.

The reason for this is that changes in mortality save human lives at all ages; the age pyramid is therefore enlarged without appreciably changing shape. Changes in births, on the other hand, modify the number of entrants of new generations into the pyramid, thus altering both the present and future structure of the population.

Investigations of this kind are naturally only possible *a posteriori*, when exact computations can be made.

It now remains to examine the differences existing between the three populations under review on 1 January 1959 (see Table 25.3).

Table 25.3 *Population of France on 1 January 1959*
(distribution by major age groups)

	Men	Women	Both sexes
0–19 years	33·4	30·3	31·8
20–59 years	53·3	50·0	51·6
60 years and over	13·3	19·7	16·6
All ages	100·0	100·0	100·0

The last column of the table is a weighted mean of the first two columns, with the proportions of men and women in the total population of France as weights. As women outnumber men, the percentages in the last column are closer to the percentages for women than to those for men.

Compare next the age structures of the male and female populations.

The sex ratio at birth in the two populations is fairly constant (105 to 100); fluctuations in fertility therefore affect males and females to a similar degree, and so cannot explain the differences between the age structures of these two populations.

Excess male mortality, on the other hand, which exists at every age, produces a progressive reduction in the sex ratio as age increases; there are therefore relatively fewer elderly men than elderly women. Table 25.3 shows the male population as younger than the female.

This explanation seems at variance with the reason suggested for the differences in age structure between the populations of 1851 and 1959. In the earlier case it was stated that mortality had no appreciable effect upon population structure, yet mortality differences are adduced as reasons for differences in the age structures of male and female populations.

However, the fundamental explanation remains the same, subject to certain reservations. Mortality alone is put forward as an explanation here, simply because it is not customary to distinguish between male and female birth rates (male births per 1000 males, and similarly for females). Such an exercise would lack any demographic significance. However, if these rates were computed in France for 1959, for instance, the result obtained is

for men:
$$b_m = \frac{422\,335}{21\,878\,000} = 0{\cdot}0193,$$

for women:
$$b_f = \frac{403\,268}{23\,219\,000} = 0{\cdot}0174.$$

The difference is quite plain and is responsible (subject to certain minor reservations) for the differences in age structure; the male age pyramid receives larger additions than does the female.

If there were no differential mortality between the sexes, would this suffice to ensure that the age structure of the two populations is identical? In such a case, however, the value of at least one of the sex-specific birth rates would be altered, and their difference would be reduced to near zero.

On the other hand, it is possible to imagine a sex ratio at birth which would yield the same birth rate for men and women. In that case, whatever the differences in mortality between the sexes, their age structures would be almost identical.

The possibility that differences in age-specific male and female mortality rates may account for differences in age structure cannot be dismissed. This point, which seems worthy of note, does not appear to have received the attention it deserves; examination has so far been limited to the effects of changes in the mortality of both sexes together.

In France, for example, after the First World War, excess male mortality constitutes a possible additional cause of differential ageing. This is certainly true in the present case because the 'over 60s' of 1959 represent almost all the generations decimated by the First World War. This population is distinguished by an exceptional scarcity of older men, and an extremely low percentage of 'over 60s' in the male population (13·3%) compared with the female population (19·7%). In this case, then, the difference between male and female fertility rates is insufficient by itself to explain this difference in the percentages.

26

Ageing of the population, and deaths from various causes

Occasionally statistical tables in demography display relationships that are deceptive; the interpretations they suggest seem reasonable but do not stand up to closer examination.

In the following example, involving different groups of populations, the pattern of cause mortality is related to the health situation and the degree of ageing. The correct relationship can only be established by a study of the nature of the ageing process.

Problem 1

Comment on Table 26.1, which is based on data taken from Table 14 of the UN *Demographic Yearbook* for 1959, relating to countries where registration of the causes of death is considered to be 'satisfactory or adequate'.

Table 26.1

Percentages of deaths at all ages from certain selected causes	Level of infant mortality (rate per 1000)					
	112–125	81–88	48–59	32–43	20–26	17
Tuberculosis (all forms)	5·6	4·0	2·9	2·1	2·3	0·8
Other infectious or parasitic diseases	3·0	4·7	1·4	1·3	0·8	0·6
Neoplasms	9·2	9·0	12·8	14·8	18·0	19·0
Diseases of the circulatory system	13·5	12·7	21·0	28·5	30·9	28·6
Diseases of the alimentary system	2·9	7·6	2·8	1·0	0·5	0·4
Respiratory diseases	15·4	9·8	9·6	6·3	5·8	6·9
Senility and unknown causes	10·3	16·5	9·8	7·5	2·5	3·4
Crude death rate	0·0115	0·0104	0·0102	0·0100	0·0093	0·0084

Answer

This table contains three types of data:

1 The infant mortality rate
2 The crude death rate
3 The distribution of 100 deaths at all ages by certain cause groups.

The comments that follow will compare fluctuations in these three variables. The first step will be to compare the infant mortality rate with the crude death rate.

The crude death rate depends on:

1 The level of mortality, defined so as to be independent of the age structure of the population. This level may be measured by some function of age-specific death rates, or probabilities of dying at certain ages or age groups; alternatively, some simpler though reliable index can be used, such as the rate of infant mortality. The expectation of life at birth is also a good index. In what follows, we shall refer to the 'intrinsic level of mortality' when using the term in this sense.
2 The age structure of the population, which depends primarily on the level of fertility (and indirectly on migration) and to a much lesser extent on the 'intrinsic level of mortality'.

In the populations considered here a low level of infant mortality is associated with low fertility; therefore the populations with the largest proportions of old people exhibit the lowest infant mortality rates. Low infant mortality also corresponds to a high expectation of life at birth.

Ranking the populations in descending order of infant mortality rates is equivalent to ranking them by increasing expectations of life at birth and increasing proportions of old people. These factors are almost independent of each other and affect the crude death rate in opposite ways. Here the influence of expectation of life at birth is stronger, and low infant mortality is associated with low values of the crude death rate. But this is not invariably the case; and there are some national populations (not groups of populations as in this case) in which the relationship looks quite different.

The next step in the comparison is to consider the distribution of deaths by cause. To simplify matters, these will now be reduced to three main groups:

1 Senility, and unknown causes.
2 Infectious and parasitic diseases, diseases of the alimentary and respiratory systems.
3 Neoplasms and diseases of the circulatory system.

The relative importance of group 1 is a good index of the quality of information on causes of death. In a society in which infant mortality is falling (due to a rise in the economic or social level of the population, improved social conditions, etc.) it is clear that as a general rule, low infant mortality is matched by a low percentage of deaths due to unknown or ill-defined causes, and vice versa. This is borne out by the present table – apart from one exception (unlikely to be important) – in the group with an infant mortality of 81–88 per 1000.

With minor exceptions, group 2 diminishes in importance whenever the proportion in group 3 increases (with a parallel decline in infant mortality). These inverse variations in groups 2 and

3 are apparent in the percentages (cause-specific distribution of 100 deaths) and also in the absolute frequencies for the same population total (these may be obtained by multiplying the percentage for the appropriate group of causes by the corresponding crude death rate; at an infant mortality level of 112–125, for example, $0.269 \times 0.0115 = 309$ per 100 000). Table 26.2 shows the figures for the different groups:

Table 26.2 *Level of infant mortality and (grouped) causes of death*

Level of infant mortality (rate per 1000)	Causes (group 2)		Causes (group 3)	
	Per 100 deaths	Per 100 000 inhabitants	Per 100 deaths	Per 100 000 inhabitants
112–125	26·9	309	22·7	261
81–88	26·1	271	21·7	226
48–59	16·7	170	33·8	345
32–43	10·7	107	43·3	433
20–26	9·4	87	48·9	455
17	8·7	73	47·6	400

Group 2 consists of death from causes that can be considerably reduced by economic or social progress and current therapeutic measures. The level of infant mortality in a population is closely related to the level of knowledge of hygiene and to medical and therapeutic measures; so infant mortality rates are normally positively correlated with the proportion of deaths in group 2.

Group 3 consists of causes of death attributable to degenerative disease; their frequencies have varied little with medical or social progress. These causes predominate in populations with a high proportion of elderly persons, and it has just been demonstrated that these are precisely the populations in which infant mortality is low. Though the relation is convincing, the series of circumstances that led to it is not inevitable. In populations where current fertility remains high and therefore the age structure is young (though this may be the result of immigration, as in Israel), and infant mortality is low, the relationship is not present. A marked decrease in mortality in underdeveloped countries would in the immediate future produce many examples of countries with a low infant mortality and a relatively low percentage of deaths from cancer or circulatory diseases.

It is clear that the table reflects a fairly complex situation in which mortality is not the only factor. In other words, the table applies only to the countries shown; it cannot be generalized to prove a universally valid law linking the infant mortality rate and the pattern of cause mortality or the crude death rate.

This would only be the case if the age structure of the population (a very important factor in determining the pattern of cause mortality) depended primarily upon the 'intrinsic level of mortality'. And this is not the case in the present instance. On the other hand, the pattern of cause mortality, in particular *birth cohorts*, may legitimately be compared with the 'intrinsic level of mortality' in these cohorts. For in that case the age structure of the population is not involved as a disturbing factor in the relationship which it is hoped to establish.

27

Contraception in Great Britain and the USA

The data used in this example come from surveys in which the comment is based solely on a diagram. Two essential points have been established; the analysis attempts to separate the effect of marriage duration and birth cohort.

This study thus resembles that of Chapter 15, and the data have been collected in the same way in both cases.

Data

Investigations undertaken in Great Britain at the beginning of 1947 and in the USA at the beginning of 1955 yielded the following percentages of couples who stated that they had already practised contraception.

Great Britain		USA	
Marriage duration	*Percentage*	*Marriage duration*	*Percentage*
Under 8 years	55	Under 5 years	65
8–12 years	66	5– 9 years	75
13–17 years	63	10–14 years	73
18–22 years	61	15–19 years	65
23–27 years	58		

The data in both cases refer to first marriages, and marriage durations are computed in single years, as differences between the year of survey and year of marriage.

The replies are assumed to be accurate.

Problem 1

Represent the data in the form of a graph, showing year of marriage on the x-axis.

Answer

The appropriate years of marriage have to be substituted for marriage durations in the table. Then for each group of years of marriage, the median date will have to be determined, to give the point on the x-axis against which the percentage of couples in the relevant groups who have practised contraception will have to be plotted.

Consider the following example, relating to the group in Great Britain at marriage duration 18–22 at the beginning of 1947. As these durations are expressed as differences between years, they refer to couples married between 1925 (1947: 22) and 1929 (1947: 18). The median date is 1 July 1927, and it is against this date that the figure of 61% (the proportion of couples in the group of marriage cohorts under review who have practised contraception) is plotted.

Table 27.1 illustrates the relationship between marriage durations and marriage dates, and forms the basis of Fig. 27.1.

Table 27.1   Marriage durations and marriage dates

Survey date, beginning of 1947 (Great Britain)

Marriage duration	Cohorts	Median date	Proportion of contraceptors*
Under 8 years	1940–1946	1 July 1943	55%
8–12 years	1935–1939	1 July 1937	66%
13–17 years	1930–1934	1 July 1932	63%
18–22 years	1925–1929	1 July 1927	61%
23–27 years	1920–1924	1 July 1922	58%

Survey date, beginning of 1947 (USA)

Marriage duration	Cohorts	Median date	Proportion of contraceptors*
Under 5 years	1951–1954	1 January 1953	65%
5– 9 years	1946–1950	1 July 1948	75%
10–14 years	1941–1945	1 July 1943	73%
15–19 years	1936–1940	1 July 1938	65%

* More accurately, the proportion of couples who had already practised contraception at the two survey dates.

Problem 2

Comment on each of the two curves obtained by joining the points relating to the two countries.

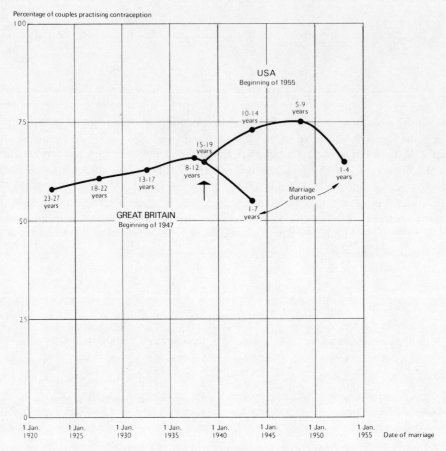

Fig. 27.1 *Proportion of couples having already practised contraception at the time of the two inquiries*

Answer

The proportion practising contraception is studied (1) in different marriage cohorts, and (2) at different marriage durations; and the more recent the cohort observed, the shorter the marriage duration. This being the case, it is worth noting:

(*a*) That the proportion of couples in a cohort or cohort group who have *already* practised contraception can only increase as the marriage duration lengthens.

(*b*) That comparisons between the *final* proportion of couples who had ever practised contraception in different cohorts or cohort groups may well yield very different values; and these differences may reveal a trend – an increase, for instance – as one passes from older to more recent cohorts. So there are grounds for suggesting that the trend in final proportions may also be apparent in the proportions at different marriage durations.

Given the present data in which duration of marriage and cohorts differ from group to group, both these variables will influence the proportion, and it is the task of demographic analysis to attempt to quantify the effect of each variable.

Begin with the British data. Excluding the younger cohorts (1940–6), it is obvious that the more recent the cohort (and therefore the shorter the marriage duration), the larger is the proportion of contracepting couples. But whereas this factor (of marriage durations) alone would have caused proportions to decline as the age of the cohort increases, the observations point in the opposite direction. There must therefore be a cohort effect: the younger the cohort, the larger the proportion of contracepting couples (except for the 1940–6 group). In other words, the practice of contraception becomes more common in the marriage cohorts from 1924 to 1935. Indeed, the proportions shown in the table (58%, 61%, 63%, 66%) underestimate the rate of dissemination; for the more recent the group (and so the shorter the marriage duration), the greater will be the gap between the percentage shown and the final percentage.

The youngest group of all (the 1940–6 cohort, at marriage duration under 8) is not affected by this general trend. Does this mark a change in trend (a final proportion of contracepting couples below that of the older cohorts), or is the intervention of the first factor (marriage duration) predominant here? The second explanation seems more likely, since the mean marriage duration for the cohort is very low (3·5 years). Moreover, investigations in the USA yield similar results (a decline in the percentage for the 1–4 marriage duration group), though the cohort involved is a totally different one (1951–4). It is therefore possible to conclude that in all probability the results for the most recent marriages do not contradict the effect of the cohort trend (progressive increase in the use of contraceptives by more recent cohorts). It must be added, however, that this effect does not alter the percentages calculated at the time of the survey. At that date an appreciable proportion of couples had not yet had families of the desired size and were therefore not yet practising contraception.

The comments and conclusions on the British inquiry are directly applicable to corresponding results in the USA.

Finally, it may be emphasized that the data to be analysed are of a type very common in demography, in which comment is best postponed until after classification by duration or age has been supplemented by division into different cohorts.

Problem 3

Comment on the differences between the two curves.

Answer

Comparison of the situation in the two countries is bound to be awkward, for the surveys took place at different times. It follows that the same marriage cohorts in the two countries were observed at different marriage durations.

However, the graph suggests that the cohorts of about 1938 in Great Britain probably contain a higher proportion of couples than in the USA who have at some time in their lives practised contraception. The 1938 cohort (indicated on the graph by an arrow) shows the same proportion at marriage duration 17 in the USA as at marriage duration 9 in Great Britain.

On the whole, however, the curves are very similar; in the older cohorts (observed in Great Britain only) and in the most recent ones (observed in the USA), the level is uniform and the trend consistent.

28

Capacity to reproduce and
level of mortality

Demographers must constantly keep check on their data, lest the existence of unsuspected correlations should vitiate the value of the results they obtain.

The present example is designed to show how to guard against this risk of error, and how the results of observations and calculation may be combined with deductive methods to reach fruitful conclusions.

Data

A population contains married women with different capacities to reproduce. No form of birth control is practised in the population; the risk of death following confinement is appreciable, but it is the same *per confinement* for all the women.

The data relate to women married before birthday 25 and dying after birthday 30 (and before the death of their spouse), and it distinguishes between (*A*) those who die between birthday 30 and birthday 50, and (*B*) those who die after birthday 50.

Problem 1

In which of these groups (*A* or *B*) would fertility be highest at ages 25–29, assuming that mortality from all causes except puerperal deaths is the same for all the women?

Answer

The two groups (*A* and *B*) are differentiated according to the women's age at death (see Fig. 28.1).

All the deaths in group *A* occur before age 50, and those in group *B* after that age. Mortality in group *A* is therefore higher than in group *B*.

This excess mortality in group *A* must be due to causes connected with childbirth, since it has been assumed that mortality from other causes is the same for all the women.

As the risk of dying per confinement is the same for all the women, this higher mortality must be the result of a larger number of births (during the same period) in group *A* than in group *B*. In other words, fertility is higher in group *A* than in group *B*.

Note that this reasoning assumes (as in the survey) that all the women predecease their husbands – or in other words that they are at risk of conceiving throughout their reproductive lives (until age 50). If this were not the case, group *B* might include women prematurely widowed; these women would consequently be subject to a lower risk of puerperal mortality – though nothing at all can be stated about their fertility.

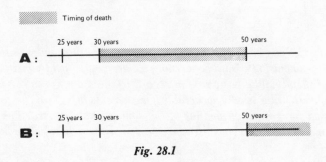

Fig. 28.1

This reasoning discloses a risk which it is impossible to eliminate *a priori* – that of underestimating the fertility of a population, especially if puerperal mortality is high. This risk is present if fertility is measured on women still married at the end of their reproductive lives. The following problem shows that the situation can be still more complex.

Problem 2

Given that fertility in group *B* exceeds that in group *A*, what is the differential mortality between women with higher and those with lower capacities to reproduce?

Answer

If it has been shown that fertility in group *B* does in fact exceed that in group *A*, it must be assumed that excess mortality resulting from the larger number of confinements in group *B* is compensated – and more than compensated – by lower mortality from other causes. Moreover, it is possible that the risk of dying per confinement, is also smaller for the women in group *B* than for those in group *A*.

In this example a high capacity to reproduce is associated with lower mortality; and inversely, greater likelihood of dying is matched by lower fertility. This is in fact true of many ancient populations.

29

Infant mortality and birth order

Demographic statistics can be extremely difficult to interpret; for, unless care is taken, they can easily lead to false conclusions. Data concerning children classified by birth order offer a classic example of this difficulty. The basic rule in regard to these data is that evidence based on the ultimate effect of birth order is only acceptable if movements in a given variable, at different birth orders, are studied for groups of families of the same completed size. The following example involving infant mortality has been constructed to demonstrate how necessary such a precaution may be.

Data

In a population in which health conditions are stable, it has been found that infant mortality was related to the size of completed family but not to birth order. A sample from this population was selected, consisting of 100 families whose completed sizes are as follows:

Family size	Number of families of this size	Infant mortality per 1000
1 child	25	80
2 children	25	100
3 children	20	120
4 children	15	140
5 children	10	160
6 children	5	180
from 1 to 6 children	100	

The table also gives the mortality rate for the different completed sizes of families.

Problem 1

Compute:

1 The average number of children per family.
2 The infant mortality rate for all children.
3 The infant mortality rate at each birth order for all families with children of that order.

Answer

The 100 families comprise:

25 families with 1 child	or	$25 \times 1 = 25$ children
25	2 children	$25 \times 2 = 50$
20	3	$20 \times 3 = 60$
15	4	$15 \times 4 = 60$
10	5	$10 \times 5 = 50$
5	6	$5 \times 6 = \underline{30}$
This gives a total of . . .		275 children

or, in other words, an average of 2·75 children per family.

The next calculation establishes the number of infant deaths among these 275 children:

Among the 25 children from families of	1 child there are	$25 \times 0.08 = 2$ deaths
50	2 children	$50 \times 0.10 = 5$
60	3	$60 \times 0.12 = 7.2$
60	4	$60 \times 0.14 = 8.4$
50	5	$50 \times 0.16 = 8$
30	6	$30 \times 0.18 = 5.4$
Thus, among the 275 children, there are . . .		36 deaths.

The infant mortality rate for all the children is thus $36/275 = 0.131$.

It is possible to check that the infant mortality rate for all the children is a weighted mean of the rates for children in families of different sizes. Thus

$$80 \times \frac{25}{275} + 100 \times \frac{50}{275} + 120 \times \frac{60}{275} + 140 \times \frac{60}{275} + 160 \times \frac{50}{275} + 180 \times \frac{30}{275}.$$

The weights show the relative importance of children in families of different sizes (25 out of 275 belong to families with 1 child, 50 out of 275 to families with 2 children, etc.).

Table 29.1 gives the number of children of a given birth order belonging to a given size of family.

The total number of children (275) in these 100 families here appears as the total of the last column and of the second last line. The bottom line of the table gives the infant mortality rates for children in families of different sizes.

The data in Table 29.1 will now be used, as an example, to calculate the rate of infant mortality among children of birth order 4. The 30 children in this category comprise:

15 belonging to families of 4 children (rate: 0·140)
10   5   0·160)
 5   6   0·180)

The number of deaths among these 30 children is therefore

$$15 \times 0.14 + 10 \times 0.16 + 5 \times 0.18 = 4.6,$$

giving an infant mortality rate of 4·6/30 = 0·153.

Table 29.1   *Children of different birth orders, by size of family*

Birth order	Size of family (number of children)						
	1	*2*	*3*	*4*	*5*	*6*	*All sizes*
1	25	25	20	15	10	5	100
2		25	20	15	10	5	75
3			20	15	10	5	50
4				15	10	5	30
5					10	5	15
6						5	5
All orders	25	50	60	60	50	30	275
Infant mortality rate	*0·080*	*0·100*	*0·120*	*0·140*	*0·160*	*0·180*	

Here, too, it is worth noting that the rate may be obtained by calculating the weighted mean of rates:

$$140 \times \frac{15}{30} + 160 \times \frac{10}{30} + 180 \times \frac{5}{30}.$$

Similarly, the infant mortality rate (per 1000) for children of birth order 1 is equal to

$$80 \times \frac{25}{100} + 100 \times \frac{25}{100} + 120 \times \frac{20}{100} + 140 \times \frac{15}{100} + 160 \times \frac{10}{100} + 180 \times \frac{5}{100} = 115.$$

The final results obtained are as follows:

Infant mortality for children of birth order 1: 0·115
                                            2: 0·127
                                            3: 0·140
                                            4: 0·153
                                            5: 0·167
                                            6: 0·180

This shows that the overall infant mortality rate (0·131) is a weighted mean of these rates, with the proportion of children of different birth orders as weights (100/275, 75/175, etc.).

Problem 2

Assume that the birth-order-specific infant mortality rates are as computed. What *a priori* interpretations must be avoided?

Answer

The data and calculations in Problem 1 have shown that *for a given completed size of family* infant mortality rates in a population remain the same whatever the birth order. If *all sizes of families* are involved, however, the rates calculated for the different birth orders increase with parity. Consequently, though birth-order-specific infant mortality rates appear to increase (0·115 for parity 1, 0·127, for parity 2, etc.), it would not be right, without further analysis, to conclude that birth order produces an effect by itself. For it can be seen from Problem 1 that constant infant mortality for each parity may be compatible with an appearance of increasing mortality rates when families of different sizes are combined.

Problem 3

What importance should be attached in general to relationships between birth intervals and birth order, or between IQ and birth order, when family size has not been taken into account?

Answer

In general, if variations by birth order in variables such as infant mortality, birth intervals, IQ, etc., are studied in families of different sizes, the comparison refers to groups with different total numbers. An index relating to parity order n can refer only to families of completed size either equal to or in excess of n. It follows that, in the case of the higher birth orders, only the families of large sizes will be included; and the relationship may not show the effect of birth order but simply the specific characteristics of these families (high infant mortality, for example, which is observable even among the first-born in these families).

30

Replacement of the last-born

The greatly simplified example given here illustrates the importance of choosing the correct method of analysis. In the present example, difficulties arise because there are no general principles that would lead one to anticipate possible errors, and because (as has been demonstrated in earlier examples) there exist no established methods for treating certain types of statistical data.

The demographer must always be capable of a critical approach; and the more extensive his past experience has been, the more successful he will be in dealing with any unexpected difficulties he may encounter.

Data

In a group of families, the probability of dying before birthday 1 is the same for all children – namely 0·100.

It is assumed that all children who die before birthday 1 are replaced, and that at the outset half the families wish to have one child and the other half two children.

Problem 1

Calculate the proportion of families in which the completed total of live births is 1, 2, 3 and over.

Answer

The basis of calculation throughout will be 1000 families.

Beginning with the 500 families who wish to have one child only: in 450 cases one live birth will suffice, for these are the 450 out of 500 families ($450 = 500 \times 0.9$) in which the first-born survives at least to 1st birthday. Fifty families have lost their first-born before birthday 1 and therefore have a second child; in 45 (50×0.9) of these 50 families this second child has survived at least to birthday 1. Finally, the five remaining families lost their first two children before birthday 1 and produce a third child.

Turning now to the 500 families who wish to have two children; in 450 of these, the first-born survived beyond birthday 1; and of these 450, 405 (450 × 0·9) have a second child over 1 year old. Thus in 405 of the 500 families, two live births have been sufficient to ensure two surviving children over 1 year old. It follows that there have been at least three live births in the remaining 95 families.

Table 30.1 *Families by number of wanted children and number of live births*

Number of children wanted	Families, by number of live births			
	1	*2*	*3 and over*	*Total*
1 child	450	45	5	500
2 children		405	95	500
Total	450	450	100	1000

Problem 2

Calculate the infant mortality rate by birth order in families with one and two births respectively.

Answer

Families with one birth consist of those who wish to have one child only; a single birth has been enough, since the child has survived to birthday 1 at least. The infant mortality rate in these families is therefore zero.

Families with two live births fall into two categories:

1 Those who wish to have one child, whose first child did not survive to birthday 1 and who therefore have a second child, aged 1 year at least.
2 Those who wish to have two children, and whose first two live-born children survive to birthday 1 at least. This is the case with 405 families.

Taking 1 and 2 together, there are 450 families (45 + 405) with two live births, 45 first births ending in death before birthday 1 (infant mortality rate 45/450 = 0·100), and no second births ending in death before birthday 1 (infant mortality rate zero).

Table 30.2 summarizes these results.

Table 30.2 *Infant mortality rate by birth order*

	Infant mortality rate in families with	
	1 live birth	*2 live births*
First births	0	0·1
Second births		0

Problem 3

What lessons can be drawn from this very simple example for analysis and interpretation of results?

Answer

The simplified example chosen illustrates the difficulty of estimating the infant mortality of last-born children in so far as they are wanted children. In these conditions, if a child is the last-born, this simply means that it has survived; otherwise it would have been replaced.

This argument holds true for the example given above, and the infant mortality rate for the last-born is indeed zero.

In practice, however, there is no society in which every birth represents a wanted child. Besides, replacement is not always possible; the couple may have become sterile in the meantime. So although a simple decline in the infant mortality rate is observable, this must not be interpreted as a fall in the risk of dying run by these children.

STATISTICAL APPENDIX

This appendix contains all the statistical data necessary for the discussion of the various problems, which could not be included in the text without unduly lengthening it. The collection of tables is therefore rather heterogeneous.

Personal search for demographic data has pedagogic value and is one of the stages in the study of demography. However, in this book reference is made to a variety of data, and it is likely that many readers would find access to the various statistical publications (such as yearbooks, journals with limited circulation, and old foreign publications) difficult. This book must therefore be self-sufficient in this respect.

The main sources from which the statistical material in this book is drawn are the following:

1 All data concerning French populations, with minor exceptions, come from the statistics published by the *Statistique générale de la France* (SGF), the *Institut national de la statistique et des études économiques* (INSEE), or from studies undertaken by statisticians working in these organizations.

2 The sources of some statistics given in the text are as follows:

Chapter 1: Bureau universitaire de statistique, Paris.

3-4: Various Soviet publications.

5: *Statistical Bulletin* of the Metropolitan Life Insurance Company, June 1962.

6: G. Mortara, *Rivista Italiana di Economica Demografia e Statistica*, 14, No. 12.

14: L. Henry, Mesure de la fréquence des divorces, *Population* No. 2, 1952.

15: K. Dandekar, Widow Remarriage in Six Rural Communities in Western India. *Proceedings of the International Union for the Scientific Study of Population.* New York, 1961.

17: Publications of the Statistical Bureau of Norway.

20: *Etude démographique par sondage en Guinée* (1954–5). Paris.

21: D. Breznik, *Sterility of First Marriages. Studies on Fertility and Social Mobility.* Budapest, 1964.

24: K. G. Basavarajappa, Effect of declines in mortality on the birth rate and related measures. *Population Studies*, 16, 3, March 1963.

27: R. Freedman, P. K. Whelpton and A. A. Campbell, *Family Planning, Sterility and Population Growth.* New York, 1959.

3 Statistics in the Appendix that have not been taken from the periodical publications of the SGF or the INSEE come from the following sources:

Table 1: W. H. Grabill, C. V. Kiseer and P. K. Whelpton, *The Fertility of American Women*. 1958.

2: *Tables de mortalité du Comité des Compagnies d'Assurances à primes fixes sur la vie.* Paris, 1895.

3: P. Delaporte, *Evolution de la mortalité en Europe depuis l'origine des statistiques de l'etat civil.* Paris, 1941.

6: Census of the USSR, 1959.

9–12: *Population Studies* Nos. 22 and 25 of the Population Division of the United Nations. Our gratitude is due to the United Nations for permission to reproduce these tables to which frequent reference is made in the text.

Table 1 Total number of live births by birth order for 1000 white native-born women in the United States at different ages and periods

Age group* (years)	Birth order							
	1	2	3	4	5	6	7	8 and higher
1 January 1910								
15–19	44	6						
20–24	349	151	50	14	3			
25–29	632	394	228	119	52	19	6	3
30–34	759	545	380	256	163	95	48	36
35–39	812	632	486	367	270	192	125	167
1 January 1915								
15–19	43	5						
20–24	349	146	48	12	2			
25–29	629	389	220	109	46	17	5	2
30–34	757	544	362	230	136	76	40	30
35–39	809	630	464	335	235	162	103	135
40–44	828	662	521	399	300	231	171	312
1 January 1920								
15–19	38	5						
20–24	339	138	44	10	2			
25–29	619	372	194	91	37	15	5	2
30–34	747	533	340	209	118	68	35	26
35–39	802	615	438	305	204	140	90	112
40–44	824	654	494	367	265	199	144	260
45–49	830	666	526	405	308	239	181	360
1 January 1925								
15–19	45	5						
20–24	358	144	44	11	2	1		
25–29	618	373	191	91	37	14	5	2
30–34	742	521	326	198	113	62	31	23
35–39	791	597	414	280	184	125	79	98
40–44	816	636	467	337	238	174	123	218
45–49	826	657	498	372	273	207	153	307
50–54	830	666	526	405	308	240	181	365
1 January 1930								
15–19	43	5						
20–24	340	133	40	10	2	1		
25–29	604	357	178	83	34	13	4	2
30–34	724	510	310	183	105	57	29	20
35–39	780	581	393	260	168	111	69	86
40–44	803	616	440	309	213	154	106	186
45–49	817	639	471	342	244	182	131	258
50–54	826	657	498	372	273	207	153	312

Table 1 (continued)

Age group*	Birth order							
(years)	1	2	3	4	5	6	7	8 and higher
1 January 1935								
15–19	36	4						
20–24	300	112	32	8	2			
25–29	567	320	151	69	28	10	3	2
30–34	704	478	277	159	88	48	23	17
35–39	760	563	366	234	149	97	60	71
40–44	791	597	414	283	191	133	91	156
45–49	805	618	443	313	218	159	113	217
50–54	817	639	471	342	244	182	132	261
1 January 1940								
15–19	39	5						
20–24	308	108	29	7	1			
25–29	555	293	127	55	22	8	3	1
30–34	689	445	238	129	69	37	18	14
35–39	745	533	327	201	123	78	47	58
40–44	770	579	384	254	168	115	76	125
45–49	792	599	417	286	195	138	96	180
50–54	805	618	443	313	218	160	113	221
1 January 1945								
15–19	39	5	1					
20–24	348	125	36	9	2			
25–29	621	337	140	57	22	8	3	1
30–34	715	462	230	115	59	30	15	12
35–39	748	524	299	172	100	61	36	46
40–44	761	554	348	219	140	93	60	100
45–49	772	581	387	257	172	119	81	143
50–54	792	599	417	286	195	138	96	182
1 January 1950								
15–19	57	9	1					
20–24	427	159	39	9	2			
25–29	715	415	163	60	22	8	3	1
30–34	789	554	274	126	60	29	14	11
35–39	782	567	316	168	91	53	30	38
40–44	770	557	331	196	118	75	47	79
45–49	764	557	352	223	143	96	63	114
50–54	772	581	387	257	172	110	81	144
1 January 1955								
15–19	65	11	1					
20–24	479	222	67	17	4	1		
25–29	757	519	233	87	30	10	3	2
30–34	845	648	346	158	69	32	15	12
35–39	839	653	376	195	99	53	29	35
40–44	799	597	350	196	111	66	40	64
45–49	773	561	335	200	122	78	50	89
50–54	764	557	352	224	144	96	63	115

* An annual age group consists of the number of births in a year centred on 1 January; the age shown in the table is therefore nearly the mean age of the group on 1 January.

Table 2 *Duvillard's life table*

Age x	l_x	e_x	Age x	l_x	e_x	Age x	l_x	e_x
0	1000	28·8	30	438	28·5	60	214	12·0
1	768	36·3	31	431		61	204	
2	672	40·4	32	425		62	195	
3	625	42·4	33	418		63	186	
4	599	43·3	34	411		64	176	
5	583	43·4	35	404	25·7	65	166	9·6
6	573	43·2	36	397		66	157	
7	566	42·7	37	390		67	147	
8	560	42·1	38	383		68	137	
9	555	41·5	39	376		69	127	
10	551	40·8	40	369	22·9	70	118	7·6
11	547		41	362		71	108	
12	543		42	355		72	99	
13	538		43	348		73	89	
14	534		44	341		74	80	
15	529	37·4	45	334	20·0	75	72	5·9
16	524		46	327		76	63	
17	519		47	320		77	56	
18	514		48	312		78	48	
19	508		49	305		79	41	
20	502	34·3	50	297	17·2	80	35	4·6
21	496		51	289		81	29	
22	490		52	282		82	24	
23	484		53	274		83	19	
24	478		54	265		84	15	
25	471	31·3	55	257	14·5	85	12	4·2
26	465		56	249		86	9	
27	458		57	240		87	7	
28	452		58	231		88	6	
29	445		59	223		89	5	
						90	4	3·9
						91	3	
						92	2	
						93	2	
						94	1	

Table 3   *Survivors of the French female birth cohort of 1820*

Age x	l_x	Age x	l_x	Age x	l_x
0	1 000 000	25	613 824	40	529 264
		26	608 140	41	523 611
5	731 675	27	602 466	42	517 951
		28	596 809	43	512 285
10	692 520	29	591 163	44	506 557
15	668 336	30	585 517	45	500 745
16	663 551	31	579 873	46	494 851
17	658 508	32	574 236	47	488 864
18	653 266	33	568 609	48	482 753
19	647 851	34	562 985	49	476 516
20	642 298	35	557 378	50	470 164
21	636 659	36	551 782	60	393 270
22	630 942	37	546 165	70	266 928
23	625 226	38	540 539	80	103 356
24	619 517	39	534 907	90	11 504

Table 4   *Male survivors according to French life tables of the period*

Age (years)	1908–1913	1920–1923	1928–1933	1933–1938	1950–1951
0	100 000	100 000	100 000	100 000	10 000
1	86 601	89 177	90 982	92 383	9 479
5	81 851	85 658	88 164	89 992	9 386
10	80 552	84 496	87 200	89 164	9 352
15	79 627	83 650	86 447	88 517	9 319
20	77 919	81 923	84 900	87 197	9 264
30	72 653	76 736	80 470	83 103	9 079
40	66 552	71 248	74 988	77 478	8 794
50	58 320	63 839	66 861	69 087	8 198
60	46 539	52 122	54 391	56 084	6 990
70	29 482	34 355	35 436	36 650	4 946
80	9 724	11 949	12 496	13 483	2 039
90	764	878	965	1 185	194

	Males		Age x (in years)	Females	
	l_x	q_x		l_x	q_x

For live-born children

Males l_x	q_x	Age x	Females l_x	q_x
100 000	0·04567	0	100 000	0·03502
95 433		1	96 498	

For children registered as live-born

Males l_x	q_x	Age x	Females l_x	q_x
100 000	0·04076	0	100 000	0·03141
95 924	0·00454	1	96 859	0·00400
95 489	0·00170	2	96 472	0·00150
95 327	0·00105	3	96 327	0·00091
95 227	0·00080	4	96 239	0·00069
95 151	0·00066	5	96 173	0·00054
95 088	0·00057	6	96 121	0·00045
95 034	0·00051	7	96 078	0·00039
94 986	0·00048	8	96 041	0·00035
94 940	0·00046	9	96 007	0·00032
94 896	0·00046	10	95 976	0·00031
94 852	0·00048	11	95 946	0·00031
94 806	0·00051	12	95 916	0·00034
94 758	0·00057	13	95 883	0·00038
94 704	0·00065	14	95 847	0·00042
94 642	0·00077	15	95 807	0·00047
94 569	0·00090	16	95 762	0·00052
94 484	0·00107	17	95 712	0·00057
94 383	0·00126	18	95 657	0·00062
94 264	0·00140	19	95 598	0·00067
94 132	0·00151	20	95 534	0·00072
93 990	0·00159	21	95 465	0·00078
93 841	0·00166	22	95 391	0·00084
93 685	0·00171	23	95 311	0·00090
93 525	0·00176	24	95 225	0·00096
93 360	0·00181	25	95 134	0·00102
93 191	0·00186	26	95 037	0·00108
93 018	0·00191	27	94 934	0·00114
92 840	0·00197	28	94 826	0·00121
92 657	0·00205	29	94 711	0·00128
92 467	0·00215	30	94 590	0·00136
92 268	0·00227	31	94 461	0·00144
92 059	0·00240	32	94 325	0·00154
91 838	0·00255	33	94 180	0·00164
91 604	0·00271	34	94 026	0·00176

Males l_x	q_x	Age x	Females l_x	q_x
91 356	0·00288	35	93 861	0·00189
91 093	0·00307	36	93 684	0·00203
90 813	0·00327	37	93 494	0·00217
90 516	0·00349	38	93 291	0·00231
90 200	0·00374	39	93 075	0·00246
89 863	0·00404	40	92 846	0·00261
89 500	0·00440	41	92 604	0·00277
89 106	0·00486	42	92 347	0·00296
88 673	0·00537	43	92 074	0·00320
88 197	0·00594	44	91 779	0·00346
87 673	0·00660	45	91 461	0·00377
87 094	0·00730	46	91 116	0·00413
86 458	0·00804	47	90 740	0·00451
85 763	0·00884	48	90 331	0·00490
85 005	0·00969	49	89 888	0·00530
84 181	0·01060	50	89 412	0·00572
83 289	0·01150	51	88 901	0·00615
82 331	0·01250	52	88 354	0·00660
81 302	0·01360	53	87 771	0·00710
80 196	0·01480	54	87 148	0·00760
79 009	0·01600	55	86 486	0·00820
77 745	0·01730	56	85 777	0·00890
76 400	0·01870	57	85 005	0·00960
74 971	0·02010	58	84 189	0·01030
73 464	0·02160	59	83 322	0·01120
71 877	0·02320	60	82 389	0·01210
70 209	0·02490	61	81 392	0·01320
68 461	0·02670	62	80 318	0·01440
66 633	0·02880	63	79 161	0·01590
64 714	0·03110	64	77 902	0·01760
62 701	0·00337	65	76 531	0·00193
60 588	0·00366	66	75 054	0·00214
58 370	0·00398	67	73 448	0·00235
56 047	0·00434	68	71 722	0·00260
53 615	0·00474	69	69 857	0·00289
51 074	0·00519	70	67 838	0·00323
48 423	0·00569	71	65 647	0·00362
45 668	0·00624	72	63 271	0·00406
42 818	0·00685	73	60 702	0·00453
39 885	0·00753	74	57 952	0·00508

Table 5 (continued)

| Males | | Age | Females | | Males | | Age | Females | |
l_x	q_x	x (in years)	l_x	q_x	l_x	q_x	x (in years)	l_x	q_x
36 882	0·00829	75	55 008	0·00572	2 241	0·00305	90	6 644	0·00257
33 824	0·00915	76	51 862	0·00642	1 557	0·00330	91	4 936	0·00280
30 729	0·01010	77	48 532	0·00718	1 043	0·00355	92	3 554	0·00305
27 625	0·01100	78	45 047	0·00800	673	0·00380	93	2 470	0·00332
24 586	0·01210	79	41 443	0·00890	417	0·00407	94	1 650	0·00361
21 611	0·01330	80	37 755	0·00985	247	0·00435	95	1 054	0·00391
18 731	0·01440	81	34 036	0·01090	140	0·00466	96	642	0·00422
16 039	0·01580	82	30 326	0·01200	75	0·00499	97	371	0·00455
13 505	0·01730	83	26 687	0·01320	38	0·00534	98	202	0·00491
11 169	0·01880	84	23 164	0·01450	18	0·00570	99	103	0·00528
9 069	0·00205	85	19 805	0·00160	8	0·00607	100	49	0·00566
7 210	0·00223	86	16 636	0·00176					
5 602	0·00244	87	13 708	0·00194	e_0 for births			Males 65·04	
4 235	0·00261	88	11 049	0·00214	registered as				
3 130	0·00284	89	8 685	0·00235	live-born			Females 71·15	

Table 6 Survivors according to the USSR life table for 1958–9

Age	Males	Females	Both sexes
0	100 000	100 000	100 000
1	95 576	96 323	95 940
5	94 029	94 823	94 416
10	93 425	94 370	93 885
15	92 966	94 044	93 497
20	92 244	93 601	92 917
25	91 170	93 013	92 084
30	89 845	92 340	91 090
35	88 258	91 550	89 937
40	86 324	90 554	88 565
45	83 851	89 256	86 805
50	80 604	87 587	84 502
55	75 958	85 210	81 236
60	69 452	81 825	76 693
65	61 058	76 875	70 429
70	50 920	69 236	61 762
e_0	64·42 years	71·68 years	68·59 years
e_{70}	11·28 years	13·35 years	12·63 years

Table 7 French population by age groups

Age	1 January 1955 Males Total	Males Single	Females Total	Females Single	1 January 1959 (in 000s) Males	Females	Age	1 January 1955 Males Total	Males Single	Females Total	Females Single	1 January 1959 (in 000s) Males	Females
0–4	2 002 936	2 002 936	1 927 281	1 927 281	2005·3	1929·4	35	205 511	28 459	206 369	22 420	321·2	320·1
5–9	1 958 869	1 958 869	1 887 369	1 887 369	2033·2	1962·8	36	184 745	24 991	185 540	19 823	322·1	321·6
10–14	1 367 221	1 367 221	1 319 323	1 319 323	1844·6	1779·8	37	160 317	21 398	164 174	16 934	335·5	336·6
							38	151 763	20 020	155 573	15 798	341·8	341·6
15	283 998	283 998	279 494	279 122	297·4	285·4	39	188 229	24 024	193 628	19 153	206·1	206·9
16	285 373	285 373	280 911	278 998	276·1	264·3							
17	289 212	289 117	282 600	275 167	248·3	241·4	40	287 970	35 490	297 435	28 719	185·1	186·2
18	294 154	292 651	287 937	267 217	265·0	255·3	41	296 710	35 663	299 847	28 427	160·9	165·0
19	296 875	290 756	290 881	244 862	291·9	281·8	42	300 623	35 299	303 224	28 838	153·0	156·3
							43	282 901	32 741	287 829	27 421	188·6	193·9
20	312 239	294 693	300 562	219 543	296·2	283·6	44	300 140	34 148	304 199	29 054	286·1	296·2
21	309 898	283 737	299 307	181 082	303·3	285·7							
22	324 398	258 903	313 694	153 941	309·8	291·1	45	299 009	33 710	304 557	29 704	293·9	298·1
23	326 919	219 168	316 765	127 303	314·1	294·3	46	299 234	32 969	307 416	30 352	296·9	301·3
24	334 961	178 487	323 330	103 568	329·2	304·0	47	295 114	31 695	300 423	29 970	278·4	285·6
							48	297 194	31 114	303 361	30 594	294·3	301·4
25	316 339	139 235	307 548	81 829	324·6	302·5	49	295 088	29 992	300 697	30 659	292·0	301·2
26	321 914	118 327	311 933	69 364	338·0	316·8							
27	319 348	101 758	309 910	60 141	340·9	319·9	50–54	1 430 621	131 550	1 480 349	155 975	1426·6	1487·5
28	322 866	90 573	317 396	55 713	347·4	326·4	55–59	1 128 305	86 884	1 358 062	155 597	1319·4	1419·8
29	322 636	80 543	318 657	50 512	326·7	310·3	60–64	832 272	56 712	1 209 745	140 981	953·9	1276·8
							65–69	722 439	46 934	1 074 372	114 914	709·7	1098·1
30	317 461	70 354	314 382	46 064	331·2	314·4	70–74	549 812	34 798	876 157	87 451	560·2	918·9
31	316 732	61 600	318 979	43 076	327·8	312·4	75–79	387 955	23 605	626 381	62 345	368·4	661·3
32	318 802	55 709	320 978	40 277	330·3	319·3	80 and over	256 673	15 005	500 752	49 803	287·3	582·0
33	333 143	52 175	336 414	39 715	328·9	320·4	All ages	20 769 411	9 672 335	22 347 589	8 944 446	21 714·5	23 073·6
34	340 492	48 951	341 848	38 047	322·9	315·9							

Sources: Population on 1 January 1955: Annuaire statistique de la France, 1956.
Population on 1 January 1959: Bulletin mensuel de statistique, January 1959.

Table 8 *Projected French population (in 000s on 1 January)*

Age	1960 Males	1960 Females	1961 Males	1961 Females	1962 Males	1962 Females	1963 Males	1963 Females	1964 Males	1964 Females	1965 Males	1965 Females
0–4	2030·0	1957·8	2031·5	1955·9	2021·9	1946·1	2003·8	1926·5	1983·6	1905·0	1952·1	1873·0
5–9	2020·5	1949·1	1998·5	1929·8	2001·1	1928·5	2000·1	1931·3	2008·2	1937·4	2018·7	1949·1
10–14	1982·2	1912·9	2093·9	2021·8	2084·6	2016·8	2068·8	1997·1	2039·7	1971·5	2015·5	1945·9
15	297·0	288·6	306·9	295·3	406·8	392·0	419·5	406·3	421·9	406·9	423·4	409·8
16	299·2	287·6	296·8	288·5	306·7	295·2	406·5	391·8	419·2	406·1	421·5	406·8
17	277·9	265·8	298·9	287·4	296·4	288·3	306·3	295·0	406·0	391·6	418·7	405·8
18	250·9	243·0	277·6	265·7	298·5	287·3	296·1	288·2	306·0	294·9	405·6	391·4
19	268·8	257·1	250·6	242·8	277·2	265·5	298·2	287·1	295·7	288·0	305·6	294·7
20	296·5	284·0	268·4	256·9	250·2	242·7	276·8	265·3	297·7	286·9	295·3	287·8
21	300·8	285·8	296·1	283·8	268·0	256·7	249·8	242·5	276·4	265·1	297·3	286·7
22	306·0	287·9	300·3	285·6	295·6	283·6	267·5	256·5	249·4	242·3	275·9	264·9
23	312·0	293·4	305·5	287·7	299·8	285·3	295·1	283·3	267·1	256·3	249·0	242·1
24	317·5	296·4	311·4	293·1	304·9	287·4	299·3	285·1	294·5	283·1	266·6	256·1
25–29	1695·0	1579·1	1659·5	1545·7	1625·7	1515·8	1588·5	1483·7	1558·0	1463·7	1519·2	1440·3
30–34	1653·1	1583·3	1669·2	1587·4	1676·5	1586·2	1684·1	1589·0	1675·9	1576·0	1677·0	1568·5
35–39	1647·8	1640·7	1630·2	1616·6	1620·8	1596·6	1622·7	1584·7	1629·4	1576·5	1629·8	1568·9
40–44	896·0	911·8	1044·6	1056·9	1221·7	1283·6	1376·3	1386·2	1505·6	1515·7	1615·1	1619·9
45–49	1446·5	1482·7	1331·8	1369·9	1199·5	1236·8	1059·6	1097·9	948·7	984·8	867·9	895·2
50–54	1428·9	1489·4	1424·0	1486·8	1401·5	1466·7	1399·2	1464·7	1390·3	1453·2	1374·1	1442·2
55–59	1335·9	1434·4	1342·6	1440·2	1339·5	1439·3	1329·0	1431·8	1325·6	1433·7	1321·5	1430·5
60–64	1016·1	1291·8	1077·8	1306·5	1120·1	1314·8	1157·1	1329·5	1182·0	1342·0	1192·0	1351·3
65–69	712·3	1111·2	716·1	1125·3	741·4	1147·0	777·8	1162·9	812·7	1167·0	861·6	1175·3
70–74	565·3	928·4	557·6	923·4	557·8	927·0	551·6	928·7	553·2	940·1	551·0	948·5
75–79	371·5	677·4	374·3	686·6	373·1	689·3	373·4	693·1	373·5	698·0	374·0	701·1
80–84	206·8	396·5	200·4	397·3	195·7	399·8	192·7	405·5	190·4	409·4	190·4	415·9
85–89	69·8	158·9	70·9	163·0	73·3	169·8	73·4	171·1	72·4	172·6	71·2	173·6
90 and over	13·0	42·4	13·5	40·6	13·0	37·4	13·5	37·8	13·8	37·4	14·0	37·7
All ages	22017·3	23337·4	22148·9	23440·5	22271·3	23535·5	22386·7	23622·6	22496·9	23705·2	22604·0	23783·0

Age	1966 Males	1966 Females	1967 Males	1967 Females	1968 Males	1968 Females	1969 Males	1969 Females	1970 Males	1970 Females	1971 Males	1971 Females
0–4	1933·8	1855·4	1928·5	1850·2	1935·1	1856·5	1953·4	1874·2	1981·7	1901·4	2016·9	1935·3
5–9	2020·0	1947·2	2010·8	1937·6	1992·7	1918·2	1972·7	1896·6	1941·4	1864·8	1923·1	1847·2
10–14	1993·7	1926·7	1996·0	1925·4	1995·2	1928·1	2003·2	1934·3	2013·6	1945·9	2014·9	1944·0
15	418·6	404·1	397·5	386·9	403·9	386·9	392·6	381·3	399·2	384·2	396·7	384·9
16	423·1	409·6	418·3	403·9	397·2	386·7	403·5	386·7	392·3	381·1	398·9	384·1
17	421·1	406·5	422·6	409·4	417·8	403·7	396·8	386·5	403·1	386·5	391·9	380·9
18	418·2	405·6	420·6	406·3	422·1	409·2	417·3	403·5	396·3	386·3	402·7	386·3
19	405·1	391·2	417·7	405·4	420·1	406·1	421·6	408·9	416·8	403·2	395·8	386·1
20	305·1	294·5	404·4	390·9	417·1	405·1	419·4	405·8	420·9	408·6	416·2	402·9
21	294·8	287·6	304·7	294·2	403·8	390·6	416·5	404·8	418·8	405·5	420·3	408·3
22	296·8	286·4	294·3	287·3	304·2	294·0	403·2	390·3	415·8	404·5	418·1	405·1
23	275·5	264·7	296·3	286·2	293·9	287·1	303·7	293·8	402·5	389·9	415·1	404·1
24	248·5	241·9	275·0	264·4	295·7	285·9	293·3	286·8	303·1	293·5	401·8	389·6
25–29	1468·5	1400·0	1405·8	1348·8	1376·3	1326·1	1372·8	1327·1	1371·8	1330·8	1408·1	1368·2
30–34	1641·8	1535·5	1608·3	1505·6	1571·4	1473·8	1541·7	1453·9	1503·1	1430·7	1453·0	1390·7
35–39	1645·5	1572·8	1652·9	1571·6	1660·4	1574·6	1652·5	1561·5	1653·3	1554·1	1618·7	1521·4
40–44	1597·9	1596·2	1588·6	1576·4	1590·6	1564·7	1597·1	1556·4	1597·5	1548·9	1613·1	1553·0
45–49	1012·8	1038·0	1184·8	1211·7	1334·2	1361·4	1458·7	1488·1	1563·9	1590·0	1547·3	1566·7
50–54	1264·4	1332·2	1137·8	1202·2	1004·7	1067·1	900·2	957·4	824·8	870·7	964·0	1010·4
55–59	1316·9	1428·1	1296·0	1408·5	1294·0	1406·7	1285·9	1395·5	1270·8	1385·0	1168·3	1278·7
60–64	1197·8	1356·6	1195·1	1355·8	1185·8	1348·8	1182·7	1350·6	1179·1	1347·7	1175·0	1345·4
65–69	913·3	1188·5	949·0	1196·5	980·4	1209·7	1000·9	1220·9	1009·1	1229·1	1013·8	1234·1
70–74	553·7	960·4	574·2	978·9	603·0	992·3	630·3	995·6	668·2	1002·7	707·6	1013·9
75–79	368·6	697·0	368·9	699·6	364·6	701·1	365·9	710·3	364·7	717·1	366·5	725·6
80–84	191·7	421·4	191·1	422·8	191·4	425·1	191·4	427·9	191·5	430·0	188·6	427·3
85–89	68·8	173·9	67·4	175·3	66·5	178·2	65·8	179·5	65·8	182·5	66·4	184·8
90 and over	14·3	38·3	14·7	39·2	14·8	39·4	14·6	39·5	14·3	39·7	13·9	39·9
All ages	22710·3	23860·3	22821·3	23941·0	22936·9	24027·1	23057·7	24117·7	23183·4	24214·4	23316·7	24318·9

Table 8 (continued)

Age	1972 Males	1972 Females	1973 Males	1973 Females	1974 Males	1974 Females	1975 Males	1975 Females	1976 Males	1976 Females
0–4	2 055·2	1 972·1	2 094·9	2 010·2	2 134·7	2 048·1	2 174·4	2 086·2	2 213·2	2 123·3
5–9	1 917·7	1 842·0	1 924·1	1 848·3	1 942·4	1 865·8	1 970·5	1 892·9	2 005·6	1 926·5
10–14	2 005·7	1 934·5	1 987·6	1 915·1	1 967·6	1 893·4	1 936·5	1 861·7	1 918·2	1 844·2
15	400·0	385·6	402·9	389·6	400·5	387·4	409·7	395·8	398·2	383·0
16	396·4	384·7	399·7	385·4	402·6	389·4	400·2	387·3	409·4	395·7
17	398·5	383·8	396·0	384·4	399·3	385·2	402·2	389·2	399·8	387·0
18	391·4	380·7	398·0	383·6	395·6	384·2	398·8	385·0	401·7	389·0
19	402·2	386·0	390·9	380·4	397·5	383·4	395·1	384·0	398·3	384·8
20	395·2	385·8	401·5	385·8	390·3	380·1	396·9	383·1	394·5	383·7
21	415·5	402·6	394·6	385·5	400·9	385·4	389·8	379·9	396·3	382·8
22	419·6	408·0	414·8	402·3	393·9	385·2	400·3	385·2	389·1	379·6
23	417·4	404·8	419·0	407·7	414·2	402·0	393·3	384·9	399·6	384·8
24	414·3	403·8	416·7	404·4	418·2	407·3	413·4	401·6	392·6	384·5
25–29	1 560·8	1 515·6	1 699·5	1 654·6	1 819·9	1 772·6	1 943·8	1 892·6	2 053·0	2 000·1
30–34	1 391·0	1 339·8	1 361·5	1 317·2	1 358·3	1 318·1	1 357·3	1 322·0	1 393·3	1 359·1
35–39	1 585·6	1 491·9	1 549·2	1 460·2	1 519·7	1 440·5	1 481·9	1 417·6	1 432·3	1 377·9
40–44	1 620·3	1 551·8	1 627·5	1 554·5	1 619·5	1 541·8	1 620·8	1 534·4	1 586·6	1 502·0
45–49	1 538·6	1 547·5	1 540·5	1 535·9	1 546·8	1 528·0	1 547·2	1 520·3	1 562·3	1 524·4
50–54	1 127·5	1 179·4	1 269·2	1 324·7	1 386·7	1 447·8	1 485·5	1 546·4	1 469·9	1 523·7
55–59	1 050·3	1 153·5	927·2	1 023·7	831·2	918·6	763·1	836·3	893·7	971·4
60–64	1 156·2	1 326·8	1 154·4	1 325·1	1 147·1	1 314·6	1 133·8	1 304·7	1 041·2	1 203·9
65–69	1 011·4	1 233·2	1 003·6	1 226·9	1 001·0	1 228·6	997·8	1 226·0	994·5	1 223·9
70–74	735·2	1 021·1	759·3	1 032·5	774·4	1 042·0	780·4	1 049·0	783·8	1 052·6
75–79	381·0	739·8	400·5	749·5	419·2	752·1	444·2	757·4	469·5	765·4
80–84	188·8	428·2	186·5	429·8	187·4	436·0	186·9	440·5	187·6	445·3
85–89	66·0	185·3	66·1	186·3	66·1	187·3	66·2	188·4	65·1	186·9
90 and over	13·7	40·5	13·6	41·2	13·5	41·4	13·5	42·0	13·5	42·4
All ages	23 455·5	24 428·8	23 599·3	24 544·8	23 748·5	24 666·3	23 903·2	24 794·4	24 062·8	24 927·9

Table 9 *Probabilities of dying for males*

Level	e_0	e_0^{-1}	0	1–4	0–4	5–9	10–14	15–19	20–24	25–29
					Probabilities of dying for age groups					
1	69·25	0·01440	0·02250	0·00424	0·02657	0·00306	0·00260	0·00453	0·00578	0·00627
2	68·48	0·01460	0·02812	0·00623	0·03412	0·00354	0·00293	0·00505	0·00656	0·00700
3	67·66	0·01478	0·03375	0·00829	0·04171	0·00407	0·00331	0·00565	0·00745	0·00784
4	66·88	0·01495	0·03937	0·01042	0·04935	0·00461	0·00367	0·00621	0·00828	0·00863
5	66·04	0·01514	0·04500	0·01262	0·05704	0·00521	0·00409	0·00688	0·00927	0·00957
6	65·22	0·01533	0·05062	0·01487	0·06477	0·00581	0·00450	0·00751	0·01020	0·01047
7	64·33	0·01554	0·05625	0·01721	0·07255	0·00646	0·00496	0·00822	0·01125	0·01147
8	63·59	0·01573	0·06157	0·01941	0·07960	0·00695	0·00527	0·00872	0·01208	0·01238
9	62·55	0·01599	0·06677	0·02163	0·08689	0·00744	0·00559	0·00924	0·01294	0·01332
10	61·67	0·01622	0·07215	0·02388	0·09402	0·00793	0·00592	0·00976	0·01381	0·01430
11	60·77	0·01646	0·07770	0·02642	0·10182	0·00865	0·00641	0·01053	0·01494	0·01543
12	59·91	0·01669	0·08325	0·02906	0·10965	0·00941	0·00693	0·01132	0·01611	0·01661
13	58·90	0·01698	0·08823	0·03146	0·11679	0·01007	0·00732	0·01197	0·01717	0·01762
14	58·06	0·01722	0·09299	0·03389	0·12391	0·01074	0·00772	0·01263	0·01824	0·01864
15	57·11	0·01751	0·09810	0·03634	0·13099	0·01141	0·00812	0·01330	0·01932	0·01967
16	56·20	0·01779	0·10355	0·03920	0·13886	0·01227	0·00869	0·01419	0·02062	0·02093
17	55·20	0·01812	0·10845	0·04200	0·14608	0·01313	0·00920	0·01500	0·02175	0·02224
18	53·36	0·01874	0·11962	0·04804	0·16122	0·01492	0·01033	0·01672	0·02424	0·02490
19	51·47	0·01943	0·12960	0·05419	0·17641	0·01678	0·01150	0·01851	0·02679	0·02765
20	49·58	0·02021	0·13993	0·06091	0·19158	0·01889	0·01287	0·02046	0·02956	0·03062
21	47·68	0·02097	0·15008	0·06789	0·20679	0·02108	0·01428	0·02246	0·03237	0·03357
22	45·82	0·02182	0·16006	0·07505	0·22168	0·02336	0·01576	0·02435	0·03500	0·03646
23	43·93	0·02276	0·16995	0·08273	0·23693	0·02587	0·01736	0·02646	0·03788	0·03968
24	42·10	0·02375	0·18020	0·09063	0·25258	0·02846	0·01902	0·02862	0·04081	0·04306
25	40·30	0·02481	0·19017	0·09914	0·26830	0·03131	0·02083	0·03097	0·04377	0·04647
26	38·57	0·02593	0·19989	0·10793	0·28409	0·03425	0·02269	0·03336	0·04683	0·05002
27	36·76	0·02720	0·21000	0·11699	0·29994	0·03729	0·02461	0·03578	0·05000	0·05373
28	35·14	0·02846	0·22050	0·12679	0·31688	0·04062	0·02670	0·03839	0·05302	0·05731
29	33·50	0·02985	0·23100	0·13708	0·33401	0·04413	0·02889	0·04108	0·05637	0·06132
30	31·90	0·03135	0·24150	0·14784	0·35130	0·04782	0·03117	0·04381	0·05971	0·06540
31	30·35	0·03295	0·25117	0·15899	0·36819	0·05166	0·03353	0·04642	0·06258	0·06924
32	28·86	0·03465	0·26052	0·17049	0·38516	0·05561	0·03593	0·04902	0·06539	0·07307
33	27·40	0·03650	0·27040	0·18232	0·40222	0·05967	0·03839	0·05162	0·06815	0·07689
34	26·02	0·03843	0·28080	0·19517	0·42012	0·06413	0·04107	0·05442	0·07130	0·08095
35	24·68	0·04052	0·29120	0·20858	0·43818	0·06871	0·04380	0·05724	0·07441	0·08502
36	23·39	0·04275	0·30160	0·22264	0·45641	0·07354	0·04667	0·06003	0·07743	0·08903
37	22·15	0·04515	0·31200	0·23731	0·47482	0·07859	0·04963	0·06280	0·08037	0·09294
38	20·95	0·04773	0·32240	0·25268	0·49340	0·08387	0·05270	0·06555	0·08323	0·09680
39	19·82	0·05045	0·33280	0·26872	0·51215	0·08931	0·05582	0·06820	0·08594	0·10050
40	18·74	0·05336	0·34320	0·28551	0·53107	0·09499	0·05905	0·07082	0·08854	0·10408

272

Probabilities of dying for age groups

30–34	35–39	40–44	45–49	50–54	55–59	60–64	65–69	70–74	75–79	80–84
0·00756	0·00999	0·01497	0·02432	0·03877	0·06012	0·09461	0·14653	0·22542	0·33783	0·48263
0·00825	0·01064	0·01569	0·02522	0·03988	0·06145	0·09642	0·14881	0·22824	0·34111	0·48610
0·00906	0·01151	0·01662	0·02624	0·04112	0·06308	0·09842	0·15134	0·23154	0·34491	0·49025
0·00979	0·01222	0·01739	0·02713	0·04223	0·06448	0·10018	0·15354	0·23412	0·34791	0·49347
0·01067	0·01315	0·01834	0·02823	0·04361	0·06618	0·10235	0·15628	0·23748	0·35180	0·49760
0·01151	0·01396	0·01930	0·02931	0·04484	0·06779	0·10439	0·15882	0·24065	0·35550	0·50151
0·01251	0·01500	0·02048	0·03072	0·04657	0·06930	0·10722	0·16236	0·24492	0·36036	0·50679
0·01339	0·01593	0·02147	0·03186	0·04787	0·07111	0·10891	0·16452	0·24771	0·36331	0·51040
0·01430	0·01690	0·02253	0·03309	0·04923	0·07276	0·11070	0·16679	0·25063	0·36631	0·51408
0·01523	0·01790	0·02362	0·03439	0·05065	0·07426	0·11257	0·16918	0·25367	0·36960	0·51792
0·01633	0·01905	0·02485	0·03579	0·05241	0·07656	0·11546	0·17275	0·25806	0·37466	0·52328
0·01748	0·02025	0·02621	0·03731	0·05417	0·07869	0·11813	0·17605	0·26214	0·37924	0·52829
0·01856	0·02140	0·02752	0·03884	0·05591	0·08083	0·12053	0·17907	0·26593	0·38326	0·53301
0·01967	0·02259	0·02891	0·04045	0·05772	0·08302	0·12299	0·18215	0·26983	0·38738	0·53788
0·02080	0·02384	0·03037	0·04215	0·05959	0·08526	0·12551	0·18531	0·27380	0·39159	0·54289
0·02216	0·02525	0·03196	0·04390	0·06171	0·08791	0·12875	0·18927	0·27856	0·39695	0·54852
0·02346	0·02668	0·03360	0·04579	0·06394	0·09046	0·13174	0·19272	0·28287	0·40148	0·55395
0·02625	0·02969	0·03704	0·04911	0·06862	0·09601	0·13839	0·20059	0·29243	0·41184	0·56548
0·02918	0·03287	0·04068	0·05401	0·07363	0·10189	0·14546	0·20891	0·30246	0·42266	0·57750
0·03238	0·03638	0·04481	0·05874	0·07913	0·10849	0·15302	0·21800	0·31300	0·43464	0·59004
0·03562	0·03998	0·04903	0·06360	0·08481	0·11525	0·16072	0·22720	0·32356	0·44661	0·60254
0·03893	0·04380	0·05353	0·06879	0·09081	0·12230	0·16832	0·23635	0·33424	0·45847	0·61464
0·04259	0·04804	0·05849	0·07454	0·09747	0·13010	0·17698	0·24650	0·34621	0·47120	0·62784
0·04646	0·05255	0·06379	0·08070	0·10457	0·13837	0·18613	0·25714	0·35868	0·48437	0·64143
0·05041	0·05721	0·06953	0·08748	0·11216	0·14714	0·19589	0·26788	0·37097	0·49723	0·65463
0·05457	0·06217	0·07570	0·09481	0·12035	0·15651	0·20615	0·27911	0·38377	0·51050	0·66823
0·05894	0·06742	0·08230	0·10268	0·12913	0·16647	0·21701	0·29085	0·39706	0·52418	0·68221
0·06327	0·07267	0·08870	0·11018	0·13761	0·17612	0·22743	0·30205	0·40924	0·53675	0·69519
0·06812	0·07863	0·09600	0·11868	0·14718	0·18676	0·23881	0·31408	0·42208	0·54969	0·70851
0·07316	0·08491	0·10379	0·12786	0·15740	0·19804	0·25063	0·32636	0·43496	0·56296	0·72209
0·07803	0·09115	0·11166	0·13729	0·16754	0·20897	0·26168	0·33734	0·44684	0·57524	0·73439
0·08294	0·09748	0·11968	0·14697	0·17789	0·22002	0·27271	0·34814	0·45848	0·58656	0·74568
0·08788	0·10391	0·12787	0·15689	0·18845	0·23121	0·28371	0·35876	0·46967	0·59693	0·75594
0·09317	0·11087	0·13679	0·16742	0·19976	0·24302	0·29526	0·36992	0·48088	0·60794	0·76709
0·09859	0·11817	0·14624	0·17865	0·21179	0·25544	0·30716	0·38118	0·49202	0·61875	0·77799
0·10396	0·12544	0·15569	0·18989	0·22372	0·26755	0·31856	0·39178	0·50252	0·62888	0·78824
0·10928	0·13275	0·16530	0·20127	0·23577	0·27960	0·32959	0·40180	0·51217	0·63812	0·79743
0·11466	0·14023	0·17526	0·21316	0·24816	0·29176	0·34059	0·41164	0·52151	0·64704	0·80674
0·11980	0·14747	0·18497	0·22481	0·26022	0·30340	0·35083	0·42063	0·53005	0·65504	0·81434
0·12485	0·15465	0·19465	0·23636	0·27200	0·31466	0·36059	0·42901	0·53789	0·66240	0·82164

Table 10 *Probabilities of dying for females by*

					Probabilities of dying for age groups					
Level	e_0	e_0^{-1}	0	1–4	0–4	5–9	10–14	15–19	20–24	25–29
1	73·98	0·01352	0·01750	0·00358	0·02109	0·00226	0·00196	0·00335	0·00428	0·00513
2	73·09	0·01368	0·02188	0·00525	0·02708	0·00262	0·00221	0·00373	0·00485	0·00572
3	72·14	0·01386	0·02625	0·00699	0·03311	0·00301	0·00249	0·00417	0·00551	0·00642
4	71·24	0·01404	0·03063	0·00878	0·03917	0·00341	0·00277	0·00459	0·00612	0·00706
5	70·28	0·01423	0·03500	0·01064	0·04528	0·00385	0·00309	0·00508	0·00685	0·00783
6	69·34	0·01442	0·03938	0·01254	0·05141	0·00429	0·00340	0·00555	0·00754	0·00857
7	68·32	0·01464	0·04375	0·01451	0·05759	0·00478	0·00374	0·00608	0·00831	0·00939
8	67·36	0·01485	0·04843	0·01680	0·06447	0·00550	0·00425	0·00684	0·00934	0·01036
9	66·30	0·01508	0·05313	0·01917	0·07144	0·00625	0·00479	0·00764	0·01041	0·01137
10	65·30	0·01531	0·05785	0·02160	0·07850	0·00703	0·00536	0·00848	0·01153	0·01242
11	64·29	0·01555	0·06230	0·02391	0·08500	0·00767	0·00580	0·00915	0·01248	0·01341
12	63·31	0·01580	0·06675	0·02630	0·09155	0·00835	0·00627	0·00984	0·01345	0·01443
13	62·24	0·01607	0·07177	0·02910	0·09891	0·00919	0·00692	0·01075	0·01465	0·01575
14	61·22	0·01633	0·07682	0·03198	0·10635	0·01006	0·00759	0·01169	0·01588	0·01712
15	60·17	0·01662	0·08190	0·03492	0·11385	0·01097	0·00828	0·01266	0·01714	0·01853
16	59·13	0·01691	0·08645	0·03766	0·12070	0·01179	0·00887	0·01349	0·01828	0·01971
17	58·04	0·01723	0·09137	0·04075	0·12839	0·01276	0·00960	0·01453	0·01973	0·02126
18	55·93	0·01788	0·10087	0·01625	0·14311	0·01464	0·01100	0·01648	0·02243	0·02412
19	53·83	0·01858	0·11040	0·05311	0·15801	0·01662	0·01246	0·01851	0·02523	0·02711
20	51·76	0·01932	0·12007	0·05994	0·17348	0·01885	0·01405	0·02077	0·02824	0·03047
21	49·67	0·02013	0·12977	0·06702	0·18913	0·02118	0·01570	0·02310	0·03134	0·03385
22	47·63	0·02100	0·14003	0·07461	0·20579	0·02370	0·01748	0·02572	0·03480	0·03745
23	45·57	0·02194	0·14990	0·08249	0·22174	0·02631	0·01932	0·02832	0·03817	0·04136
24	43·57	0·02295	0·15980	0·09063	0·23786	0·02904	0·02124	0·03100	0·04163	0·04572
25	41·63	0·02402	0·16983	0·09950	0·25447	0·03206	0·02334	0·03379	0·04530	0·05006
26	39·74	0·02516	0·17990	0·10868	0·27124	0·03519	0·02551	0·03664	0·04912	0·05462
27	37·81	0·02645	0·19000	0·11817	0·28818	0·03843	0·02775	0·03954	0·05310	0·05939
28	36·06	0·02773	0·19950	0·12807	0·30446	0·04186	0·03010	0·04243	0·05630	0·06335
29	34·31	0·02915	0·20900	0·13846	0·32091	0·04547	0·03257	0·04540	0·05985	0·06778
30	32·61	0·03067	0·21850	0·14932	0·33752	0·04928	0·03515	0·04843	0·06341	0·07228
31	30·97	0·03229	0·22883	0·16117	0·35499	0·05343	0·03794	0·05167	0·06739	0·07708
32	29·39	0·03403	0·23920	0·17340	0·37259	0·05771	0·04080	0·05493	0·07136	0·08189
33	27·88	0·03587	0·24960	0·18600	0·39033	0·06211	0·04373	0·05822	0·07533	0·08671
34	26·43	0·03784	0·25920	0·19911	0·40770	0·06675	0·04678	0·06136	0·07880	0·09129
35	25·02	0·03997	0·26880	0·21280	0·42522	0·07151	0·04990	0·06454	0·08225	0·09588
36	23·68	0·04223	0·27840	0·22714	0·44292	0·07654	0·05315	0·06769	0·08559	0·10039
37	22·39	0·04466	0·28800	0·24211	0·46078	0·08179	0·05653	0·07082	0·08883	0·10480
38	21·15	0·04728	0·29760	0·25778	0·47882	0·08729	0·06002	0·07391	0·09199	0·10916
39	19·97	0·05008	0·30720	0·27415	0·49701	0·09295	0·06358	0·07691	0·09498	0·11332
40	18·84	0·05308	0·31680	0·29127	0·51537	0·09887	0·06727	0·07986	0·09780	0·11736

Probabilities of dying for age groups

30–34	35–39	40–44	45–49	50–54	55–59	60–64	65–69	70–74	75–79	80–84
0·00650	0·00843	0·01188	0·01834	0·02779	0·04134	0·06711	0·11167	0·18630	0·29363	0·43667
0·00709	0·00898	0·01245	0·01902	0·02858	0·04227	0·06840	0·11341	0·18864	0·29647	0·43980
0·00780	0·00971	0·01320	0·01980	0·02948	0·04338	0·06982	0·11534	0·19136	0·29978	0·44355
0·00843	0·01030	0·01381	0·02047	0·03027	0·04434	0·07106	0·11702	0·19350	0·30239	0·44647
0·00919	0·01109	0·01456	0·02129	0·03125	0·04552	0·07261	0·11910	0·19628	0·30577	0·45021
0·00991	0·01178	0·01532	0·02211	0·03214	0·04663	0·07405	0·12104	0·19889	0·30898	0·45375
0·01077	0·01265	0·01626	0·02318	0·03337	0·04815	0·07606	0·12374	0·20242	0·31321	0·45853
0·01173	0·01358	0·01723	0·02421	0·03467	0·04994	0·07835	0·12669	0·20613	0·31792	0·46336
0·01274	0·01455	0·01825	0·02531	0·03603	0·05182	0·08074	0·12975	0·20997	0·32277	0·46829
0·01378	0·01556	0·01932	0·02647	0·03743	0·05378	0·08321	0·13292	0·21393	0·32776	0·47332
0·01477	0·01655	0·02033	0·02755	0·03873	0·05544	0·08534	0·13573	0·21762	0·33224	0·47822
0·01582	0·01760	0·02145	0·02873	0·04004	0·05699	0·08731	0·13833	0·22106	0·33630	0·48279
0·01709	0·01886	0·02268	0·03012	0·04177	0·05916	0·09034	0·14216	0·22580	0·34218	0·48875
0·01841	0·02018	0·02398	0·03158	0·04356	0·06138	0·09344	0·14608	0·23065	0·34818	0·49487
0·01978	0·02156	0·02535	0·03311	0·04541	0·06366	0·09663	0·15009	0·23560	0·35429	0·50113
0·02108	0·02285	0·02668	0·03450	0·04703	0·06565	0·09913	0·15330	0·23970	0·35915	0·50632
0·02257	0·02441	0·02826	0·03626	0·04909	0·06828	0·10252	0·15775	0·24510	0·36575	0·51308
0·02551	0·02744	0·03136	0·03966	0·05304	0·07321	0·10880	0·16586	0·25508	0·37770	0·52552
0·02860	0·03065	0·03466	0·04331	0·05727	0·07845	0·11546	0·17441	0·26554	0·39014	0·53844
0·03210	0·03430	0·03846	0·04744	0·06200	0·08414	0·12276	0·18329	0·27671	0·40258	0·55202
0·03566	0·03807	0·04236	0·05171	0·06722	0·08998	0·13008	0·19230	0·28796	0·41506	0·56559
0·03976	0·04239	0·04687	0·05669	0·07294	0·09679	0·13919	0·20276	0·30043	0·42893	0·58082
0·04393	0·04681	0·05155	0·06185	0·07879	0·10366	0·14784	0·21288	0·31223	0·44232	0·59527
0·04836	0·05151	0·05657	0·06738	0·08469	0·11095	0·15697	0·22350	0·32452	0·45615	0·61015
0·05323	0·05690	0·06211	0·07330	0·09150	0·11883	0·16634	0·23446	0·33680	0·46987	0·62483
0·05840	0·06266	0·06807	0·07971	0·09885	0·12725	0·17626	0·24594	0·34958	0·48403	0·63993
0·06386	0·06878	0·07446	0·08660	0·10673	0·13621	0·18673	0·25793	0·36286	0·49862	0·65545
0·06855	0·07413	0·08026	0·09292	0·11373	0·14410	0·19669	0·26785	0·37400	0·51057	0·66793
0·07380	0·08021	0·08686	0·10008	0·12164	0·15280	0·20549	0·27852	0·38572	0·52287	0·68073
0·07926	0·08663	0·09391	0·10782	0·13008	0·16204	0·21565	0·28942	0·39750	0·53550	0·69377
0·08514	0·09365	0·10175	0·11620	0·13947	0·17219	0·22675	0·30123	0·40976	0·54905	0·70799
0·09110	0·10083	0·10979	0·12481	0·14908	0·18252	0·23789	0·31296	0·42178	0·56173	0·72127
0·09713	0·10815	0·11803	0·13365	0·15893	0·19303	0·24907	0·32460	0·43355	0·57353	0·73360
0·10297	0·11539	0·12627	0·14262	0·16846	0·20288	0·25922	0·33469	0·44388	0·58410	0·74441
0·10897	0·12299	0·13500	0·15219	0·17861	0·21326	0·26966	0·34488	0·45418	0·59449	0·75499
0·11490	0·13056	0·14371	0·16175	0·18866	0·22337	0·27968	0·35446	0·46386	0·60422	0·76494
0·12078	0·13817	0·15258	0·17145	0·19883	0·23342	0·28935	0·36354	0·47277	0·61310	0·77387
0·12673	0·14595	0·16178	0·18158	0·20928	0·24358	0·29901	0·37244	0·48139	0·62166	0·78257
0·13240	0·15349	0·17075	0·19151	0·21944	0·25330	0·30801	0·38057	0·48927	0·62936	0·79028
0·13799	0·16097	0·17967	0·20134	0·22938	0·26270	0·31657	0·38815	0·49651	0·63642	0·79736

Sex and age (x)	Level 0 ($e_0 = 20$)	Level 5 ($e_0 = 22.5$)	Level 10 ($e_0 = 25$)	Level 15 ($e_0 = 27.5$)	Level 20 ($e_0 = 30$)	Level 25 ($e_0 = 32.5$)	Level 30 ($e_0 = 35$)	Level 35 ($e_0 = 37.5$)	Level 40 ($e_0 = 40$)	Level 45 ($e_0 = 42.5$)	Level 50 ($e_0 = 45$)	Level 55 ($e_0 = 47.5$)
Males												
0	332·31	310·55	290·49	271·93	255·59	240·38	224·65	209·25	195·73	182·39	169·09	156·53
1– 4	267·98	235·27	207·67	184·21	164·43	146·69	130·86	116·31	104·16	92·50	82·07	72·52
5– 9	89·06	77·89	68·40	60·33	53·53	47·42	42·01	37·06	33·00	29·09	25·65	22·55
10–14	55·68	49·22	43·61	38·78	34·66	30·93	27·57	24·47	21·89	19·42	17·22	15·24
15–19	68·08	62·41	57·05	52·03	47·65	43·52	39·45	35·60	32·34	29·14	26·28	23·68
20–24	85·81	79·96	74·20	68·61	63·91	59·35	54·34	49·76	45·52	41·46	37·63	34·07
25–29	100·33	92·40	84·74	77·49	71·05	64·96	58·89	53·45	48·50	43·81	39·40	35·44
30–34	119·56	108·54	98·22	88·66	80·35	72·62	65·19	58·61	52·79	47·33	42·27	37·76
35–39	147·14	131·73	117·68	104·93	94·14	84·24	75·03	67·03	60·05	53·58	47·67	42·45
40–44	184·52	163·96	145·60	129·18	115·45	102·96	91·58	81·81	73·06	65·05	58·06	51·94
45–49	224·27	199·69	177·89	158·44	141·87	126·88	113·54	102·09	91·67	82·19	74·04	66·96
50–54	259·66	234·09	210·97	190·11	172·43	156·31	141·39	128·48	116·84	106·46	96·89	88·69
55–59	302·86	277·92	254·60	232·95	214·20	196·83	180·32	165·73	152·50	140·30	129·43	119·81
60–64	350·36	328·05	306·35	285·41	266·90	249·36	231·93	216·20	201·75	188·28	176·23	165·63
65–69	420·21	400·41	380·42	360·40	342·45	325·04	306·80	289·97	274·30	259·50	245·62	233·12
70–74	529·66	510·83	491·26	471·32	452·34	433·58	414·31	396·07	378·29	361·39	345·17	330·47
75–79	654·67	636·83	618·02	598·55	580·59	561·54	541·86	523·16	504·82	487·20	470·10	454·28
80–84	813·99	796·15	777·25	757·58	739·73	720·64	700·45	681·17	662·40	644·34	626·70	610·36
Females												
0	306·76	286·66	268·15	251·01	233·73	217·48	203·25	189·25	175·59	162·01	149·05	136·40
1– 4	273·39	240·03	211·87	187·93	166·95	148·16	132·18	117·46	104·75	92·58	81·81	71·93
5– 9	92·69	81·06	71·16	62·79	55·45	48·87	43·29	38·19	33·85	29·70	26·08	22·81
10–14	63·42	56·06	49·69	44·18	39·29	34·87	31·08	27·58	24·58	21·70	19·16	16·85
15–19	76·77	70·38	64·32	58·68	53·21	48·11	43·60	39·32	35·42	31·61	28·10	24·79
20–24	94·84	88·38	82·02	75·84	69·27	63·03	57·70	52·80	47·48	42·44	37·88	33·58
25–29	113·13	104·19	95·57	87·38	79·35	71·80	65·10	59·03	52·67	46·68	41·02	36·18
30–34	132·14	119·96	108·56	97·99	87·96	78·66	70·62	63·45	56·19	49·43	43·57	38·31
35–39	153·14	137·11	122·47	109·21	97·05	85·94	76·53	68·32	60·19	52·70	46·43	40·86
40–44	170·34	151·35	134·41	119·24	105·55	93·15	82·87	73·98	65·52	57·77	51·15	45·28
45–49	191·05	170·10	151·54	134·96	120·27	106·99	95·75	86·09	76·96	68·68	61·40	54·93
50–54	218·97	197·41	177·92	160·33	144·01	129·18	116·86	106·14	95·70	86·19	78·28	70·92
55–59	252·65	232·02	212·56	194·48	177·08	161·05	147·54	135·54	123·64	112·68	103·07	94·38
60–64	307·59	288·00	268·95	250·56	232·02	214·56	199·56	185·95	172·01	159·03	147·09	135·97
65–69	380·19	362·28	344·19	326·08	306·78	288·25	272·07	257·04	241·02	225·91	212·00	199·06
70–74	488·91	471·53	453·48	435·07	415·44	396·24	378·63	361·87	344·11	327·22	311·21	296·02
75–79	629·00	611·86	593·79	575·08	555·05	534·15	515·43	497·53	477·96	459·17	441·16	424·03
80–84	789·92	772·63	754·27	735·19	714·27	692·37	672·99	654·29	633·46	613·38	594·02	575·44

Note: The expéctations of life in parentheses are the expectations of life at birth for both sexes combined, in years.

Life Tables

Level 60 ($e_0 = 50$)	Level 65 ($e_0 = 52.5$)	Level 70 ($e_0 = 55$)	Level 75 ($e_0 = 57.6$)	Level 80 ($e_0 = 60.4$)	Level 85 ($e_0 = 63.2$)	Level 90 ($e_0 = 65.8$)	Level 95 ($e_0 = 68.2$)	Level 100 ($e_0 = 70.2$)	Level 105 ($e_0 = 71.7$)	Level 110 ($e_0 = 73.0$)	Level 115 ($e_0 = 73.0$)	Sex and age (x)
												Males
143·78	130·82	118·11	102·34	84·47	66·60	50·52	38·01	29·67	24·11	20·41	17·94	0
63·56	54·98	47·22	39·88	33·21	26·78	20·56	14·55	9·75	6·55	4·42	3·00	1– 4
19·72	17·03	14·68	12·48	10·55	8·75	7·20	5·73	4·06	2·80	1·96	1·40	5– 9
13·40	11·66	10·18	8·81	7·61	6·48	5·44	4·49	3·31	2·36	1·73	1·31	10–14
21·22	18·64	16·49	14·39	12·45	10·64	8·99	7·42	5·64	4·01	2·93	2·21	15–19
30·63	27·02	23·90	20·89	17·94	15·10	12·52	10·07	7·44	5·37	3·99	3·07	20–24
31·74	28·00	24·54	21·25	18·35	15·59	12·87	10·34	7·83	5·90	4·61	3·75	25–29
33·61	29·56	25·87	22·48	19·36	16·49	13·86	11·39	9·05	7·14	5·86	5·01	30–34
37·75	33·28	29·28	25·60	22·26	19·22	16·43	13·85	11·50	9·47	8·12	7·22	35–39
46·41	41·17	36·57	32·36	28·52	25·04	22·02	19·16	16·61	14·30	12·50	11·30	40–44
60·58	54·57	48·66	44·36	40·00	36·00	32·50	29·15	26·23	23·30	20·66	18·61	45–49
81·28	74·28	67·99	62·25	57·21	52·65	48·57	44·67	41·11	37·63	34·15	31·01	50–54
111·05	102·67	95·26	88·53	82·41	76·85	71·96	67·56	63·06	58·62	54·58	50·54	55–59
155·94	146·35	137·49	129·48	122·30	115·83	109·82	104·10	98·40	92·61	87·14	82·15	60–64
221·49	209·98	199·52	190·11	181·21	173·20	165·69	158·46	151·32	143·92	137·21	130·87	65–69
317·01	303·71	291·13	279·61	268·74	258·62	249·22	240·20	231·51	222·76	214·70	207·39	70–74
439·18	424·08	4!0·44	398·05	386·23	375·29	364·86	354·98	344·87	334·57	323·99	314·24	75–79
594·78	578·98	563·92	549·84	536·52	523·97	512·30	500·96	490·21	480·19	468·67	456·23	80–84
												Females
123·75	111·54	99·58	85·99	70·59	55·19	41·33	30·55	23·37	18·58	15·39	13·26	0
62·64	53·92	45·50	38·41	31·17	24·24	18·03	12·27	8·22	5·52	3·72	2·52	1– 4
19·73	16·88	14·39	12·03	9·82	7·77	5·89	4·23	3·01	2·08	1·46	1·05	5– 9
14·68	12·65	10·81	9·05	7·40	5·86	4·53	3·36	2·49	1·79	1·32	1·01	10–14
21·65	18·78	16·22	13·74	11·43	9·24	7·25	5·48	4·17	2·99	2·20	1·67	15–19
29·42	25·59	22·06	18·63	15·54	12·61	9·89	7·44	5·51	4·01	3·01	2·35	20–24
31·75	27·51	23·73	20·09	16·74	13·55	10·88	8·47	6·41	4·83	3·78	3·08	25–29
33·45	29·01	25·11	21·44	18·04	14·91	12·25	9·81	7·79	6·12	5·00	4·26	30–34
35·73	31·08	27·03	23·23	19·81	16·69	14·11	11·68	9·70	7·99	6·85	6·09	35–39
39·94	35·11	30·94	27·06	23·62	20·48	17·76	15·21	13·19	11·49	10·17	9·29	40–44
49·06	43·80	39·20	34·93	31·17	27·71	24·78	21·99	19·79	17·94	16·28	14·99	45–49
63·98	57·83	52·50	47·53	43·06	38·91	35·37	32·01	29·47	27·15	25·41	23·85	50–54
86·36	79·12	72·54	66·29	60·76	55·65	50·91	46·47	43·37	40·78	38·84	37·38	55–59
125·54	116·32	107·95	99·95	92·57	85·61	79·59	73·84	69·81	66·61	63·41	61·01	60–64
186·71	175·46	164·76	154·38	144·98	136·09	128·27	120·77	115·32	110·49	105·77	101·05	65–69
280·98	266·86	253·73	241·01	229·29	218·09	208·12	198·52	191·33	184·00	176·35	168·88	70–74
407·31	391·61	376·08	360·75	346·50	332·80	320·43	308·53	299·75	291·47	281·04	270·15	75–79
557·17	540·05	523·83	507·96	493·16	478·85	465·91	453·25	443·51	434·43	423·99	412·71	80–84

Table 12 *Survivors in UN Model Life Tables*

Sex and age (x)	Level 0 (e₀ = 20)	Level 5 (e₀ = 22·5)	Level 10 (e₀ = 25)	Level 15 (e₀ = 27·5)	Level 20 (e₀ = 30)	Level 25 (e₀ = 32·5)	Level 30 (e₀ = 35)	Level 35 (e₀ = 37·5)	Level 40 (e₀ = 40)	Level 45 (e₀ = 42·5)	Level 50 (e₀ = 45)	Level 55 (e₀ = 47·5)
Males												
0	100 000	100 000	100 000	100 000	100 000	100 000	100 000	100 000	100 000	100 000	100 000	100 000
1	66 769	68 545	70 951	72 807	74 441	75 962	77 535	79 075	80 427	81 761	83 091	84 347
5	48 876	52 418	56 217	59 395	62 201	64 819	67 389	69 878	72 050	74 198	76 272	78 230
10	44 523	48 335	52 372	55 812	58 871	61 745	64 558	67 288	69 672	72 040	74 316	76 466
15	42 044	45 956	50 088	53 648	56 831	59 835	62 778	65 641	68 147	70 641	73 036	75 301
20	39 182	43 088	47 230	50 857	54 123	57 231	60 301	63 304	65 943	68 583	71 117	73 518
25	35 820	39 643	43 726	47 368	50 664	53 834	57 024	60 154	62 941	65 740	68 441	71 013
30	32 226	35 980	40 021	43 697	47 064	50 337	53 666	56 939	59 888	62 860	65 744	68 496
35	28 373	32 075	36 090	39 823	43 282	46 682	50 168	53 602	56 727	59 885	62 965	65 910
40	24 198	27 850	31 843	35 644	39 207	42 750	46 404	50 009	53 321	56 676	59 963	63 112
45	19 733	23 284	27 207	31 040	34 681	38 348	42 154	45 918	49 425	52 989	56 482	59 834
50	15 307	18 634	22 367	26 122	29 761	33 482	37 368	41 230	44 894	48 634	52 300	55 828
55	11 332	14 272	17 648	21 156	24 629	28 248	32 085	35 933	39 649	43 456	47 233	50 877
60	7 900	10 306	13 155	16 228	19 353	22 688	26 299	29 978	33 603	37 359	41 120	44 781
65	5 132	6 925	9 125	11 596	14 188	17 031	20 199	23 497	26 824	30 325	33 873	37 364
70	2 975	4 152	5 654	7 417	9 329	11 495	14 002	16 684	19 466	22 456	25 553	28 654
75	1 399	2 031	2 876	3 921	5 109	6 511	8 201	10 076	12 102	14 341	16 733	19 185
80	483	738	1 099	1 574	2 143	2 855	3 757	4 805	5 993	7 354	8 867	10 470
85	90	150	245	382	558	798	1 125	1 532	2 023	2 616	3 310	4 080

Note: The expectations of life in parentheses are the expectations of life at birth for both sexes combined, in years.

Table 12 (*continued*)

Sex and age (x)	Level 0 ($e_0 = 20$)	Level 5 ($e_0 = 22.5$)	Level 10 ($e_0 = 25$)	Level 15 ($e_0 = 27.5$)	Level 20 ($e_0 = 30$)	Level 25 ($e_0 = 32.5$)	Level 30 ($e_0 = 35$)	Level 35 ($e_0 = 37.5$)	Level 40 ($e_0 = 40$)	Level 45 ($e_0 = 42.5$)	Level 50 ($e_0 = 45$)	Level 55 ($e_0 = 47.5$)
Females												
0	100 000	100 000	100 000	100 000	100 000	100 000	100 000	100 000	100 000	100 000	100 000	100 000
1	69 324	71 334	73 185	74 899	76 627	78 252	79 675	81 075	82 441	83 799	85 095	86 360
5	50 372	54 212	57 679	60 823	63 834	66 658	69 144	71 552	73 805	76 041	78 133	80 148
10	45 703	49 818	53 585	57 004	60 294	63 400	66 151	68 819	71 307	73 783	76 095	78 320
15	42 805	47 025	50 913	54 486	57 925	61 189	64 095	66 921	69 554	72 182	74 637	77 000
20	39 519	43 715	47 638	51 289	54 843	58 245	61 300	64 290	67 090	69 900	72 540	75 091
25	35 771	39 851	43 731	47 399	51 044	54 574	57 763	60 895	63 905	66 933	69 792	72 569
30	31 724	35 699	39 552	43 257	46 994	50 656	54 003	57 300	60 539	63 809	66 929	69 943
35	27 532	31 417	35 258	39 018	42 860	46 671	50 189	53 664	57 137	60 655	64 013	67 263
40	23 316	27 109	30 940	34 757	38 700	42 660	46 348	49 998	53 698	57 458	61 041	64 515
45	19 344	23 006	26 781	30 613	34 615	38 686	42 507	46 299	50 180	54 139	57 919	61 594
50	15 648	19 093	22 723	26 481	30 452	34 547	38 437	42 313	46 318	50 421	54 363	58 211
55	12 222	15 324	18 680	22 235	26 067	30 084	33 945	37 822	41 885	46 075	50 107	54 083
60	9 134	11 769	14 709	17 911	21 451	25 239	28 937	32 696	36 706	40 883	44 942	48 979
65	6 324	8 380	10 753	13 423	16 474	19 824	23 162	26 616	30 392	34 381	38 331	42 319
70	3 920	5 344	7 052	9 046	11 420	14 110	16 860	19 775	23 067	26 614	30 205	33 895
75	2 003	2 824	3 854	5 110	6 676	8 519	10 476	12 619	15 129	17 905	20 805	23 861
80	743	1 096	1 566	2 171	2 970	3 969	5 076	6 341	7 898	9 684	11 627	13 743
85	156	249	385	575	849	1 221	1 660	2 192	2 895	3 744	4 720	5 835

Table 12 (continued)

Sex and age (x)	Level 60 (e₀ = 50)	Level 65 (e₀ = 52·5)	Level 70 (e₀ = 55)	Level 75 (e₀ = 57·6)	Level 80 (e₀ = 60·4)	Level 85 (e₀ = 63·2)	Level 90 (e₀ = 65·8)	Level 95 (e₀ = 68·2)	Level 100 (e₀ = 70·2)	Level 105 (e₀ = 71·7)	Level 110 (e₀ = 73·0)	Level 115 (e₀ = 73·9)
Males												
0	100 000	100 000	100 000	100 000	100 000	100 000	100 000	100 000	100 000	100 000	100 000	100 000
1	85 622	86 918	88 189	89 766	91 553	93 340	94 948	96 199	97 033	97 589	97 959	98 206
5	80 180	82 139	84 025	86 186	88 513	90 840	92 996	94 799	96 087	96 950	97 526	97 911
10	78 599	80 740	82 792	85 110	87 579	90 045	92 326	94 256	95 697	96 670	97 335	97 774
15	77 546	79 799	81 949	84 360	86 913	89 462	91 821	93 838	95 380	96 451	97 167	97 646
20	75 900	78 304	80 598	83 146	85 831	88 510	90 999	93 142	94 842	96 064	96 882	97 430
25	73 575	76 188	78 672	81 409	84 291	87 173	89 860	92 204	94 136	95 548	96 495	97 131
30	71 240	74 055	76 741	79 679	82 744	85 814	88 704	91 251	93 399	94 984	96 050	96 767
35	68 846	71 866	74 756	77 888	81 142	84 399	87 475	90 212	92 554	94 306	95 487	96 282
40	66 247	69 474	72 567	75 894	79 336	82 777	86 038	88 963	91 490	93 413	94 712	95 587
45	63 172	66 614	69 913	73 438	77 073	80 704	84 143	87 258	89 970	92 077	93 528	94 507
50	59 345	62 979	66 511	70 180	73 990	77 799	81 408	84 174	87 610	89 932	91 596	92 748
55	54 521	58 301	61 989	65 811	69 757	73 703	77 454	80 930	84 008	86 548	88 468	89 872
60	48 466	52 315	56 084	59 985	64 008	68 039	71 880	75 462	78 710	81 475	83 639	85 330
65	40 908	44 659	48 373	52 218	56 180	60 158	63 986	67 606	70 965	73 930	76 351	78 320
70	31 847	35 282	38 722	42 291	46 000	49 739	53 384	56 893	60 227	63 290	65 875	68 070
75	21 751	24 567	27 499	30 466	33 638	36 875	40 080	43 227	46 284	49 192	51 732	53 953
80	12 198	14 149	16 183	18 339	20 646	23 036	25 456	27 882	30 322	32 734	34 971	36 999
85	4 943	5 957	7 057	8 255	9 569	10 966	12 415	13 914	15 458	17 015	18 581	20 119

Table 12 (continued)

Sex and age (x)	Level 60 ($e_0 = 50$)	Level 65 ($e_0 = 52\cdot5$)	Level 70 ($e_0 = 55$)	Level 75 ($e_0 = 57\cdot6$)	Level 80 ($e_0 = 60\cdot4$)	Level 85 ($e_0 = 63\cdot2$)	Level 90 ($e_0 = 65\cdot8$)	Level 95 ($e_0 = 68\cdot2$)	Level 100 ($e_0 = 70\cdot2$)	Level 105 ($e_0 = 71\cdot7$)	Level 110 ($e_0 = 73\cdot0$)	Level 115 ($e_0 = 73\cdot9$)
Females												
0	100 000	100 000	100 000	100 000	100 000	100 000	100 000	100 000	100 000	100 000	100 000	100 000
1	87 625	88 846	90 042	91 401	92 941	94 481	95 867	96 945	97 663	98 142	98 461	98 674
5	82 136	84 055	85 945	87 890	90 044	92 191	94 139	95 755	96 860	97 600	98 095	98 425
10	80 515	82 636	84 708	86 833	89 160	91 475	93 585	95 350	96 568	97 397	97 952	98 322
15	79 333	81 591	83 792	86 047	88 500	90 939	93 161	95 030	96 328	97 223	97 823	98 223
20	77 615	80 059	82 433	84 865	87 488	90 099	92 486	94 509	95 926	96 932	97 608	98 059
25	75 332	78 010	80 615	83 284	86 128	88 963	91 571	93 806	95 397	96 543	97 314	97 829
30	72 940	75 864	78 702	81 611	84 686	87 758	90 575	93 011	94 786	96 077	96 946	97 528
35	70 500	73 663	76 726	79 861	83 158	86 450	89 465	92 099	94 048	95 489	96 461	97 113
40	67 981	71 374	74 652	78 006	81 511	85 007	88 203	91 023	93 136	94 726	95 800	96 522
45	65 266	68 868	72 342	75 895	79 586	83 266	86 637	89 639	91 908	93 638	94 826	95 625
50	62 064	65 852	69 506	73 244	77 105	80 959	84 490	87 668	90 089	91 958	93 282	94 192
55	58 093	62 044	65 857	69 763	73 785	77 809	81 502	84 862	87 434	89 461	90 912	91 946
60	53 076	57 135	61 080	65 138	69 302	73 479	77 353	80 918	83 642	85 813	87 381	88 509
65	46 413	50 489	54 486	58 627	62 887	67 188	71 196	74 943	77 803	80 097	81 840	83 109
70	37 747	41 630	45 509	49 576	53 770	58 044	62 064	65 892	68 831	71 247	73 184	74 711
75	27 141	30 521	33 962	37 628	41 441	45 385	49 147	52 811	55 662	58 138	60 278	62 094
80	16 086	18 569	21 190	24 054	27 082	30 281	33 399	36 517	38 977	41 193	43 337	45 319
85	7 123	8 541	10 090	11 836	13 726	15 781	17 838	19 966	21 690	23 298	24 963	26 615

Table 13 *Probabilities of survival by age groups in UN Model Life Tables*

Sex and age (x)	Level 0 (e₀ = 20)	Level 5 (e₀ = 22·5)	Level 10 (e₀ = 25)	Level 15 (e₀ = 27·5)	Level 20 (e₀ = 30)	Level 25 (e₀ = 32·5)	Level 30 (e₀ = 35)	Level 35 (e₀ = 37·5)	Level 40 (e₀ = 40)	Level 45 (e₀ = 42·5)	Level 50 (e₀ = 45)	Level 55 (e₀ = 47·5)
Males												
(Births)	(0·6092)	(0·6334)	(0·6622)	(0·6853)	(0·7058)	(0·7248)	(0·7440)	(0·7626)	(0·7789)	(0·7950)	(0·8107)	(0·8256)
0– 4	0·7666	0·7953	0·8200	0·8405	0·8577	0·8731	0·8868	0·8993	0·9098	0·9198	0·9287	0·9369
5– 9	0·9269	0·9359	0·9436	0·9501	0·9556	0·9606	0·9651	0·9691	0·9725	0·9757	0·9785	0·9811
10–14	0·9383	0·9444	0·9498	0·9547	0·9590	0·9629	0·9666	0·9700	0·9729	0·9758	0·9783	0·9806
15–19	0·9234	0·9291	0·9346	0·9399	0·9444	0·9487	0·9532	0·9574	0·9612	0·9648	0·9681	0·9712
20–24	0·9073	0·9141	0·9207	0·9271	0·9326	0·9379	0·9434	0·9484	0·9530	0·9574	0·9615	0·9653
25–29	0·8906	0·8999	0·9088	0·9171	0·9245	0·9313	0·9381	0·9440	0·9494	0·9545	0·9592	0·9634
30–34	0·8675	0·8805	0·8925	0·9036	0·9130	0·9218	0·9301	0·9373	0·9437	0·9496	0·9551	0·9599
35–39	0·8357	0·8533	0·8692	0·8836	0·8957	0·9068	0·9170	0·9258	0·9336	0·9408	0·9473	0·9529
40–44	0·7976	0·8198	0·8395	0·8572	0·8722	0·8857	0·8980	0·9085	0·9180	0·9267	0·9342	0·9408
45–49	0·7603	0·7850	0·8072	0·8271	0·8440	0·8594	0·8734	0·8854	0·8964	0·9062	0·9150	0·9226
50–54	0·7219	0·7469	0·7698	0·7907	0·8086	0·8251	0·8406	0·8542	0·8664	0·8776	0·8877	0·8965
55–59	0·6776	0·7011	0·7233	0·7443	0·7626	0·7798	0·7964	0·8113	0·8249	0·8375	0·8488	0·8587
60–64	0·6221	0·6428	0·6633	0·6833	0·7011	0·7182	0·7355	0·7514	0·7660	0·7798	0·7924	0·8037
65–69	0·5395	0·5582	0·5772	0·5963	0·6139	0·6312	0·6492	0·6660	0·6820	0·6972	0·7116	0·7246
70–74	0·4303	0·4478	0·4660	0·4847	0·5023	0·5202	0·5386	0·5561	0·5732	0·5896	0·6054	0·6199
75–79	0·3044	0·3207	0·3381	0·3559	0·3724	0·3900	0·4083	0·4258	0·4430	0·4595	0·4757	0·4906
80+	(0·1095)	(0·1280)	(0·1483)	(0·1678)	(0·1850)	(0·2023)	(0·2195)	(0·2355)	(0·2502)	(0·2640)	(0·2768)	(0·2882)

Note: The expectations of life in parentheses are the expectations of life at birth for both sexes combined, in years.

Table 13 (continued)

Sex and age (x)	Level 0 ($e_0 = 20$)	Level 5 ($e_0 = 22\cdot5$)	Level 10 ($e_0 = 25$)	Level 15 ($e_0 = 27\cdot5$)	Level 20 ($e_0 = 30$)	Level 25 ($e_0 = 32\cdot5$)	Level 30 ($e_0 = 35$)	Level 35 ($e_0 = 37\cdot5$)	Level 40 ($e_0 = 40$)	Level 45 ($e_0 = 42\cdot5$)	Level 50 ($e_0 = 45$)	Level 55 ($e_0 = 47\cdot5$)
Females (Births)	(0·6290)	(0·6558)	(0·6801)	(0·7024)	(0·7242)	(0·7447)	(0·7627)	(0·7802)	(0·7969)	(0·8135)	(0·8292)	(0·8443)
0– 4	0·7637	0·7932	0·8179	0·8387	0·8570	0·8732	0·8870	0·8996	0·9105	0·9209	0·9300	0·9384
5– 9	0·9212	0·9309	0·9392	0·9462	0·9524	0·9579	0·9627	0·9670	0·9707	0·9742	0·9773	0·9801
10–14	0·9301	0·9370	0·9432	0·9487	0·9539	0·9586	0·9628	0·9666	0·9701	0·9734	0·9764	0·9792
15–19	0·9146	0·9209	0·9271	0·9330	0·9390	0·9446	0·9495	0·9541	0·9587	0·9631	0·9671	0·9709
20–24	0·8965	0·9041	0·9115	0·9186	0·9259	0·9327	0·9387	0·9442	0·9500	0·9555	0·9606	0·9651
25–29	0·8779	0·8884	0·8983	0·9076	0·9165	0·9249	0·9322	0·9388	0·9456	0·9520	0·9577	0·9628
30–34	0·8581	0·8720	0·8849	0·8967	0·9077	0·9178	0·9265	0·9342	0·9419	0·9490	0·9550	0·9604
35–39	0·8390	0·8563	0·8719	0·8861	0·8989	0·9106	0·9204	0·9289	0·9372	0·9448	0·9513	0·9570
40–44	0·8203	0·8400	0·8576	0·8734	0·8875	0·9003	0·9110	0·9202	0·9290	0·9369	0·9439	0·9500
45–49	0·7965	0·8175	0·8364	0·8533	0·8686	0·8825	0·8942	0·9043	0·9140	0·9229	0·9304	0·9373
50–54	0·7663	0·7872	0·8064	0·8241	0·8407	0·8560	0·8688	0·8800	0·8910	0·9012	0·9098	0·9178
55–59	0·7238	0·7437	0·7626	0·7805	0·7981	0·8145	0·8285	0·8411	0·8538	0·8655	0·8761	0·8859
60–64	0·6627	0·6811	0·6993	0·7171	0·7355	0·7530	0·7682	0·7822	0·7967	0·8104	0·8230	0·8348
65–69	0·5782	0·5952	0·6125	0·6300	0·6487	0·6668	0·6830	0·6983	0·7145	0·7299	0·7443	0·7578
70–74	0·4636	0·4799	0·4970	0·5143	0·5330	0·5519	0·5689	0·5853	0·6029	0·6197	0·6358	0·6511
75–79	0·3275	0·3431	0·3600	0·3772	0·3959	0·4156	0·4331	0·4500	0·4687	0·4867	0·5040	0·5206
80 +	(0·1320)	(0·1508)	(0·1694)	(0·1878)	(0·2066)	(0·2251)	(0·2409)	(0·2556)	(0·2708)	(0·2850)	(0·2979)	(0·3099)

Table 13 (continued)

Sex and age (x)	Level 60 ($e_0 = 50$)	Level 65 ($e_0 = 52 \cdot 5$)	Level 70 ($e_0 = 55$)	Level 75 ($e_0 = 57 \cdot 6$)	Level 80 ($e_0 = 60 \cdot 4$)	Level 85 ($e_0 = 63 \cdot 2$)	Level 90 ($e_0 = 65 \cdot 8$)	Level 95 ($e_0 = 68 \cdot 2$)	Level 100 ($e_0 = 70 \cdot 2$)	Level 105 ($e_0 = 71 \cdot 7$)	Level 110 ($e_0 = 73 \cdot 0$)	Level 115 ($e_0 = 73 \cdot 9$)
Males												
(Births)	(0·8406)	(0·8557)	(0·8703)	(0·8877)	(0·9070)	(0·9262)	(0·9438)	(0·9580)	(0·9678)	(0·9744)	(0·9788)	(0·9817)
0– 4	0·9445	0·9518	0·9584	0·9618	0·9708	0·9765	0·9818	0·9867	0·9908	0·9936	0·9954	0·9966
5– 9	0·9834	0·9856	0·9876	0·9893	0·9909	0·9924	0·9937	0·9949	0·9963	0·9974	0·9982	0·9986
10–14	0·9827	0·9848	0·9867	0·9884	0·9900	0·9914	0·9928	0·9941	0·9955	0·9968	0·9977	0·9982
15–19	0·9741	0·9772	0·9798	0·9824	0·9848	0·9871	0·9893	0·9913	0·9935	0·9953	0·9965	0·9974
20–24	0·9688	0·9725	0·9758	0·9789	0·9819	0·9847	0·9873	0·9898	0·9924	0·9944	0·9957	0·9966
25–29	0·9673	0·9712	0·9748	0·9781	0·9811	0·9840	0·9866	0·9891	0·9916	0·9935	0·9948	0·9956
30–34	0·9644	0·9686	0·9725	0·9760	0·9792	0·9822	0·9849	0·9874	0·9897	0·9917	0·9930	0·9939
35–39	0·9580	0·9628	0·9671	0·9711	0·9746	0·9779	0·9808	0·9835	0·9860	0·9881	0·9807	0·9907
40–44	0·9467	0·9523	0·9575	0·9617	0·9658	0·9696	0·9728	0·9759	0·9786	0·9812	0·9835	0·9851
45–49	0·9294	0·9359	0·9419	0·9469	0·9516	0·9558	0·9596	0·9632	0·9664	0·9696	0·9727	0·9752
50–54	0·9045	0·9121	0·9189	0·9250	0·9306	0·9356	0·9400	0·9441	0·9481	0·9521	0·9558	0·9594
55–59	0·8678	0·8767	0·8847	0·8919	0·8985	0·9044	0·9098	0·9148	0·9198	0·9249	0·9296	0·9341
60–64	0·8141	0·8244	0·8338	0·8423	0·8502	0·8573	0·8639	0·8702	0·8765	0·8830	0·8890	0·8945
65–69	0·7367	0·7487	0·7598	0·7698	0·7794	0·7881	0·7963	0·8042	0·8119	0·8197	0·8269	0·8335
70–74	0·6334	0·6469	0·6594	0·6708	0·6816	0·6917	0·7012	0·7102	0·7192	0·7283	0·7372	0·7454
75–79	0·5049	0·5193	0·5326	0·5449	0·5566	0·5675	0·5779	0·5878	0·5976	0·6072	0·6176	0·6280
80+	(0·2988)	(0·3091)	(0·3186)	(0·3272)	(0·3352)	(0·3426)	(0·3492)	(0·3556)	(0·3613)	(0·3666)	(0·3721)	(0·3775)

Table 13 (continued)

Sex and age (x)	Level 60 (e₀ = 50)	Level 65 (e₀ = 52·5)	Level 70 (e₀ = 55)	Level 75 (e₀ = 57·6)	Level 80 (e₀ = 60·4)	Level 85 (e₀ = 63·2)	Level 90 (e₀ = 65·8)	Level 95 (e₀ = 68·2)	Level 100 (e₀ = 70·2)	Level 105 (e₀ = 71·7)	Level 110 (e₀ = 73·0)	Level 115 (e₀ = 73·9)
Females (Births)	(0·8594)	(0·8739)	(0·8882)	(0·9036)	(0·9208)	(0·9380)	(0·9535)	(0·9660)	(0·9744)	(0·9801)	(0·9838)	(0·9864)
0– 4	0·9463	0·9537	0·9607	0·9669	0·9731	0·9791	0·9844	0·9892	0·9925	0·9948	0·9963	0·9973
5– 9	0·9828	0·9852	0·9874	0·9895	0·9914	0·9932	0·9948	0·9962	0·9972	0·9981	0·9986	0·9990
10–14	0·9819	0·9843	0·9865	0·9886	0·9906	0·9925	0·9941	0·9956	0·9967	0·9976	0·9982	0·9987
15–19	0·9745	0·9778	0·9809	0·9838	0·9865	0·9891	0·9914	0·9935	0·9952	0·9965	0·9974	0·9980
20–24	0·9694	0·9735	0·9771	0·9807	0·9839	0·9869	0·9896	0·9920	0·9940	0·9956	0·9966	0·9973
25–29	0·9674	0·9718	0·9756	0·9792	0·9826	0·9858	0·9884	0·9909	0·9929	0·9945	0·9956	0·9963
30–34	0·9654	0·9700	0·9739	0·9777	0·9811	0·9842	0·9868	0·9893	0·9913	0·9929	0·9941	0·9948
35–39	0·9622	0·9669	0·9710	0·9749	0·9783	0·9814	0·9841	0·9866	0·9886	0·9903	0·9915	0·9923
40–44	0·9556	0·9606	0·9650	0·9691	0·9727	0·9759	0·9788	0·9814	0·9835	0·9853	0·9868	0·9879
45–49	0·9437	0·9493	0·9543	0·9589	0·9631	0·9668	0·9700	0·9731	0·9754	0·9775	0·9792	0·9806
50–54	0·9252	0·9318	0·9377	0·9433	0·9482	0·9529	0·9570	0·9609	0·9637	0·9661	0·9680	0·9695
55–59	0·8949	0·9030	0·9104	0·9175	0·9238	0·9298	0·9315	0·9402	0·9437	0·9466	0·9491	0·9510
60–64	0·8459	0·8559	0·8653	0·8743	0·8825	0·8903	0·8971	0·9036	0·9083	0·9122	0·9161	0·9196
65–69	0·7710	0·7832	0·7948	0·8059	0·8162	0·8259	0·8345	0·8429	0·8490	0·8549	0·8609	0·8668
70–74	0·6662	0·6804	0·6940	0·7073	0·7197	0·7316	0·7422	0·7525	0·7602	0·7677	0·7764	0·7852
75–79	0·5369	0·5523	0·5672	0·5819	0·5955	0·6088	0·6207	0·6323	0·6410	0·6493	0·6592	0·6697
80+	(0·3211)	(0·3313)	(0·3406)	(0·3495)	(0·3576)	(0·3652)	(0·3719)	(0·3781)	(0·3828)	(0·3869)	(0·3913)	(0·3957)

INDEX